I0902369

POSTCARD HISTORY SERIES

Miami

in Vintage Postcards

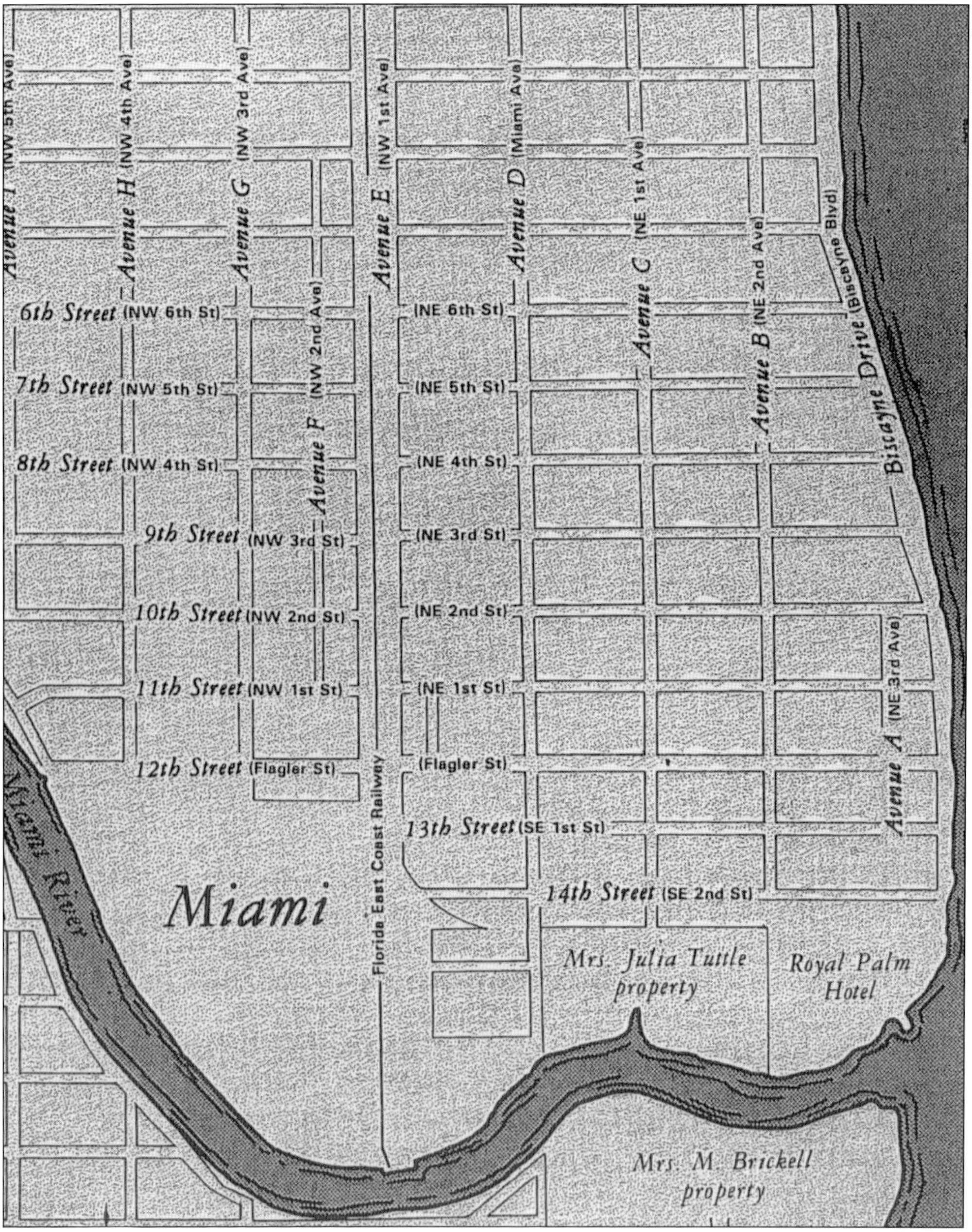

The street names originally established in the late 1800s were changed on January 1, 1921. This map shows the original street names in italics, followed by their new names in parentheses. (Courtesy of Florida State Archives.)

POSTCARD HISTORY SERIES

Miami
in Vintage Postcards

Patricia Kennedy

ARCADIA
PUBLISHING

ISBN 978-0-7385-0643-2

Published by Arcadia Publishing
Charleston, South Carolina

Printed in the United States of America

Library of Congress Catalog Card Number: 00-107238

For all general information contact Arcadia Publishing at:
Telephone 843-853-2070
Fax 843-853-0044
E-Mail sales@arcadiapublishing.com
For customer service and orders:
Toll-Free 1-888-313-2665

Visit us on the Internet at www.arcadiapublishing.com

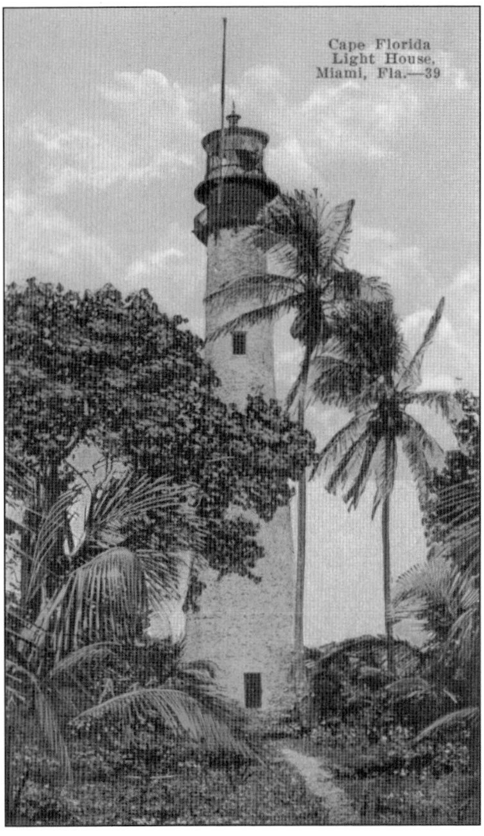

The Cape Florida Lighthouse, built in 1825, is one of the oldest original structures in Florida. The lighthouse warned ships of dangerous reefs and provided shelter for settlers during the Seminole Indian Wars. In 1966, Bill Baggs led the campaign to save the Cape Florida Lighthouse and create a state park on the surrounding land. Today, the 95-foot-tall treasure stands within the Bill Baggs Cape Florida State Recreation Area on Key Biscayne. (Published by E.C. Kropp.)

Contents

Acknowledgments

The images in this book are from my own collection with the exception of additional photographs that are acknowledged in the text. I wish to extend my gratitude to the following people who provided assistance, information, and photographs during the preparation of this book:

Sam J. Boldrick and Kenneth E. Koonce at the Miami-Dade Public Library; Dr. Dorothy Jenkins Fields, Dianne Rolle, and Stephanie Wanza at the Black Archives Foundation; Susan Franqui at the Historic Preservation Department, Coral Gables, Florida; Deborah Gust and Christine Pyle at the Curt Teich Postcard Archives, Lake County Museum; Dawn Hugh at the Historical Museum of Southern Florida; Leslie Lawhon and Joan Morris at the Florida State Archives; Dr. Joan D. Lutton at the Cushman School; and Arno Weinstein and Ginger M. Young at the Jewish Museum of Florida.

I especially thank my editor, Christine T. Riley, for her helpful assistance; my friends and loved ones who patiently listened to my idea of creating this book; and my daughter Colleen, to whom this book is dedicated.

INTRODUCTION

On July 28, 1996, Miami celebrated 100 years as a city. Incorporation as a "city" required a minimum of 300 registered voters, and on July 28, 1896, in a room over the pool hall on the city's first street, 343 voters marked the birth of the "Magic City." Julia Tuttle's dream of establishing a city on the banks of the Miami River had come true.

The strategic and beautiful location had attracted settlers before. The first humans arrived in South Florida 15,000 years ago, as part of a migration to North America from Asia. Remains of settlements dating back 10,000 years were found near the Charles Deering Estate in 1985, while in 1994 another site was uncovered in South Miami by archeologist Robert Carr and a team of excavators. The trail of human history ends around these sites until the appearance of the Tequesta Indians 4,000 years ago.

When Juan Ponce de Leon first arrived in the Miami area in 1513, two of the largest Tequesta villages were located along the Miami River at today's downtown and on Key Biscayne. The Spanish established permanent settlements in Florida in 1565, and the native populations soon suffered from a combination of violence and Old World diseases brought by the Spanish explorers. In little over a century the Tequesta no longer existed in South Florida. By the 1700s, however, their place had been taken by the Seminole Indians who migrated into Florida from the Southeastern United States. The term "Seminole," roughly translated, means "renegade."

"La Florida" had become part of Spain's New World Empire, but Spain did not reap the expected benefits. In 1763, the treaty ending the French and Indian War gave "La Florida" to the British, who traded it back to Spain following the American Revolution. The United States then acquired Florida from Spain in 1821. Hoping to attract settlers, the government offered the inducement of free land; however, the forced relocation of Indians to reservations in the West resulted in the Seminole Wars, which began in 1835. In response to the wars, Fort Dallas was established on the north bank of the Miami River in 1838. That same year Dade County was created and named for Major Francis L. Dade, who had been killed by Indians a year earlier.

Ralph Kirkpatrick, a plantation owner from Georgia, purchased land from the state with hopes of developing a plantation community like his home in Georgia. By the 1840s, discouraged by the Indian attacks, Kirkpatrick gave the land to his nephew, William F. English. As Julia Tuttle would decades later, English dreamed of creating a city. English began building but soon ran low on funds. Hearing about the California Gold Rush, he left for California with his uncle, hoping to return with enough money to build his city. English never got the chance. He accidentally shot himself while dismounting his horse and died out West. Twenty years later in 1879, William Brickell bought the land from William English's mother, Harriet English.

Ephraim T. Sturtevant had come to the area with Brickell in 1870. His daughter Julia Sturtevant Tuttle visited him in the 1870s and was very taken with the area. Mrs. Tuttle returned to Ohio to run the business of her ailing husband, Frederick Tuttle. After his death, she moved to the Miami area with her two children in 1891. By this time, pioneers had already established themselves in areas such as Coconut Grove, Cutler, Lemon City, and Buena Vista. Julia Tuttle saw the potential for a great city and bought land on the north side of the Miami River. She tried, unsuccessfully at first, to get Henry Plant or Henry Flagler to extend their railroad systems to the area. Flagler stopped the line of his Florida East Coast Railway in Palm Beach. All that changed when, in 1895, a devastating freeze destroyed all of the state's citrus groves as far south as Palm Beach. Legend has it that Mrs. Tuttle sent Flagler a twig of green leaves and white blossoms from her orange tree. She renewed her offer to give him half of her 640 acres if he would extend his railroad to the Miami area, build a first-rate hotel, and lay out streets for the future city. By October a contract sealed their agreement, and both parties kept their word. Flagler's East Coast Railway arrived on April 15, 1896 and his Royal Palm Hotel opened on January 16, 1897, built on land donated by Julia Tuttle. Henry Flagler also donated land for churches, clubs, and schools. Another man of vision, Carl Fisher, built a monument in honor of Flagler on an island in Biscayne Bay. The main business street in today's downtown Miami is named after Henry Flagler in appreciation for his role in establishing the city.

A special note should be made at this point that the street names given in the early years of Miami, such as Avenue D and Twelfth Street, were changed on January 1, 1921. Avenue D became Miami Avenue, the dividing line for the east and west sections of the city. Twelfth Street became Flagler Street, the dividing line for the north and south sections. A detailed map showing the pre-1921 street names in italics next to the current names is featured on page 2. This map will be useful since the early postcards often show the pre-1921 address of the featured scene.

At the time of its incorporation in July 1896, the first businesses were built on Avenue D, Miami's first street. On Christmas Eve of the same year, a fire destroyed most of the buildings. The merchants rebuilt, only to experience another major fire in 1898. Early Miamians prevailed through fires, epidemics, hurricanes, financial prosperity, and loss. There was no turning back—Miami was here to stay. Julia Tuttle's dream had come true, as had the dreams of those early settlers determined to build a life in the new city.

In 1898, two years after Miami was incorporated, a special one-cent postage rate was made available for "Private Mailing Cards," which were the early commercially produced postcards. Images of cities and towns across America were now captured, sent to loved ones, and collected. The postcards became valuable historic resources. This book takes the reader on a postcard journey through Miami, from the turn of the century into the 1940s. Enjoy your trip!

One

A Dream Comes True

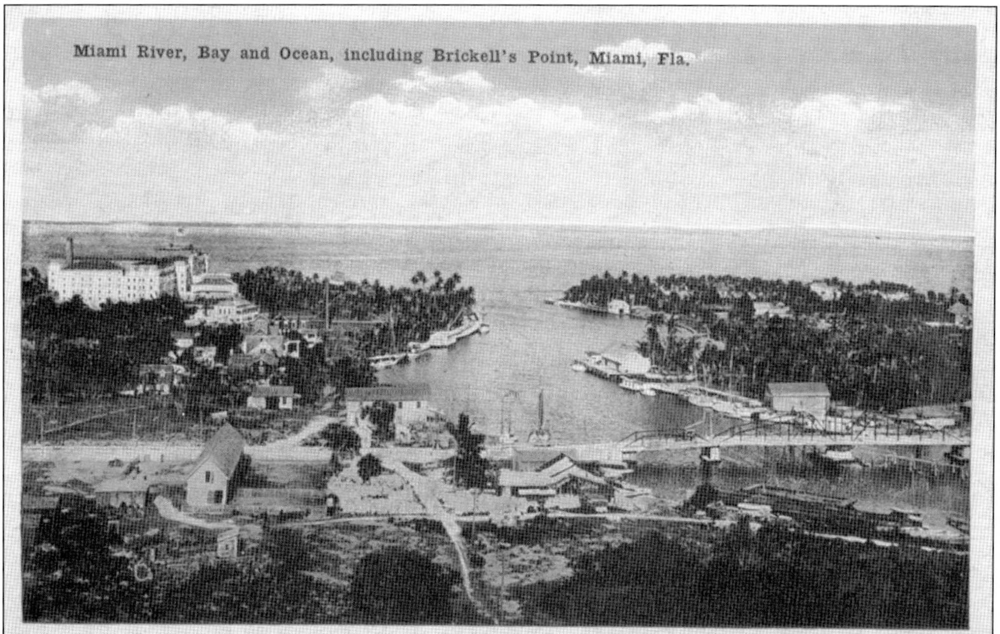

This turn-of-the-century view of Miami in its infancy shows the Avenue D (today's Miami Avenue) Bridge crossing the Miami River. At the mouth of the river on the north side, occupying the site of today's Dupont Plaza, is Henry Flagler's Royal Palm Hotel. Across the river on the south side is Brickell Point. (Published by E.C. Kropp.)

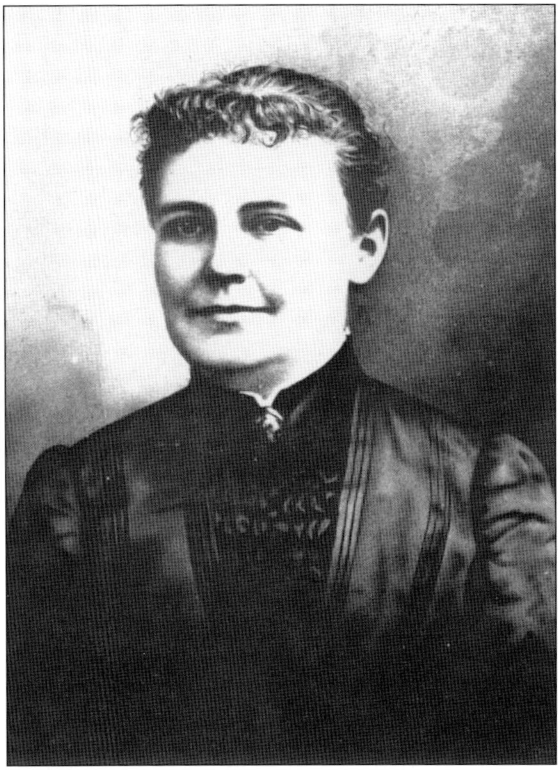

Julia Tuttle dreamed of creating a city on the shores of the Miami River. As the legend goes, when the freeze of 1894–1895 destroyed crops all over Florida, Mrs. Tuttle sent Henry Flagler orange blossoms to show that the Biscayne Bay area was unaffected. She convinced him to bring his railroad to the area and build a first-rate hotel. Julia Tuttle lived to see her dream come true. Miami was incorporated in 1896; however, the "Mother of Miami" died suddenly in 1898 at the age of 48. (Courtesy of Florida State Archives.)

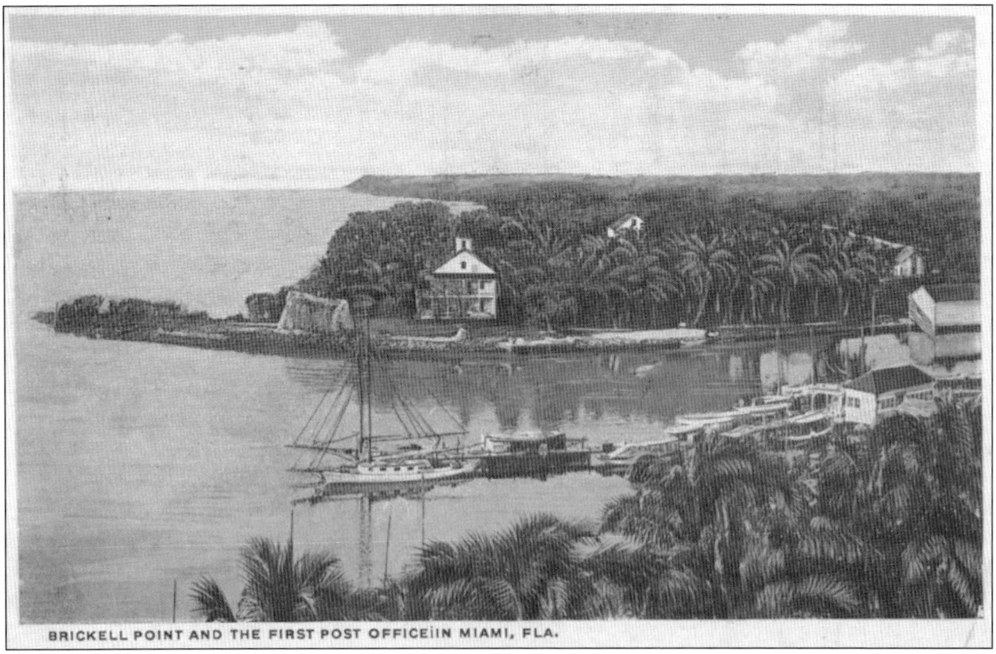

A guest looking across the Miami River from the Royal Palm Hotel in the early 1900s would have seen this view of the Brickell Trading Post and the first post office in Miami. (Published by Curt Teich.)

Henry Morrison Flagler brought his Florida East Coast Railroad to the Biscayne Bay area in 1896, laid out the streets for the new city, and opened his Royal Palm Hotel. Flagler built homes and a hospital for his employees; donated land for schools, clubs, and churches; and dredged a channel for ships in Biscayne Bay. The main business street in downtown Miami is named after him. Carl Fisher, another man of vision, built a monument in Flagler's honor on an island in Biscayne Bay. (Courtesy of Florida State Archives.)

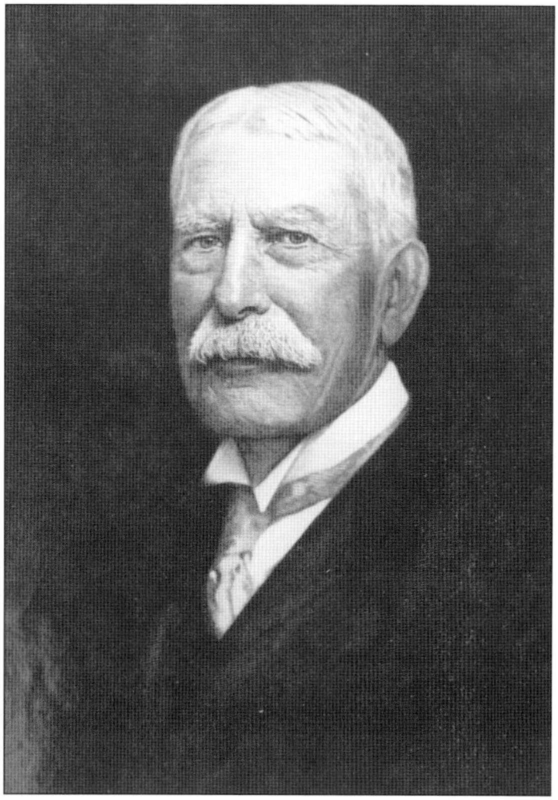

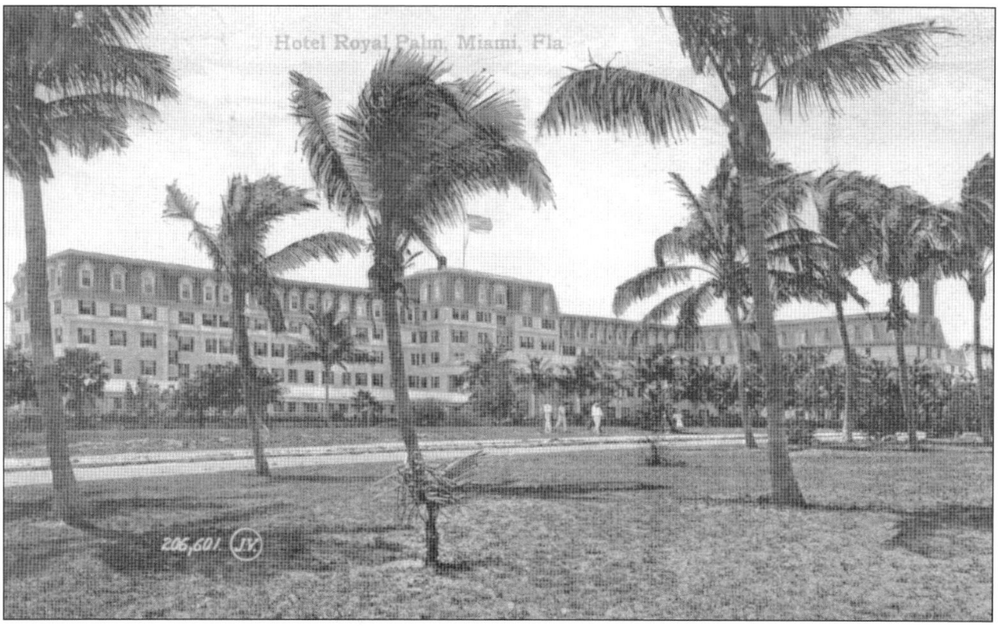

Henry Flagler built his magnificent Royal Palm Hotel on land donated by Julia Tuttle. The hotel, which contained 350 rooms and cost $750,000 to complete, opened in January 1897 for the winter season. (Published by Valentine & Sons.)

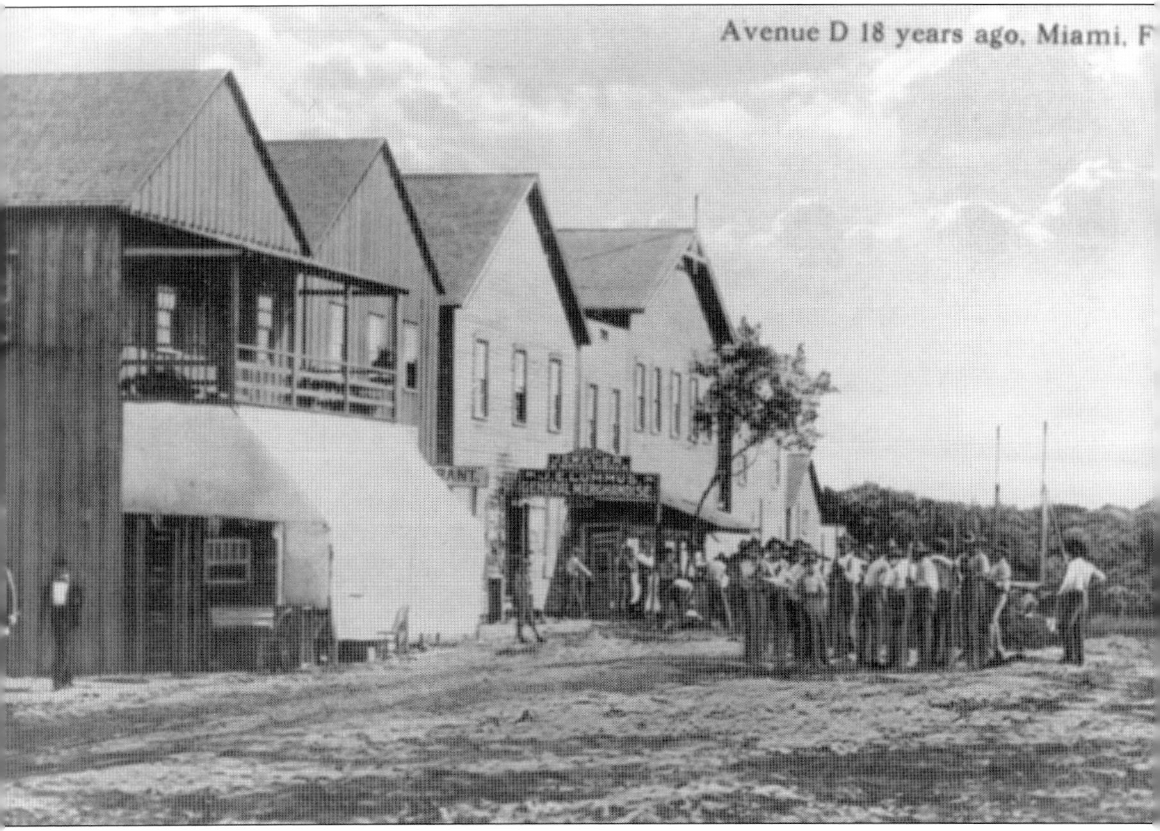

This early view of Avenue D contains a significant amount of Miami history. The two men on the far left belonged to Miami's "Tuxedo Club." Julia Tuttle built the long building shown that contained the J.E. Lummus General Merchandise Store. Mr. Lummus would become Miami's second mayor. The large group of men pictured on the right had accompanied John Sewell to Miami to build the Royal Palm Hotel. On July 28, 1896, at 2 p.m., they gathered upstairs in the Lobby Pool Hall (the building with the lightning rod). They joined a group that totaled 343 men and incorporated the city of Miami. (Courtesy of the Historical Museum of Southern Florida.)

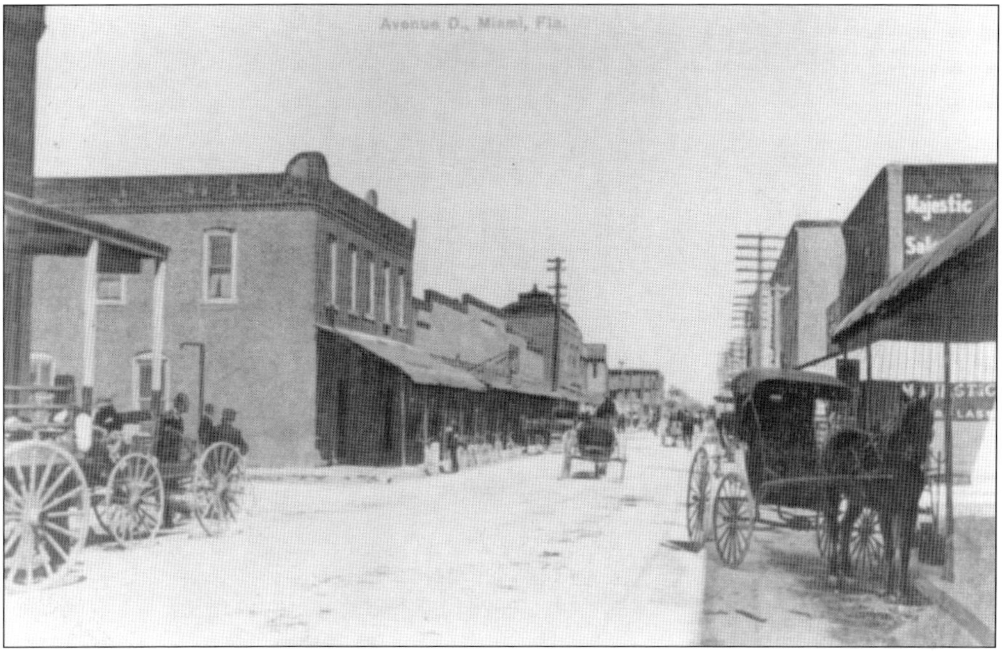

Avenue D was Miami's first street and the location of the first business district. A fire on Christmas Eve in 1896 destroyed most of the newly incorporated town. Merchants subsequently rebuilt on Twelfth Street, which was later renamed Flagler Street in honor of Henry Flagler. (Courtesy of the Historical Museum of Southern Florida.)

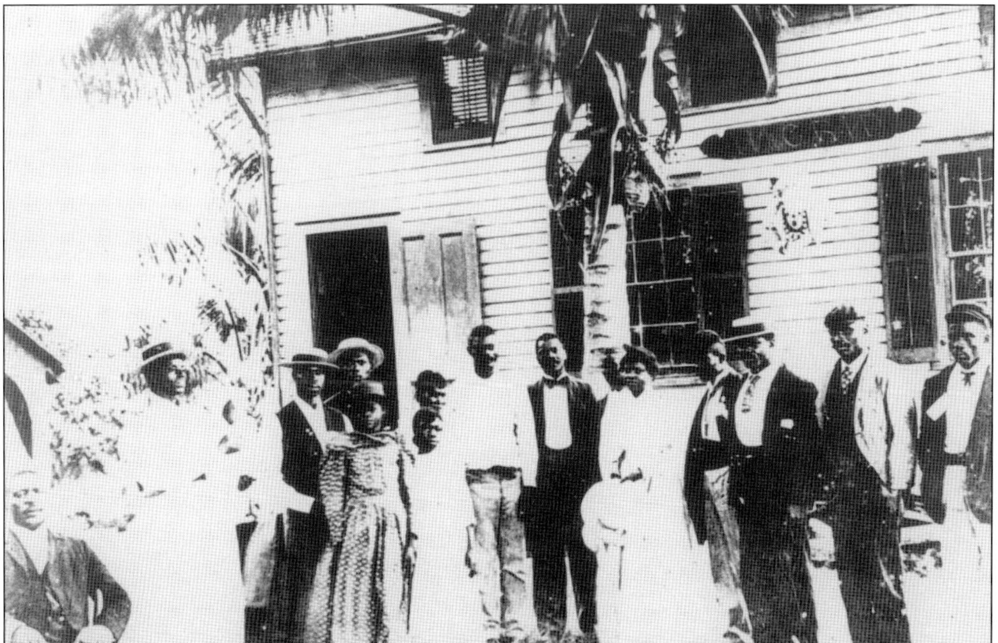

Commodore Ralph Munroe's boathouse was the setting for this photograph showing early Coconut Grove pioneers. The residents shown here, mostly Bahamians, worked at the Peacock Inn. (Courtesy of the Black Archives Foundation.)

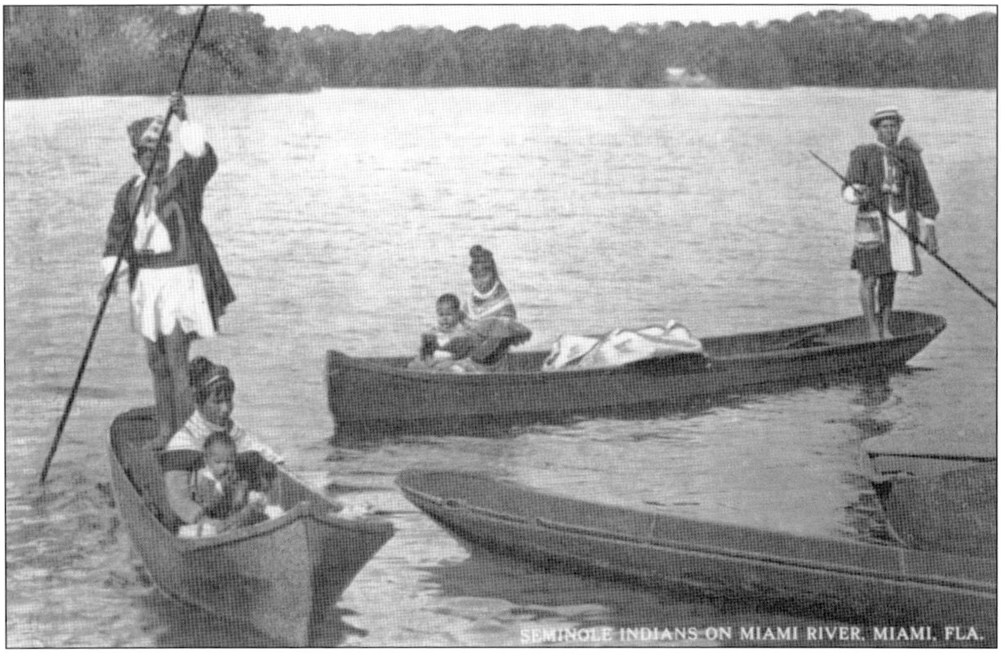

The Seminole Indians were regular visitors at the Brickell Trading Post, transporting goods for trade in their cypress canoes. (Courtesy of Florida State Archives.)

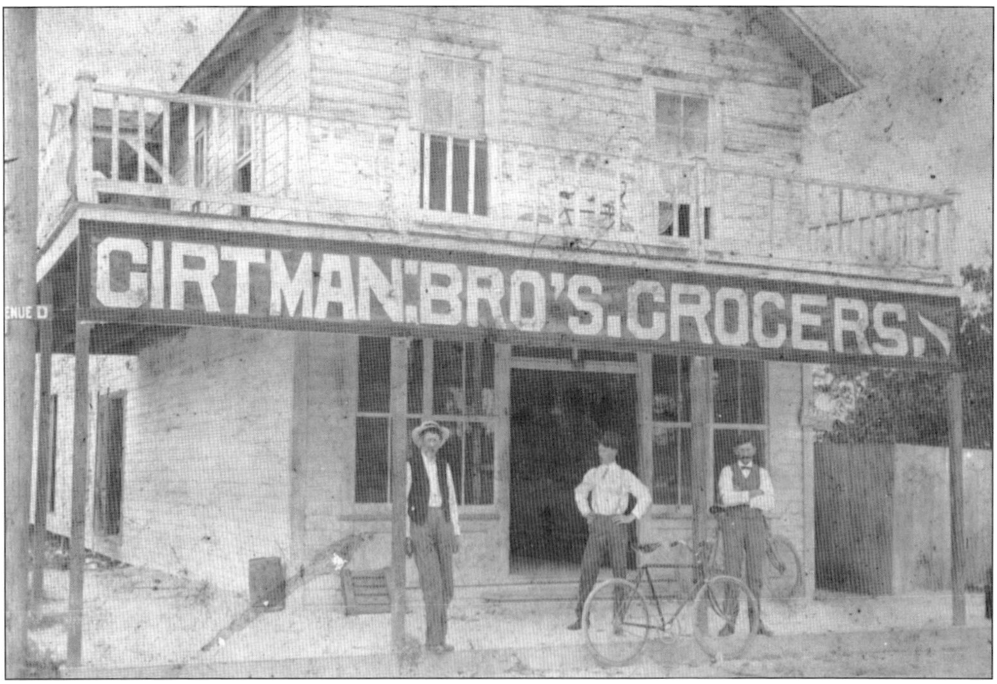

At the Girtman Brothers grocery store on Avenue D, Seminole Indians traded with their friend W.H. Girtman. James Girtman was responsible for the construction of LeJeune Road in 1901, where he built a home that still stands in the 1800 block. In 1912, James established a fur trading post with the Seminoles. (Courtesy of Florida State Archives.)

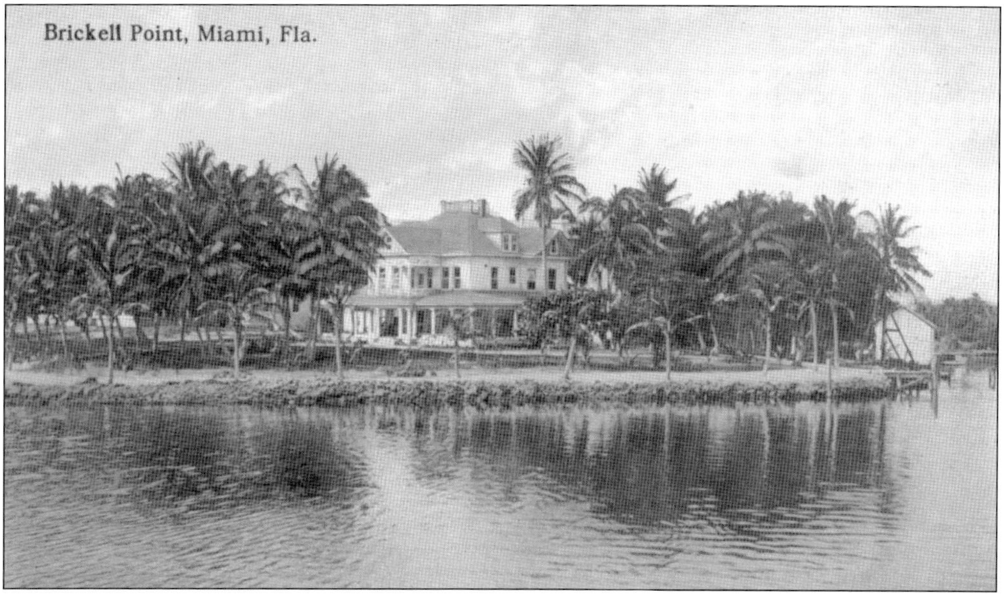

The Brickell family moved to Miami in 1879 and purchased all of the bayfront property from the Miami River to Coconut Grove. The Sheraton Biscayne Bay Hotel now occupies the site of their home on Brickell Point, where they raised their seven children. (Published by J.N. Chamberlain.)

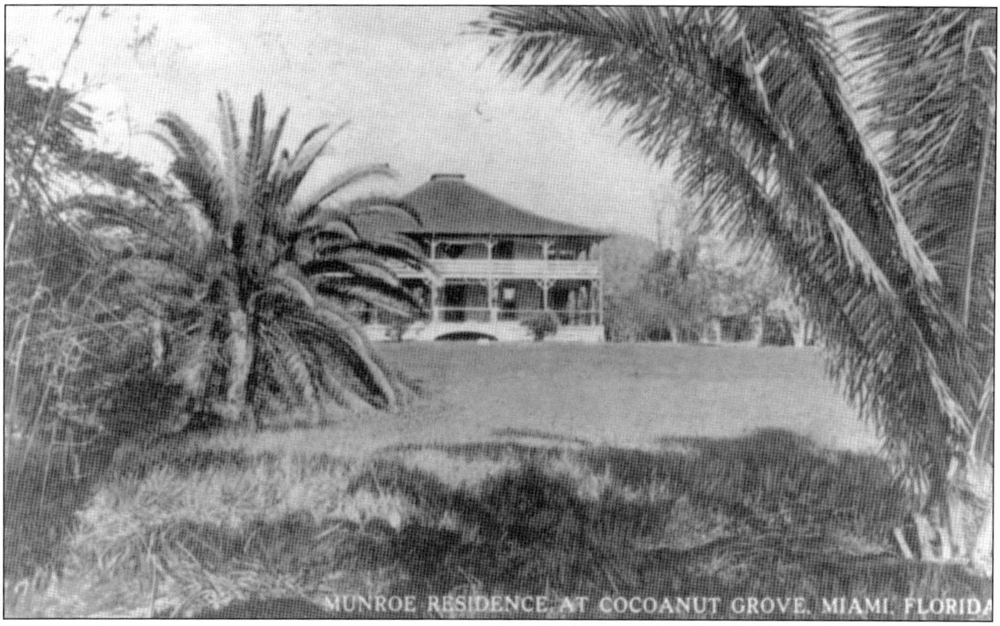

Like the Brickells, Commodore Ralph Munroe knew a great view when he saw one. The skilled boatbuilder built his home, "The Barnacle," in 1891 overlooking Biscayne Bay. The home was originally a one-story cottage, set off the ground on treated posts. In 1908, Munroe raised the entire house on stilts and added a new first floor underneath. A wing was added for his library a few years later. The Barnacle is now a state historic site. (Courtesy of the Historical Museum of Southern Florida.)

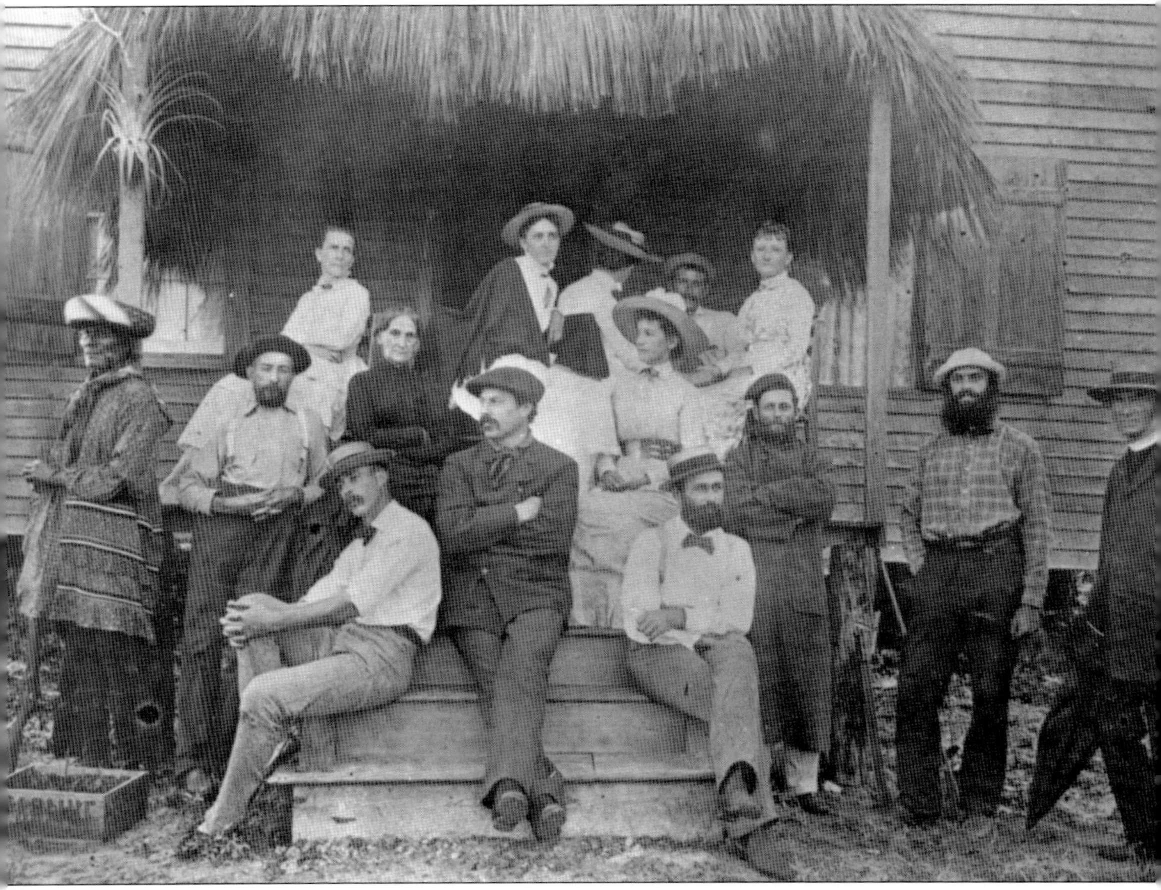

Coconut Grove residents and visitors were photographed during the winter of 1886–1887 in front of Kirk Munroe's house, "The Scrububs." Pictured from left to right are (front row) adventure story author Kirk Munroe; Count Jean d'Hedouville; and Thomas A. Hine; (middle row) Dr. Tiger, son of Seminole Chief Tigertail; Ralph Munroe, who donated the land for Union Church; Mrs. E.P. Brown; Miss ? Brown; Charles E. Stowe, son of Harriet Beecher Stowe; Count James L. Nugent; and E.P. Brown; (back row) Mrs. Thomas Munroe; Miss Flora McFarlane, Grove school teacher and founder of the Housekeeper's Club; Mrs. Kirk Munroe, who formed a literary society called the Pine Needle Club that resulted in the first Coconut Grove library; Edward A. Hine; and Mrs. Thomas A. Hine. (Courtesy of Florida State Archives.)

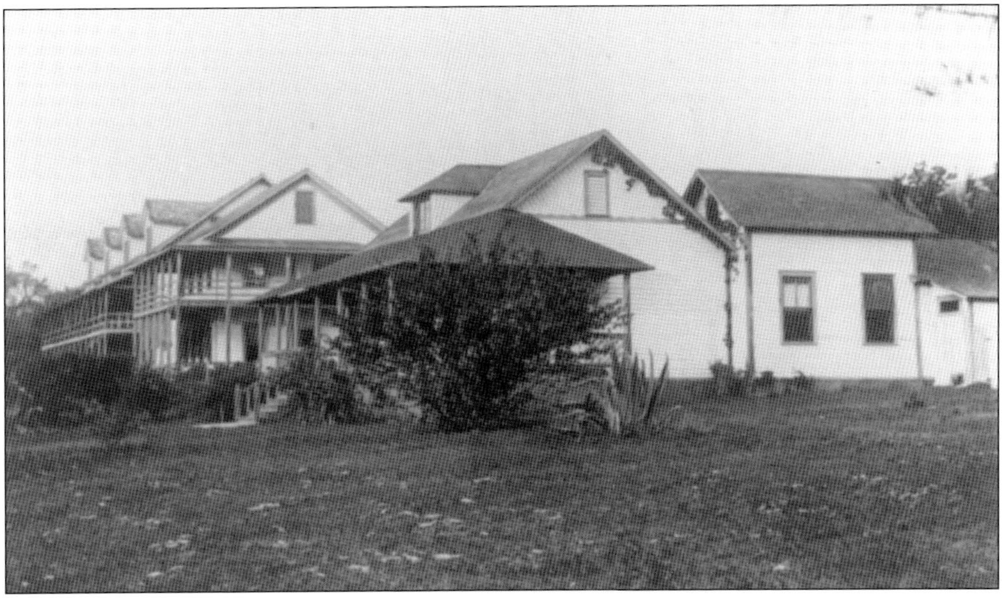

Ralph Munroe's enthusiasm for the area convinced the Charles Peacock family to build a hotel on the site of today's Peacock Park. The hotel opened as the Bayview House in 1882 and was the first hotel built in the Miami area. A few years later, the Peacock family constructed additional buildings and renamed it the Peacock Inn. The inn later became the Lake Placid School for boys. The building was torn down in 1926. (Courtesy of the Historical Museum of Southern Florida.)

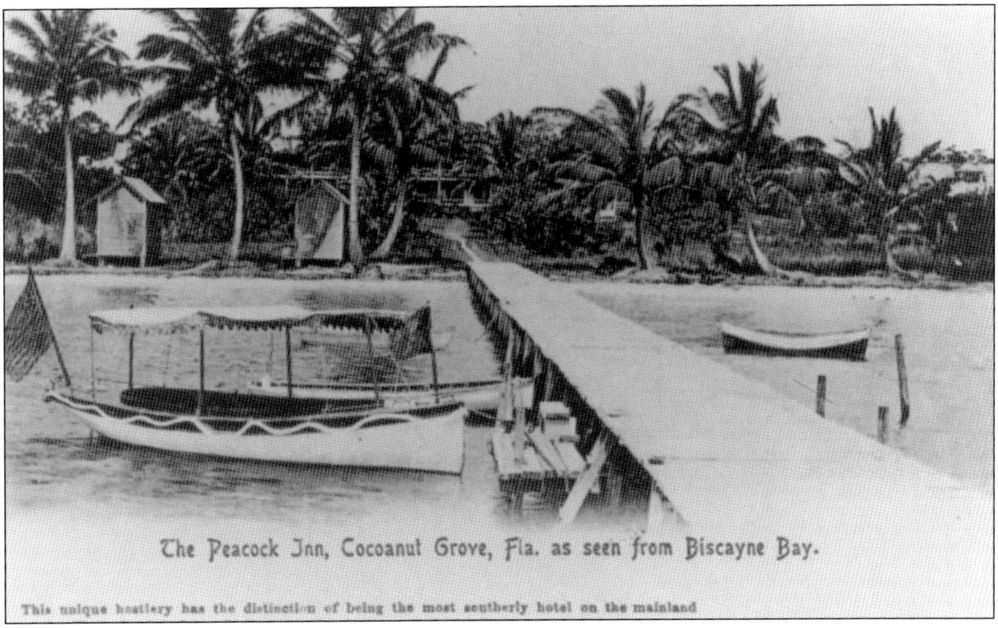

When first opened in the late 1800s, the Peacock Inn was the most southerly hotel in the continental United States. Nestled in a grove of palm trees, the hotel provided guests with beautiful views of Biscayne Bay. (Courtesy of the Historical Museum of Southern Florida.)

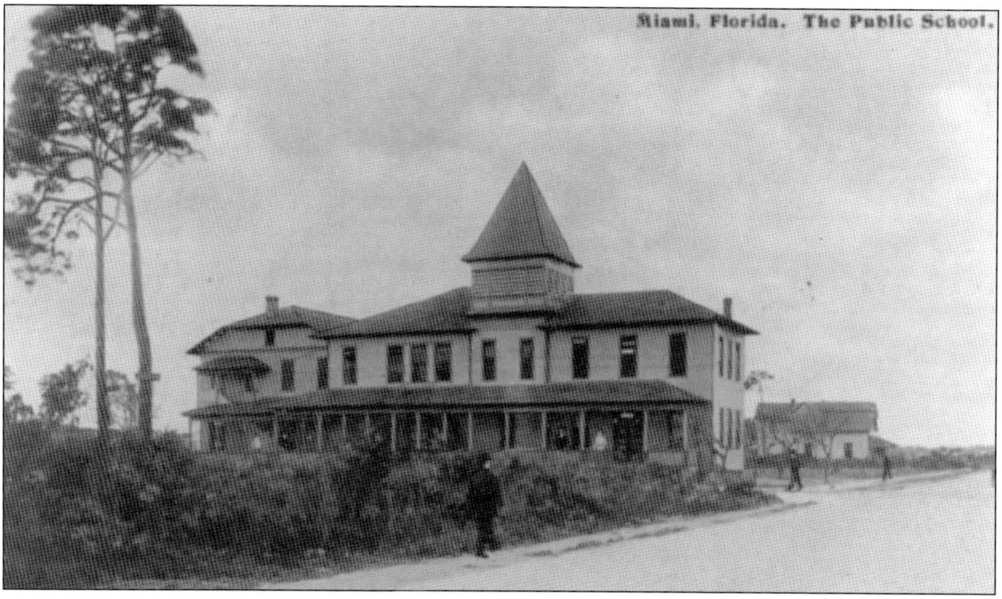

Miami's first public school, built in 1897, was a wood-frame building with four rooms. By 1904, a wing was added on the left to accommodate both high school and elementary school students. The school was located at Ninth Street and Avenue C (today's Northeast First Avenue and Third Street). In 1904, Miami had its first graduating class, made up of three graduates—Miss Grace Rader, Miss Florence Stephens, and Mr. Ralph Rader. (Courtesy of Historical Museum of Southern Florida.)

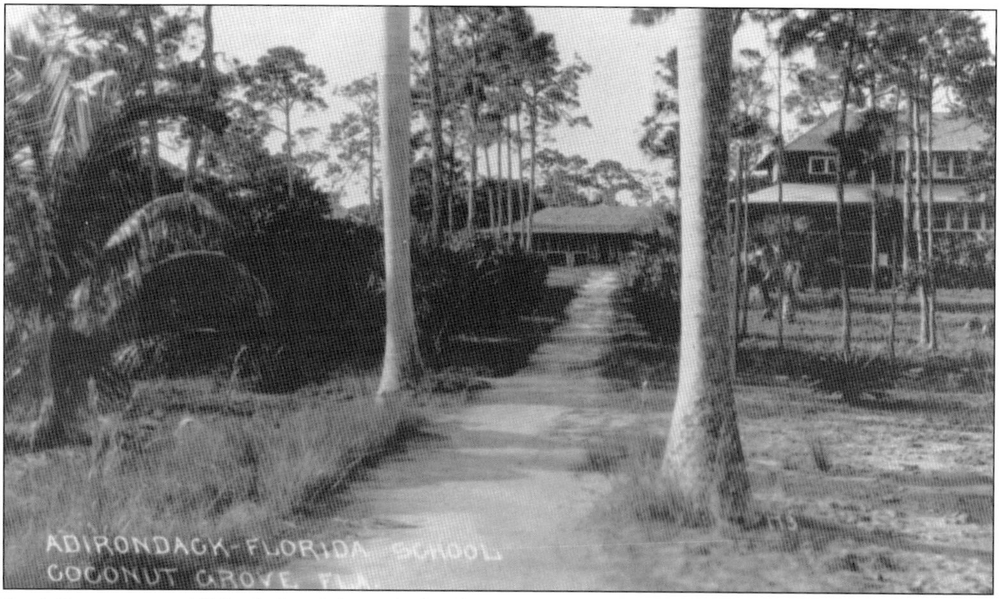

Paul Ransom established the Adirondack-Florida School with the help of Kirk Munroe. Mr. Munroe (no relation to Commodore Ralph Munroe) was a well-known author of adventure stories. The private boys school held summer classes in the Adirondacks and winter classes in Coconut Grove. The school eventually became the Ransom-Everglades School. (Courtesy of Historical Museum of Southern Florida.)

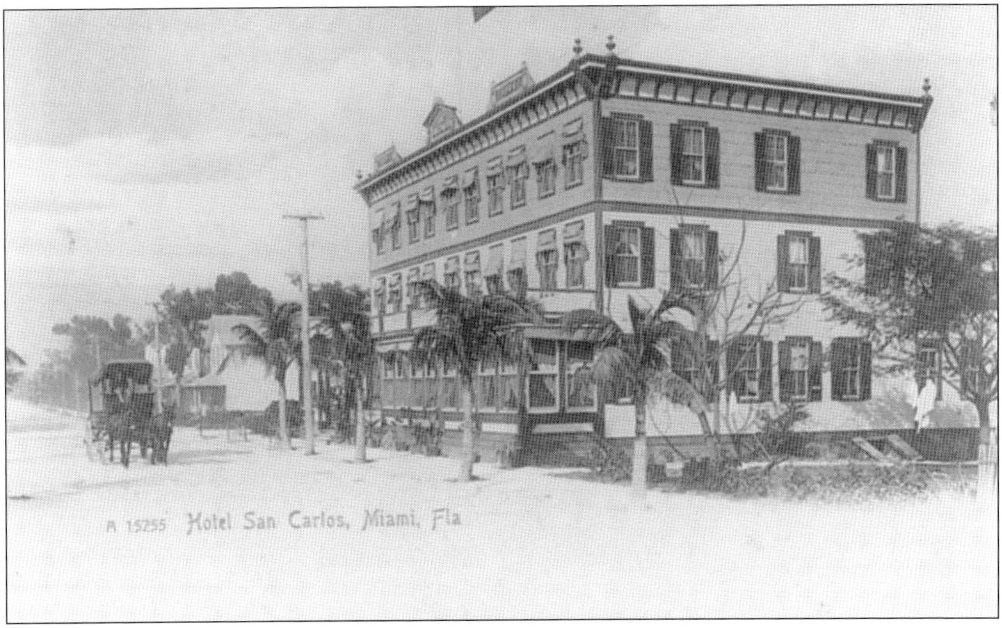

The Hotel San Carlos, run by Mr. Gus A. Muller, was named after his son Charles. Located at Avenue B and Eleventh Street, it was a favorite of visitors from Cuba. (Courtesy of Historical Museum of Southern Florida.)

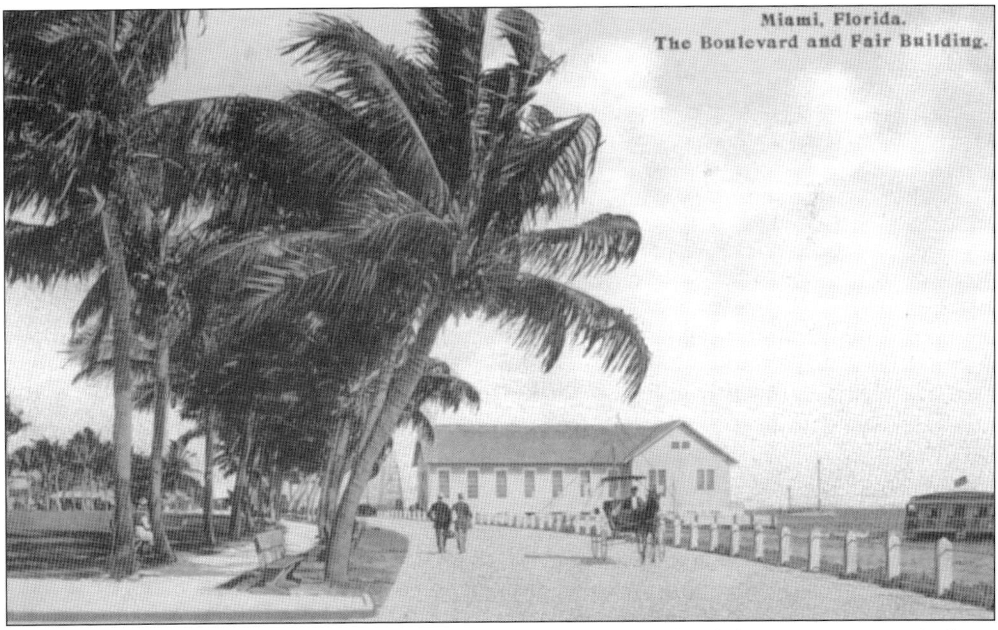

A driver and his carriage travel along the bay on the Boulevard. Behind the carriage is Horticulture Hall, more commonly called the Fair Building. The hall, a gift to the city from Henry Flagler, was built in 1903 and painted "Flagler yellow" to match the Royal Palm Hotel. It was the site of the county fair, social and cultural events, and held Miami's first library for several years. (Published by Hugh C. Leighton Co.)

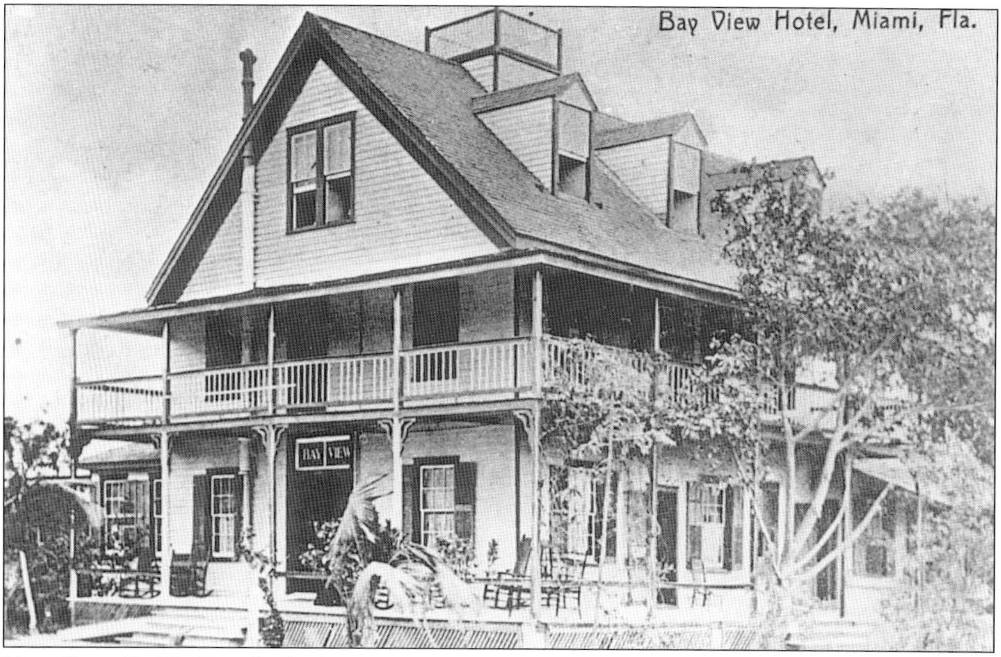

Mrs. Cornelia H. Keys built the Bayview Hotel in 1892 on Lemon Avenue in Lemon City. The hotel was moved by barge to Sixth Street in Miami in 1899. Lemon City was located along Biscayne Bay near today's Northeast Sixty-second Street. The vibrant community was the connection to the rest of Florida in 1892 when a road was cleared from Lantana to Lemon City. The weekly stagecoach run retired the "Barefoot Mailman," who previously walked the beaches to deliver the mail. (Courtesy of Florida State Archives.)

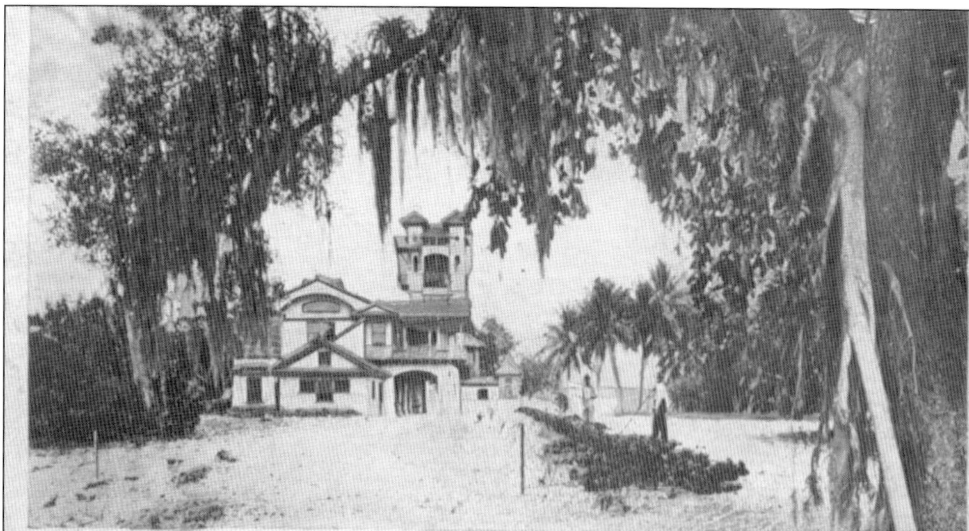

The Tee House Plantation, home of William B. Ogden, was located in Lemon City. Mr. Ogden was the owner of the Ye Wee Tappie Tavern and the Biscayne Bay Company, a fruit growing and shipping company. His 30-acre plantation was considered one of the finest grapefruit groves in the country at that time. (Published by Crandon-Hunter Co.)

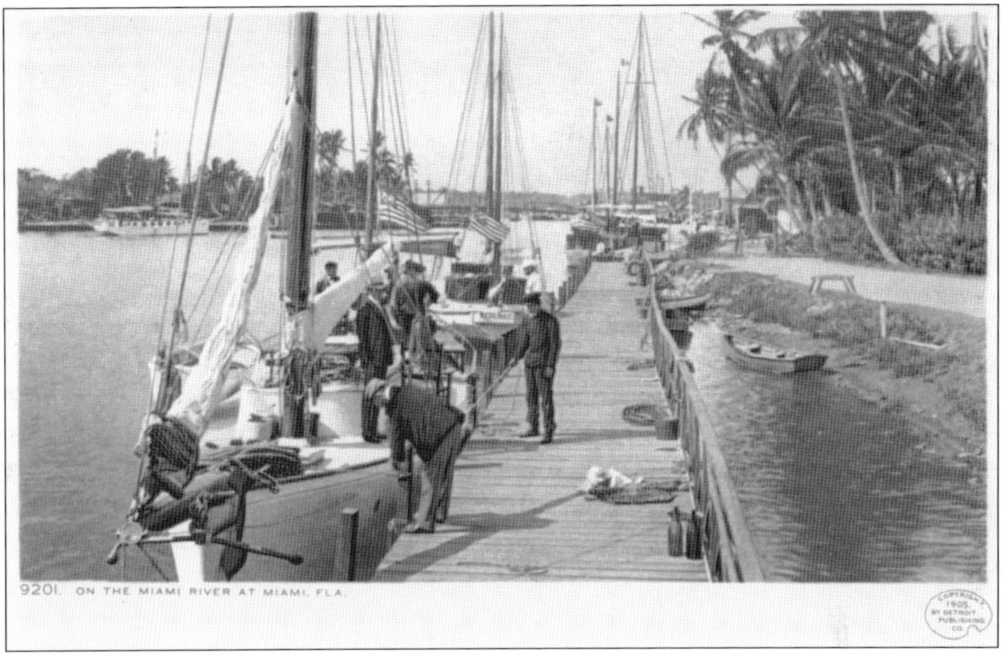

Sailing quickly became a popular pastime of Miami residents and visitors. Sailboats line the dock in this 1905 view of the Miami River. (Published by Detroit Publishing Co.)

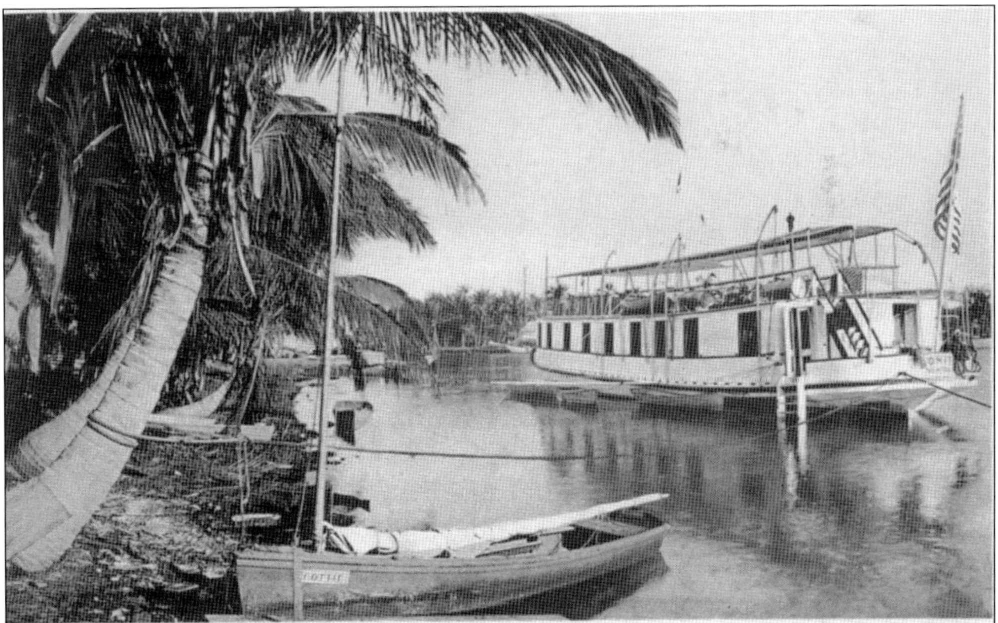

Houseboating also became popular along the Miami River because of the close proximity to the new city's "downtown." The sailboat in the foreground has the name "Tuttle" on it and sits along the shore of the Tuttle property. (Published by Detroit Publishing Co.)

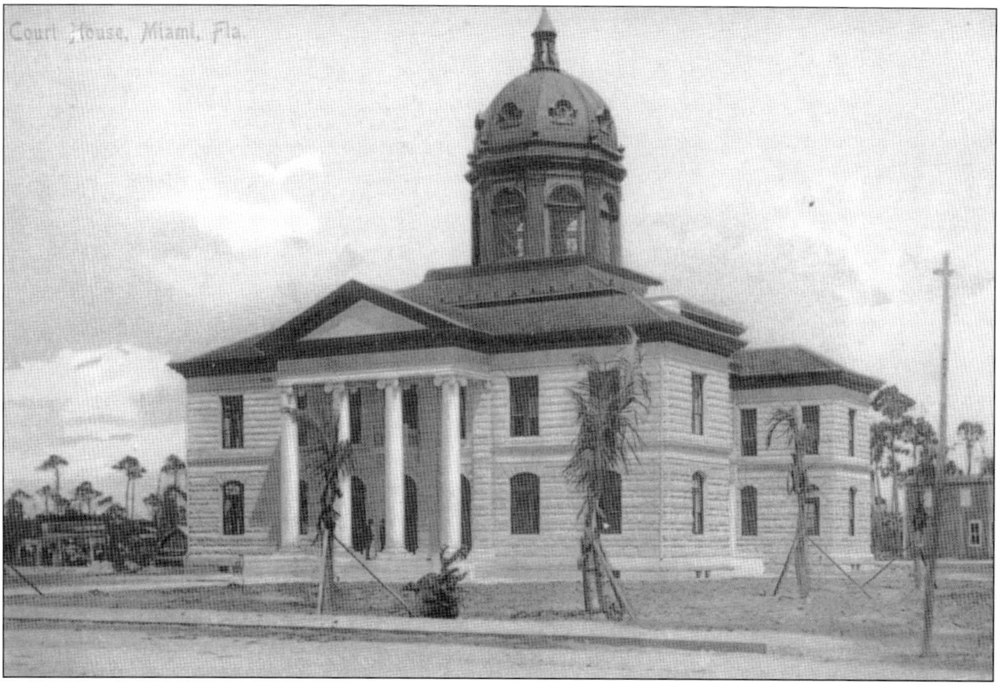

This Dade County Courthouse building was erected in 1904 on West Flagler Street. In 1925, a new 26-story courthouse (shown on page 72) was literally built around this structure. After the county records were transferred, the smaller 1904 building was dismantled. (Published by the Rotograph Co.)

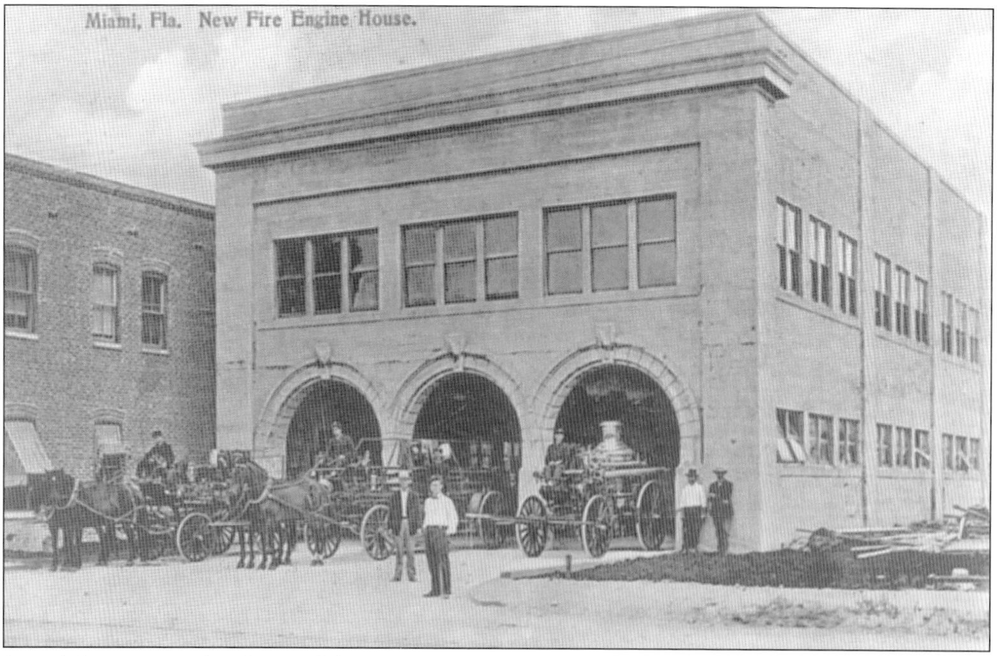

Proud firemen stand in front of the new engine house located on Twelfth Street (today's Flagler Street). (Courtesy of Historical Museum of Southern Florida.)

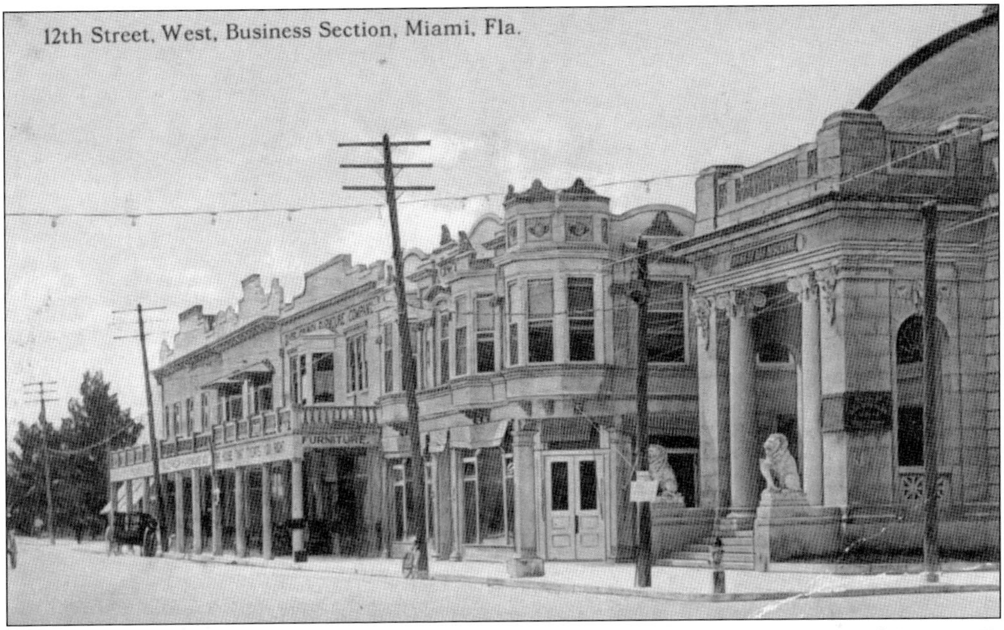

Statues of lions frame the entrance to the Bank of Bay Biscayne on the corner of Avenue D and Twelfth Street. Further down, a horse and carriage are parked in front of the Dade County Furniture Company. (Published by J.N. Chamberlain.)

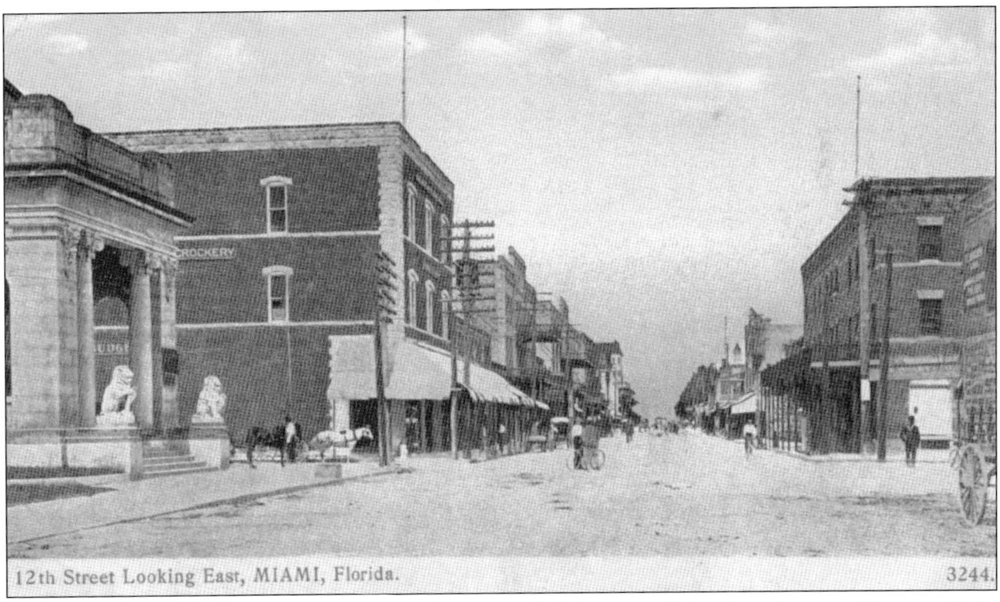

A view of Twelfth Street looking east shows probably one of the last times traffic was light enough for friends to chat in the middle of one of downtown Miami's busiest intersections. The men are shown standing in what is now the intersection of Flagler Street and Miami Avenue. (Published By A.C. Bosselman & Co.)

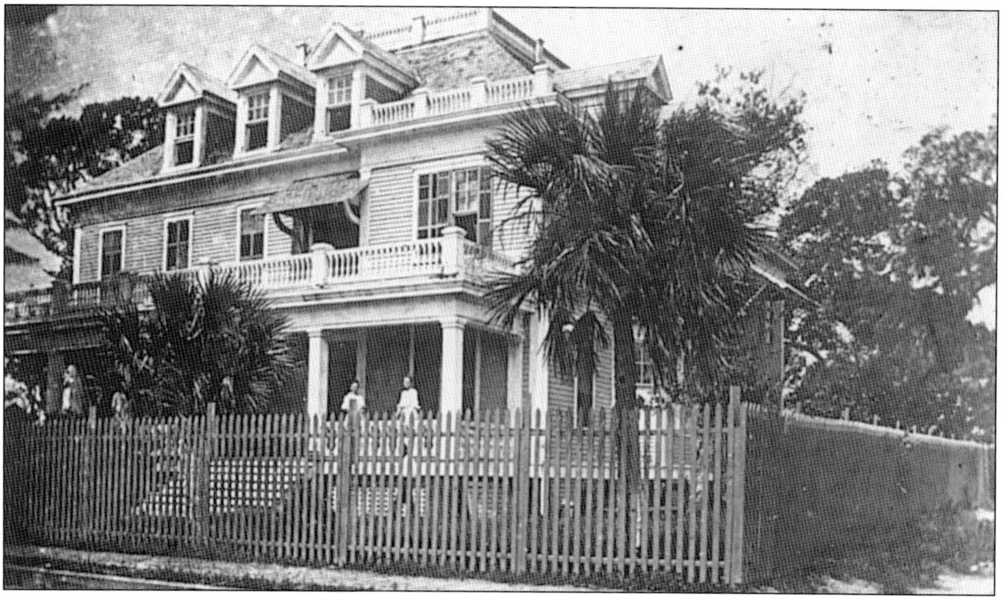

Henry Flagler built the Florida East Coast (FEC) Hospital for FEC Railway employees. Located at 300 Boulevard, it was painted "Flagler yellow," liked the Flagler hotels, and administered by Dr. James M. Jackson. In 1909, one week of hospitalization at FEC was $17.50. A patient could have minor surgery for $5 or major surgery for $10. The FEC was no longer needed once the railroad extension was completed, and the property was sold to Mrs. Charlotte Baldwin and Willis W. Hall. They opened a private school named Baldwin-Hall. (Courtesy of Florida State Archives.)

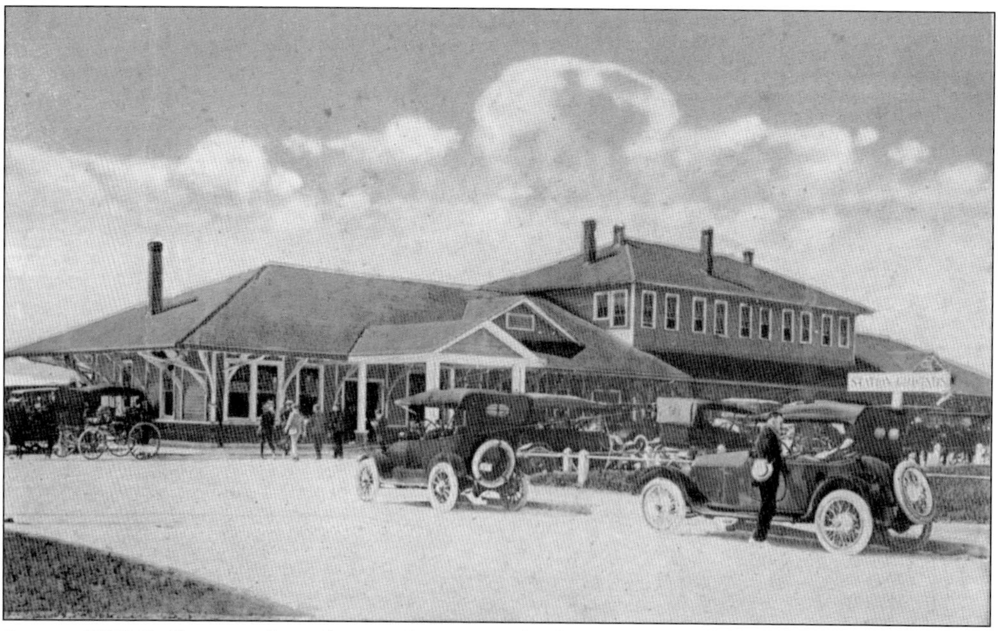

A new FEC Railway station, shown above, was built in 1912 just west of the Dade County Courthouse. This card also provides a good view of the automobiles of the time. (Published by Crandon-Hunter Co.)

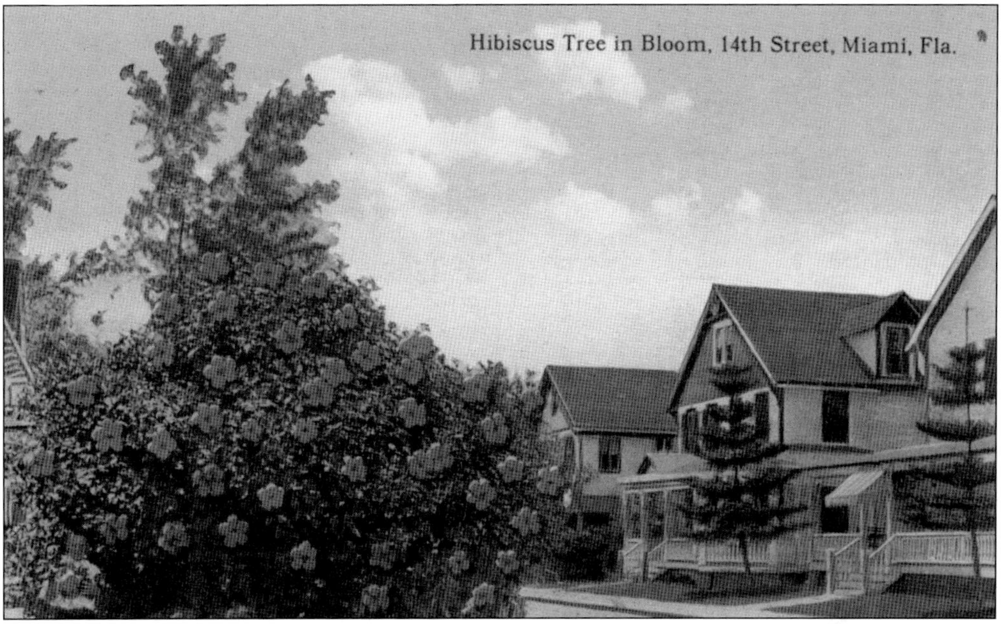

A hibiscus tree stands in full bloom on Fourteenth Street (today's Southeast Second Street) where Henry Flagler built the Royal Palm Cottages for his employees. The two-and-a-half-story wooden homes with front porches rented from $15 to $22 a month, and sold for $1,200 to $3,000. The only remaining Royal Palm Cottage has been restored by the city of Miami and moved to Fort Dallas Park. (Published By H. & W.B. Drew.)

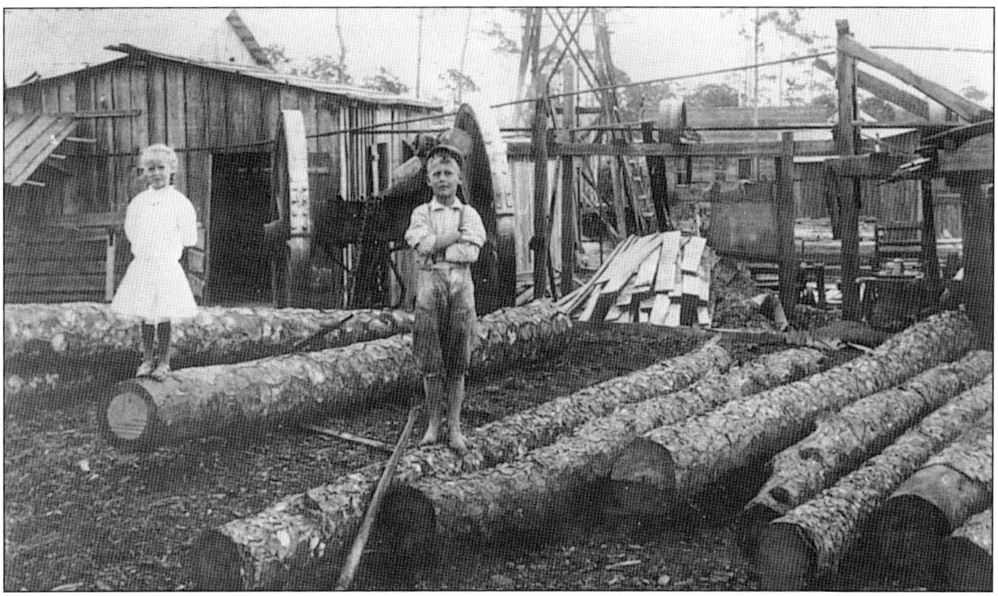

Alfred B. Hurst operated a sawmill in the Piney Woods area (Northeast Second Avenue at 103rd Street). The sawmill supplied ties for the extension of the FEC Railway. Hurst's daughter May and son John stand on the logs in this *c.* 1908 photograph. (Courtesy of Florida State Archives.)

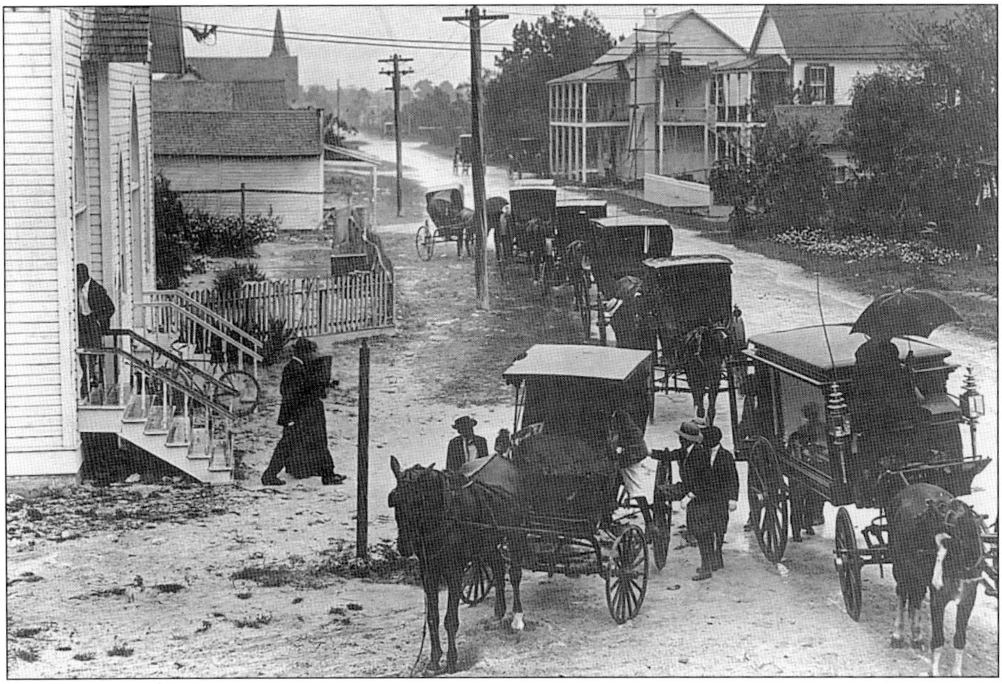

Mourners prepare to join a turn-of-the-century funeral procession at Mt. Zion Church in the Overtown section of Miami. (Courtesy of the Black Archives Foundation.)

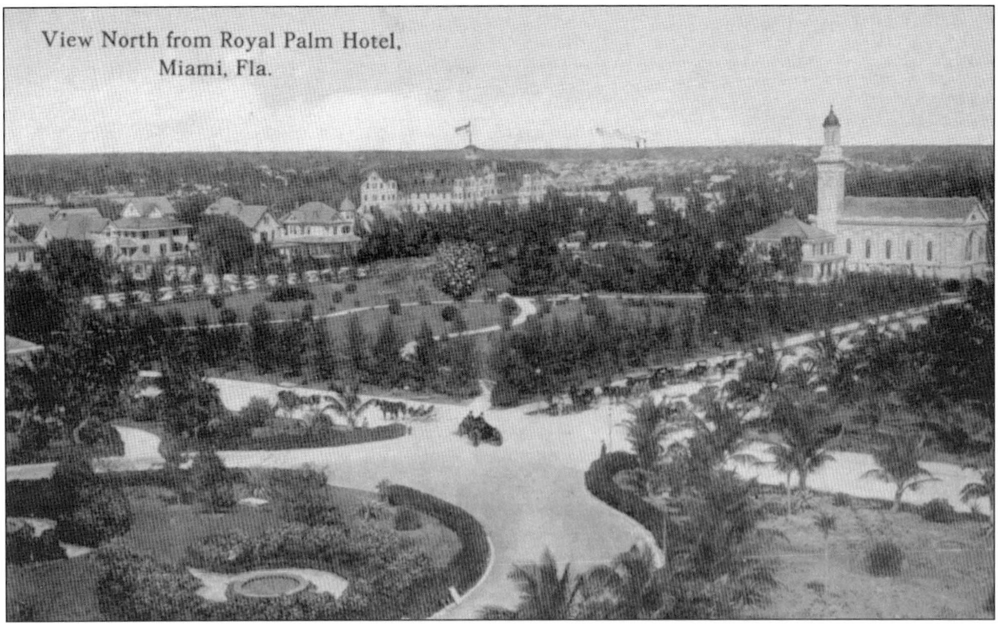

This view from the Royal Palm Hotel shows drivers and their carriages "staged" along Royal Palm Boulevard (today's Southeast Third Avenue), waiting for passengers from the hotel. The First Presbyterian Church and parsonage are shown at the far right. In the distance, with a flag on the roof, is the popular Halcyon Hotel. (Published by J.N. Chamberlain.)

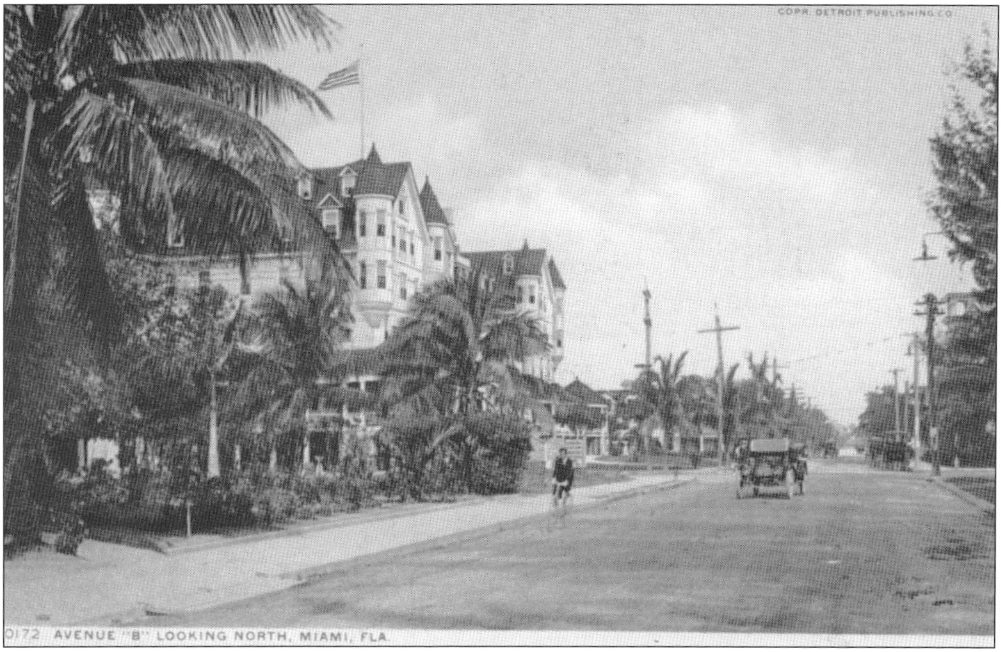

A motorist and a bicyclist pass the Halcyon Hotel in this early view of Avenue B looking north. (Published by Detroit Publishing Co.)

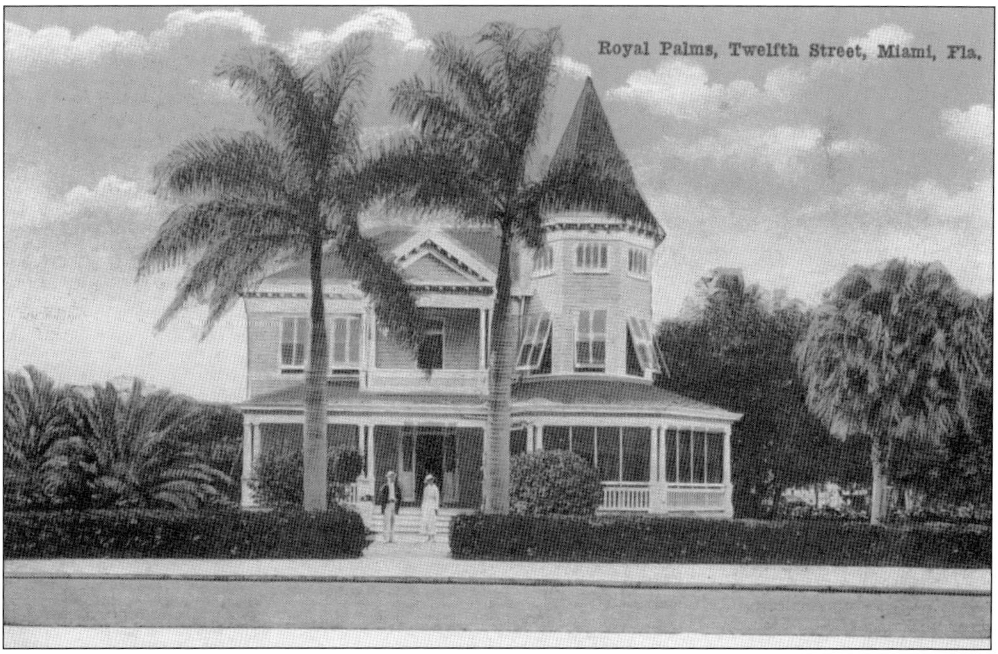

Two stately royal palms grace the entrance to this lovely home in the residential section of Twelfth Street (today's Flagler Street). (Published by E.C. Kropp Co.)

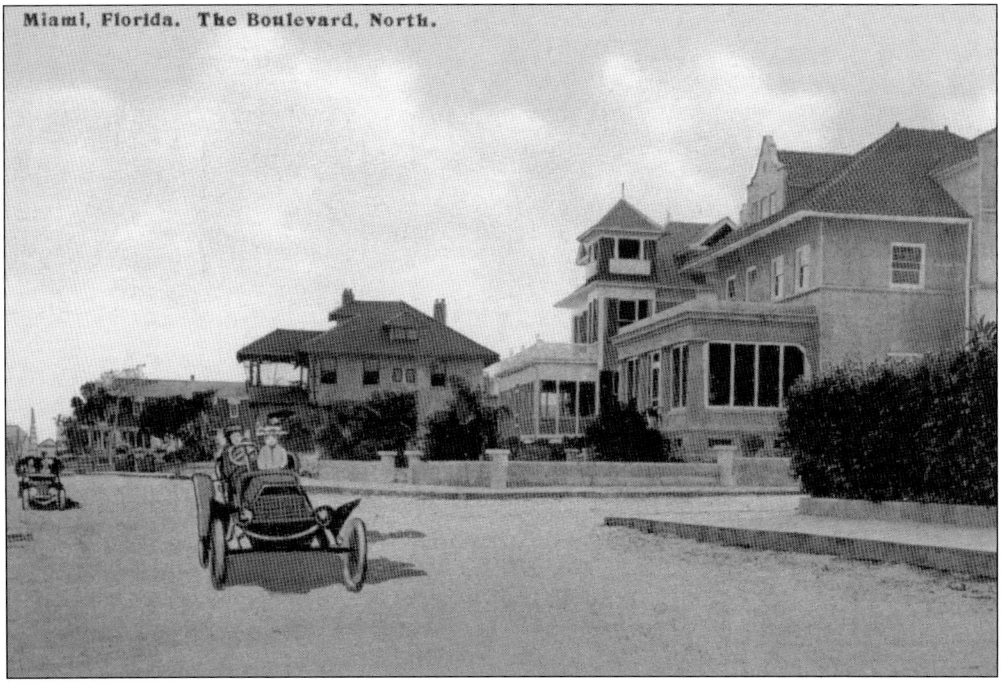

Traffic was light along the north end of the Boulevard in the early 1900s. The first speed limits were established in 1906—8 miles per hour on a straightaway and 5 miles per hour on curves. (Published by Hugh C. Leighton Co.)

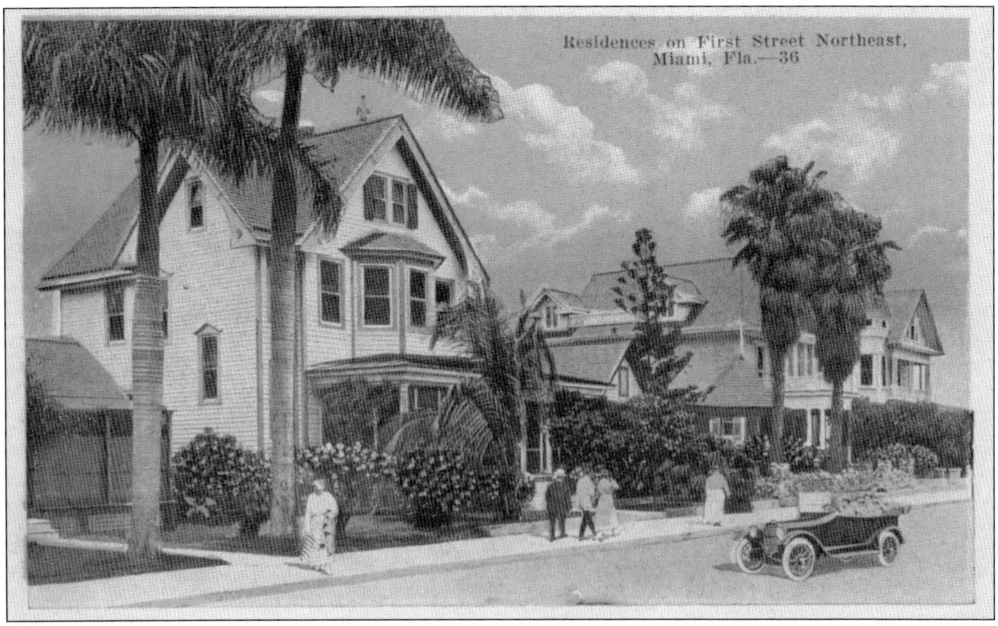

As Miami continued to grow, neighborhoods developed for year-round residents, such as this one on First Street Northeast. (Published by E.C. Kropp Co.)

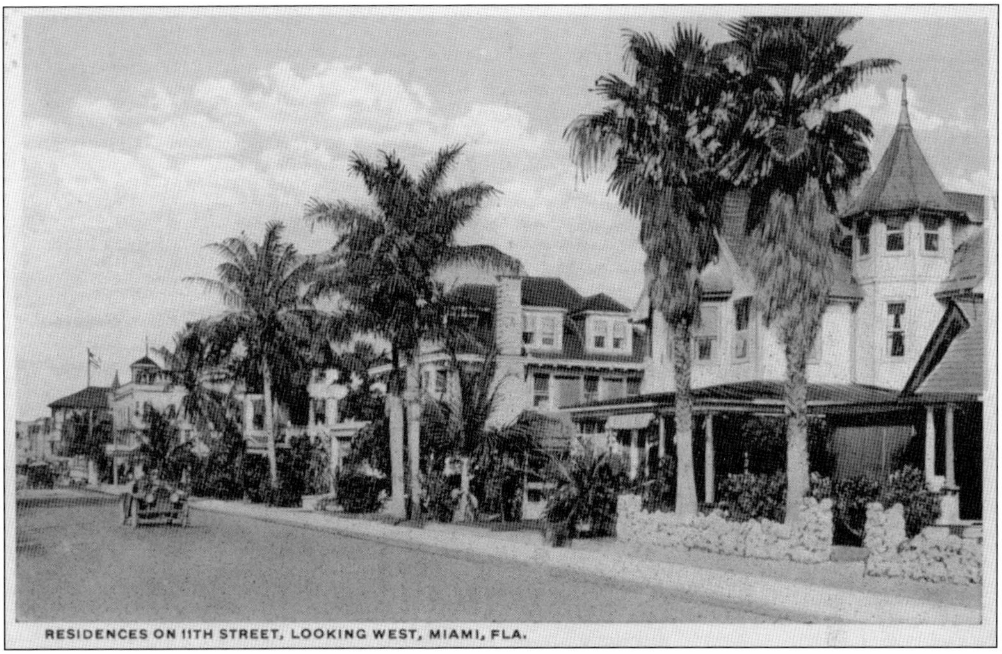

Palm trees line the sidewalk on Eleventh Street, known today as First Street. Owners of spacious homes frequently rented rooms to Northern visitors escaping the winter weather. (Published by H. & W.B. Drew Co.)

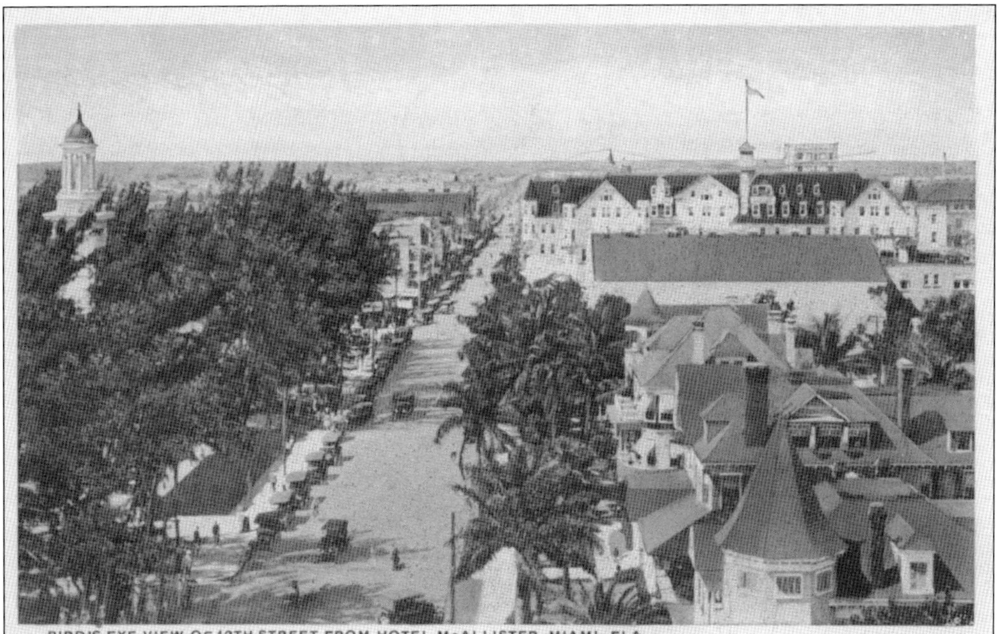

Looking out on Twelfth Street from the Hotel McAllister, one sees the turreted roof of Mr. Glen C. Frissell's home immediately to the right. The Halcyon Hotel can be seen in the distance, and the steeple of the First Presbyterian Church stands above the trees to the left. (Published by H. & W.B. Drew Co.)

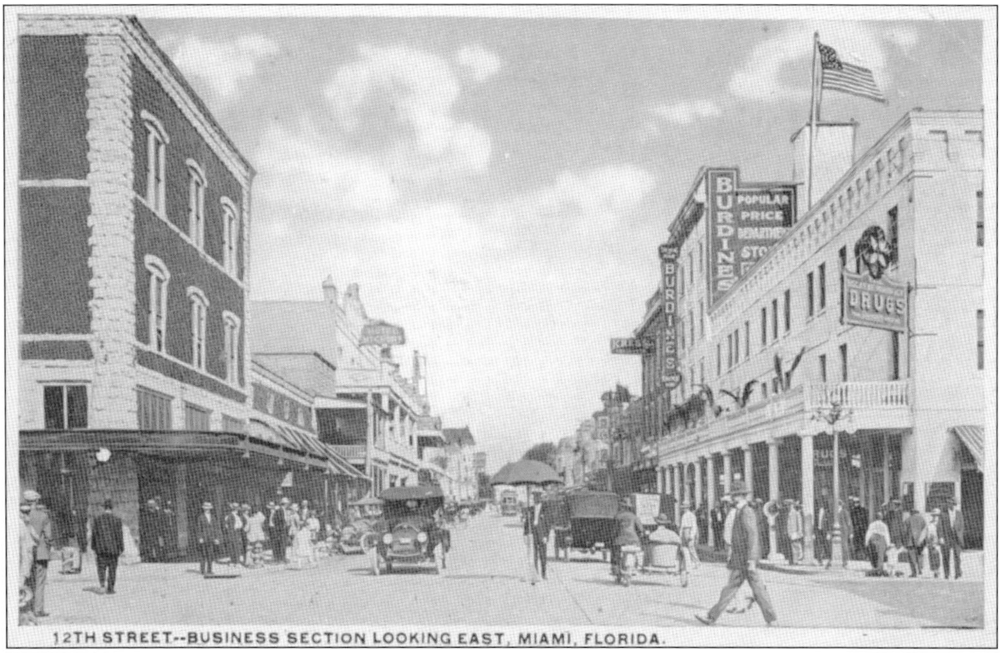

An umbrella-covered stand offers a policeman relief from the hot Florida sun in this *c.* 1920 view of Twelfth Street. Biscayne Pharmacy and Burdines Department Store are on the right. (Published by Crandon-Hunter Co.)

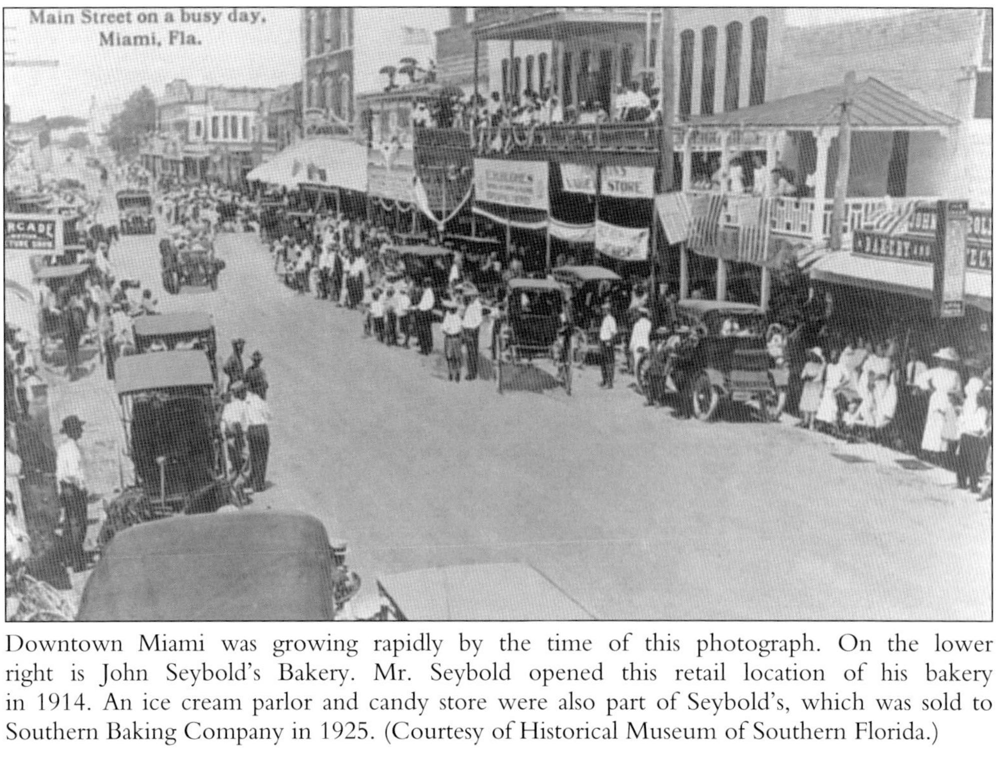

Downtown Miami was growing rapidly by the time of this photograph. On the lower right is John Seybold's Bakery. Mr. Seybold opened this retail location of his bakery in 1914. An ice cream parlor and candy store were also part of Seybold's, which was sold to Southern Baking Company in 1925. (Courtesy of Historical Museum of Southern Florida.)

Two

Early Hotels and Tourism

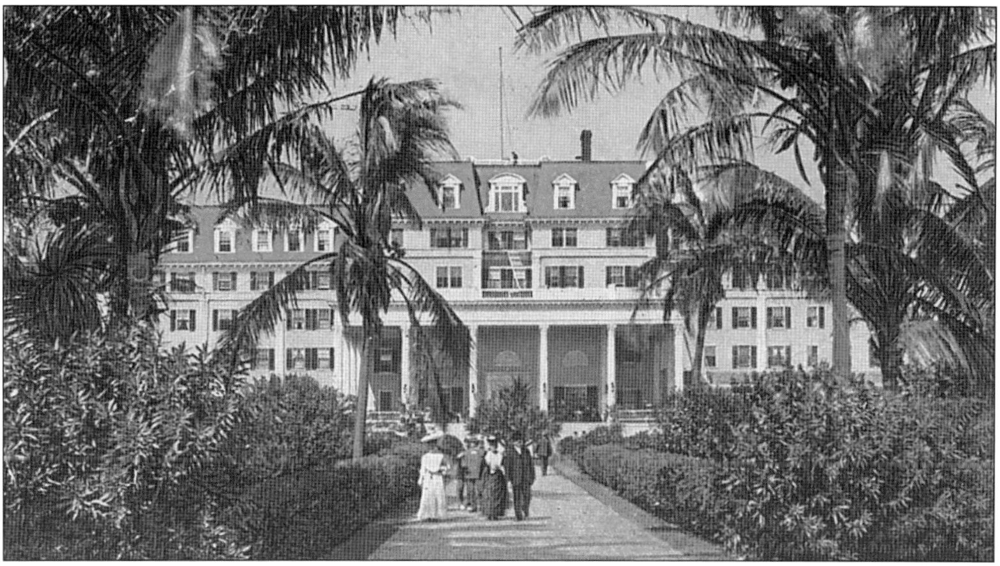

Guests stroll along the beautifully landscaped walk in front of the Royal Palm Hotel in this 1907 postcard. The hotel, painted "Flagler yellow" with green trim, opened in January 1897 for the winter season. It had 350 rooms and 200 baths, a grand ballroom, and a dining room that accommodated over 500 people. Rocking-chair verandas were in demand by guests who wanted to sit and enjoy the warm breezes, and the Royal Palm's 578-foot-long veranda overlooking the bay was the answer. The Royal Palm's importance in the development of Miami was substantial—its construction supplied jobs during the city's infancy, its luxurious accommodations attracted visitors, and its 30-year operation offered more employment. The hotel was declared a fire hazard and torn down in June of 1930, marking the end of an era. (Published by Detroit Publishing Co.)

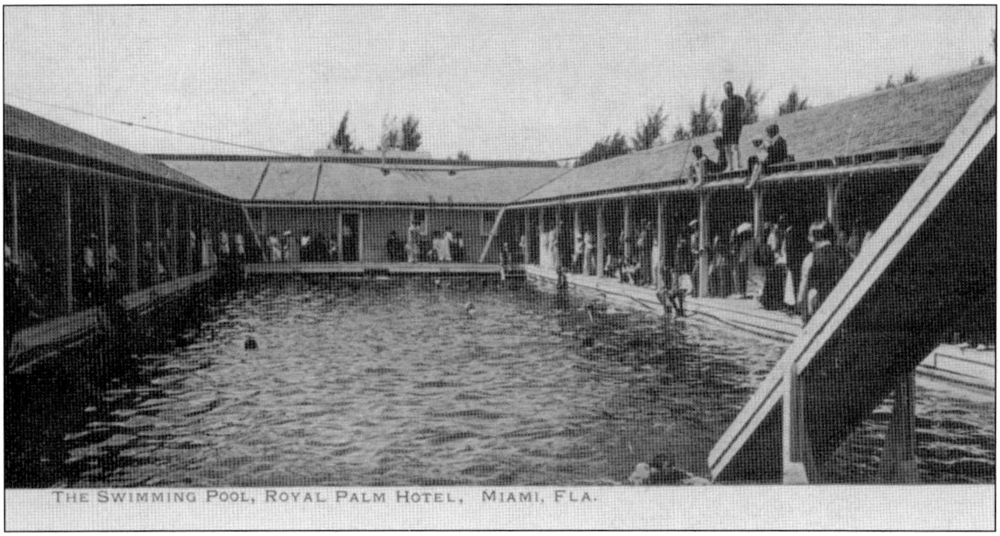

In 1898, Miami's first swimming pool opened at the Royal Palm Hotel. The 40-foot-wide and 150-foot-long pool was filled with salt water pumped in from Biscayne Bay. During the summer off-season, local residents were allowed to use the pool for a fee of 25¢ for adults and 15¢ for children. (Published by E.C. Kropp Co.)

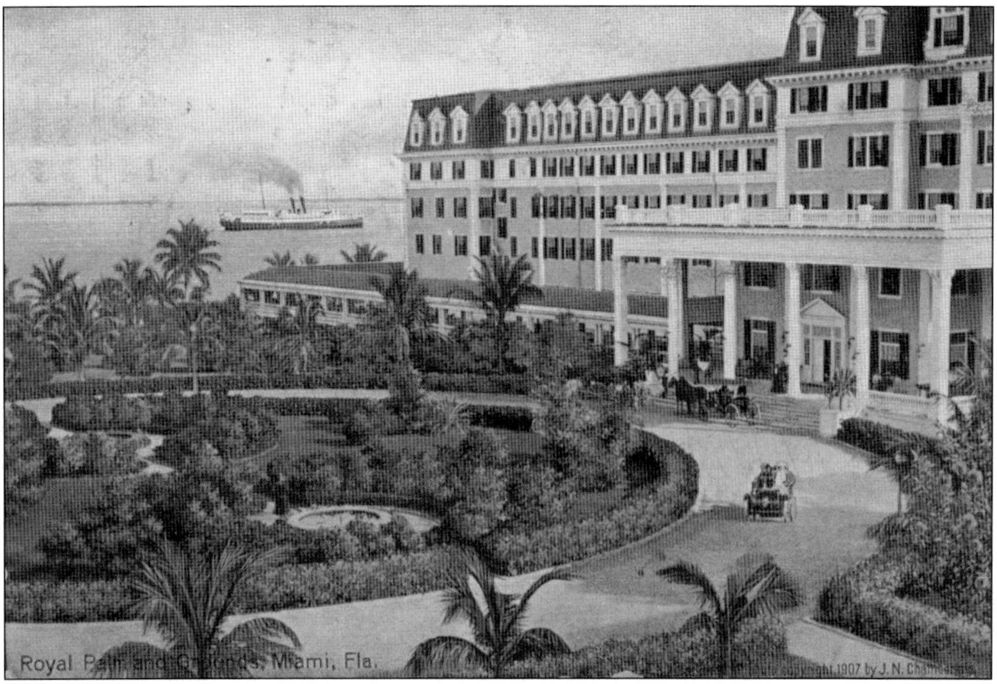

This 1907 postcard shows the changing times as some guests arrive by horse and carriage, while others depart by automobile. The S.S. *Miami* passes in the distance on the way to Key West. (Published by J.N. Chamberlain.)

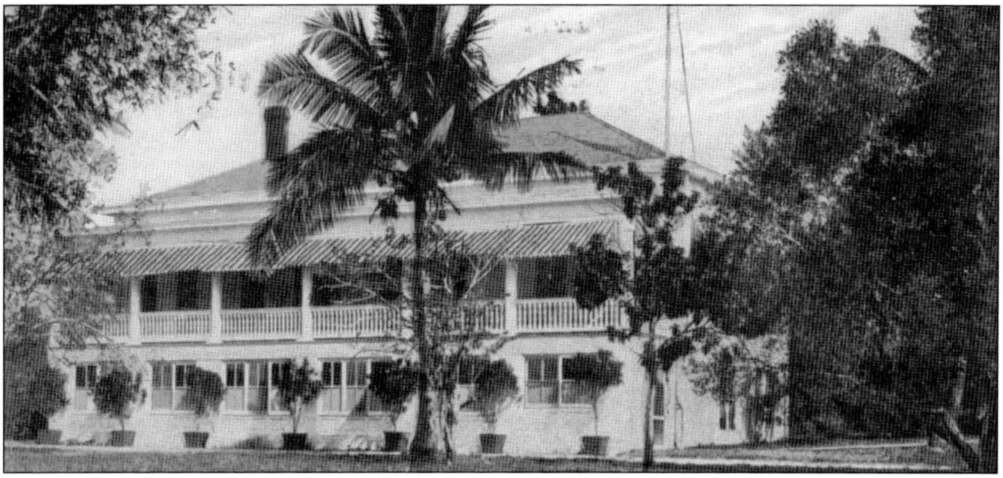

Julia Tuttle's home was originally built by William F. English as a home for his family in the 1840s. Mrs. Tuttle purchased it in 1891, along with 640 acres in today's downtown area. After her death, her son Harry leased the home to an enterprising gambler who converted it into the Seminole Club. The club functioned primarily to offer gambling for tourists, particularly guests of the Royal Palm Hotel. The building was torn down in 1925, and the Hyatt Hotel/Knight Center now occupies the site. (Published by I. Stern.)

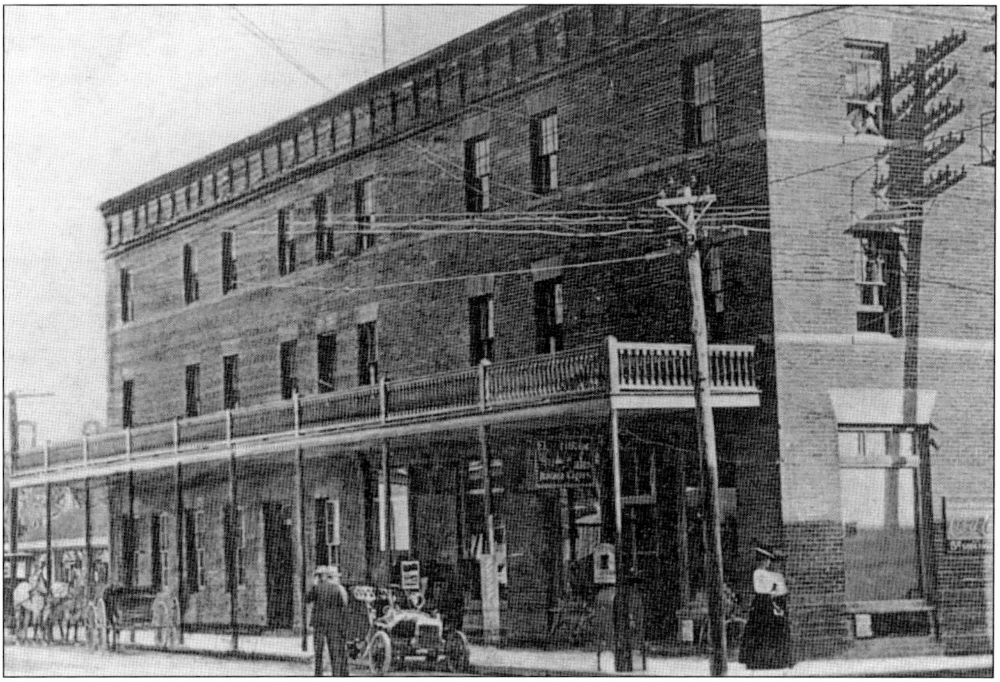

The three-story brick Hotel Biscayne sat on the corner of Twelfth Street and Avenue D. (today's Flagler Street and Miami Avenue). There were retail stores on the first floor and a veranda on the grounds between the hotel and the neighboring Burdines store. The hotel had its own "truck garden" where the public could buy any surplus of cabbage, eggplant, onions, beans, and tomatoes. (Courtesy of Historical Museum of Southern Florida.)

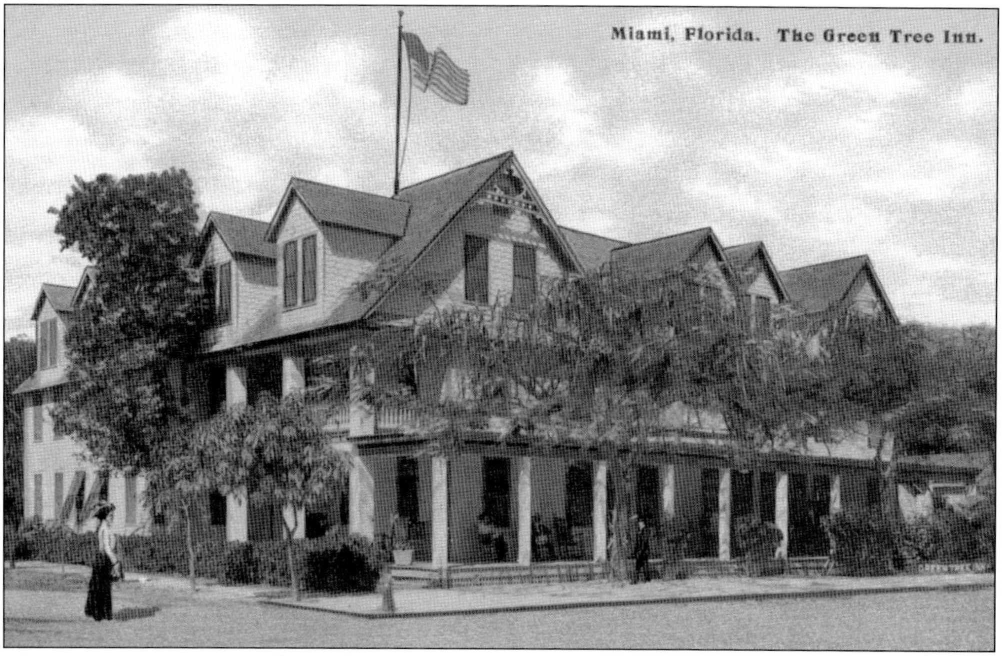

The Green Tree Inn was located at Eleventh Street and Avenue B. In 1909, the inn hosted a banquet for the entire graduating class of Miami High School—a total of five students! (Published by Hugh E. Leighton Co.)

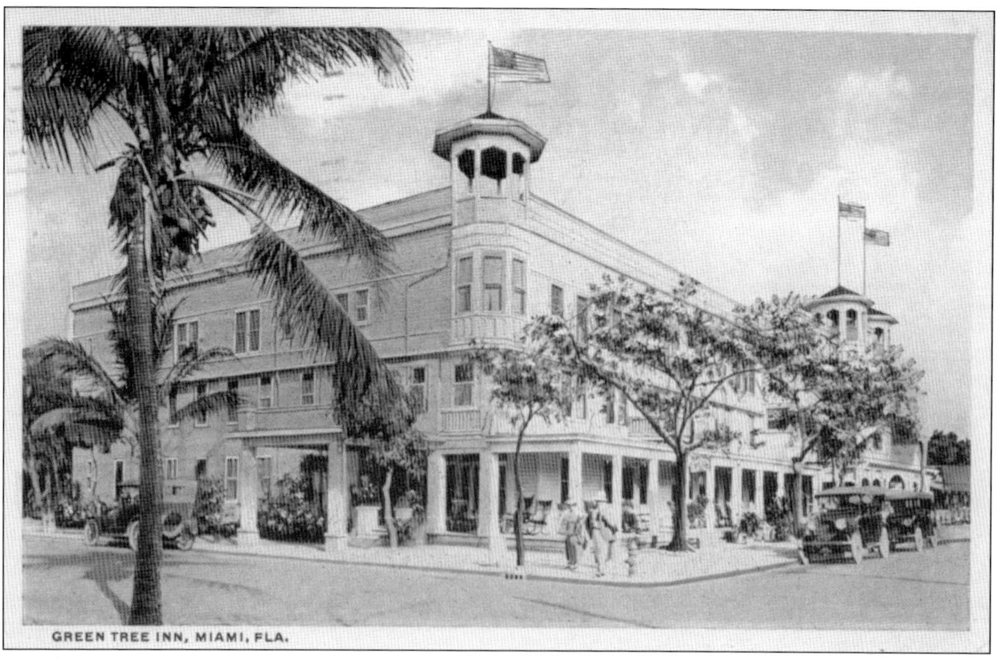

This later view of the Green Tree Inn, postmarked February 4, 1920, shows the renovation and expansion of the popular inn. (Published by H. & W.B. Drew Co.)

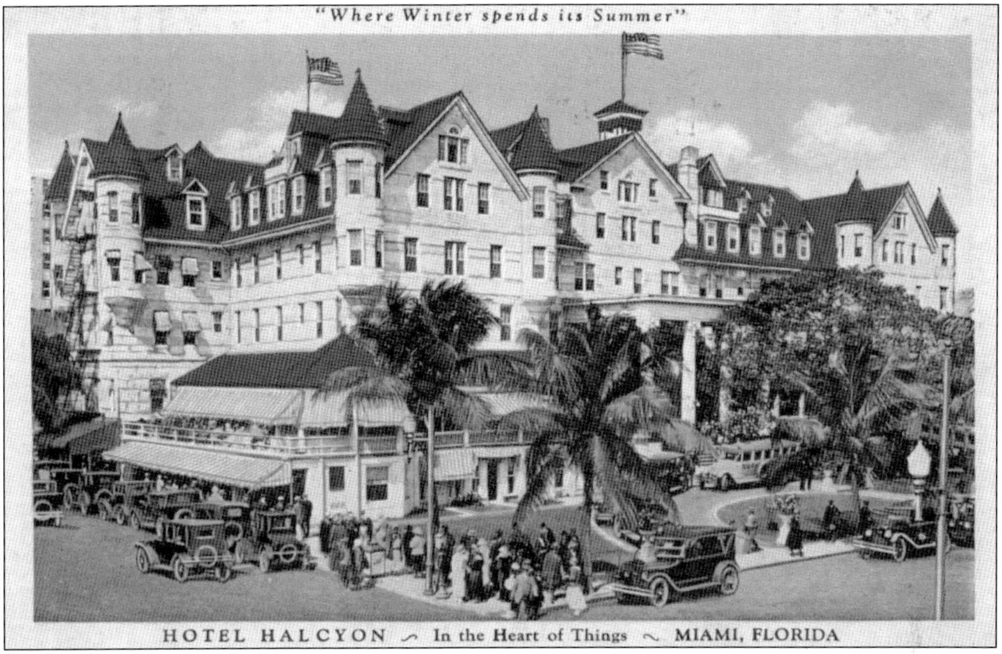

The Halcyon Hotel was built on the corner of Twelfth Street and Avenue B. Opened in 1906, it evoked an old-world charm with its spacious porches and turreted corner towers. The popular Halcyon, nicknamed the "White Palace," was demolished in 1930 to make room for the Dupont Building. (Published by Curt Teich.)

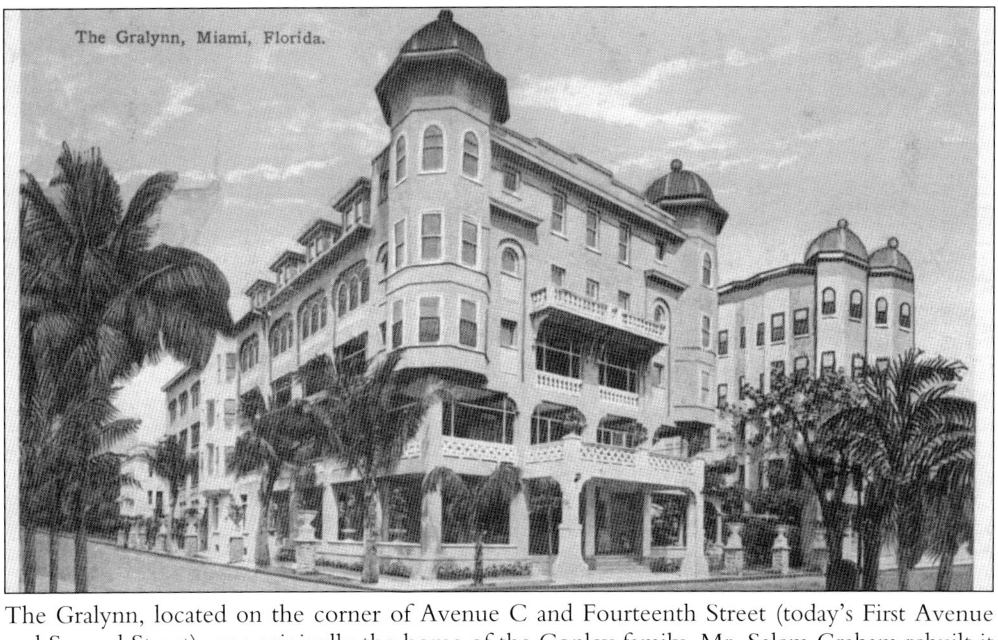

The Gralynn, located on the corner of Avenue C and Fourteenth Street (today's First Avenue and Second Street), was originally the home of the Conley family. Mr. Salem Graham rebuilt it and named it the Gralynn, using the first three letters of his last name and his wife's maiden name. The hotel was considered one of the best in the South. (Published by E.C. Kropp Co.)

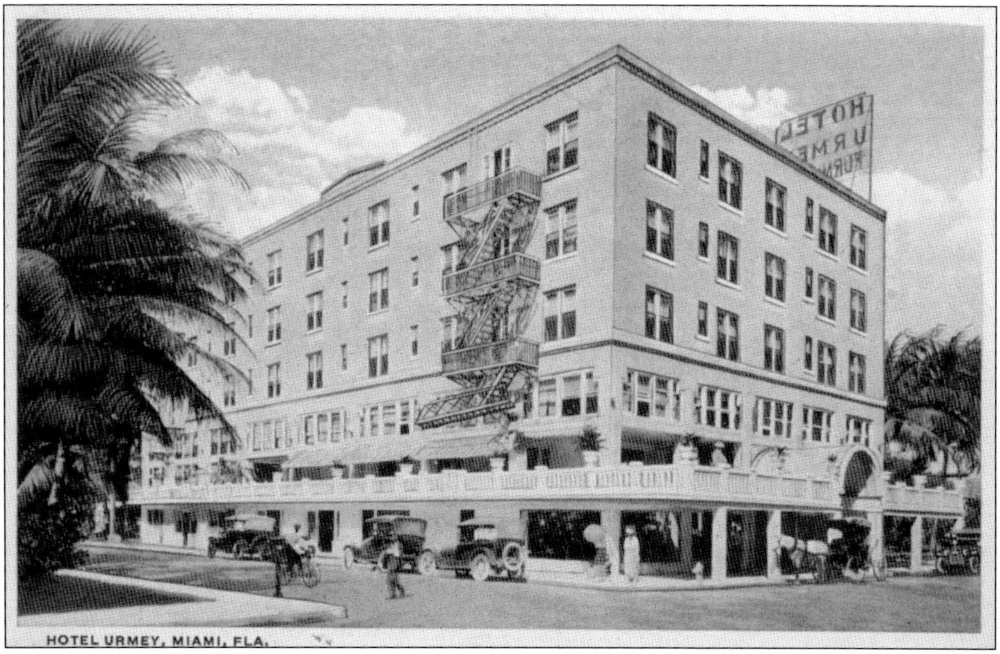

William N. Urmey came to Miami in 1911 from Indiana. After successfully operating the San Carlos Hotel for five years, he built his namesake hotel in 1916. The Urmey Hotel opened for business on January 4, 1917, and was located at Avenue B overlooking Royal Palm Park. (Published by H. & W.B. Drew Co.)

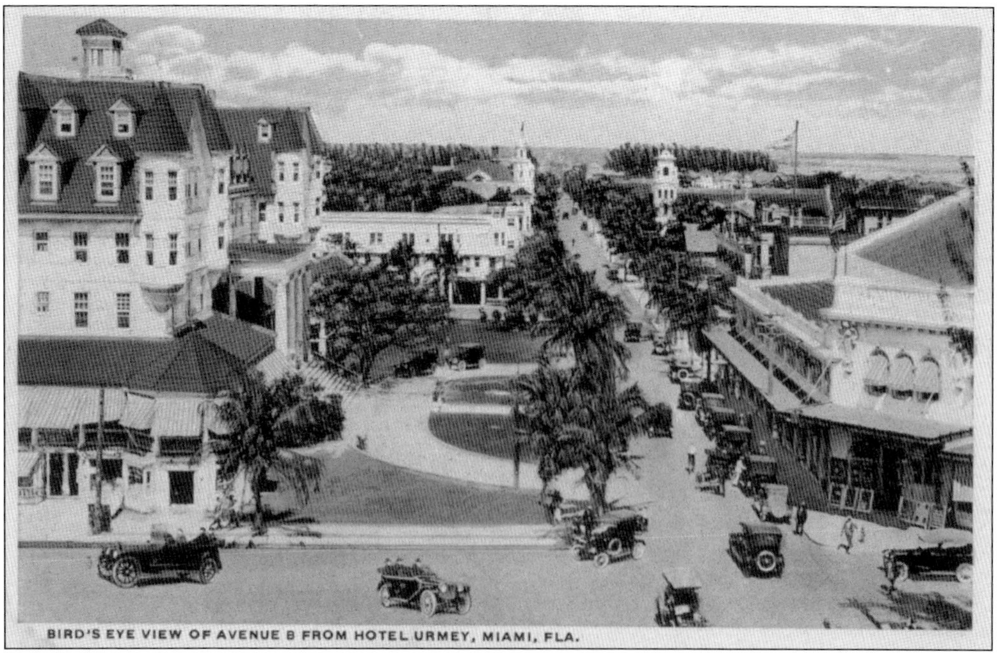

A guest looking out from the Urmey Hotel would have seen this view of Avenue B and the neighboring Halcyon Hotel with the turreted corners. (Published by H. & W.B. Drew Co.)

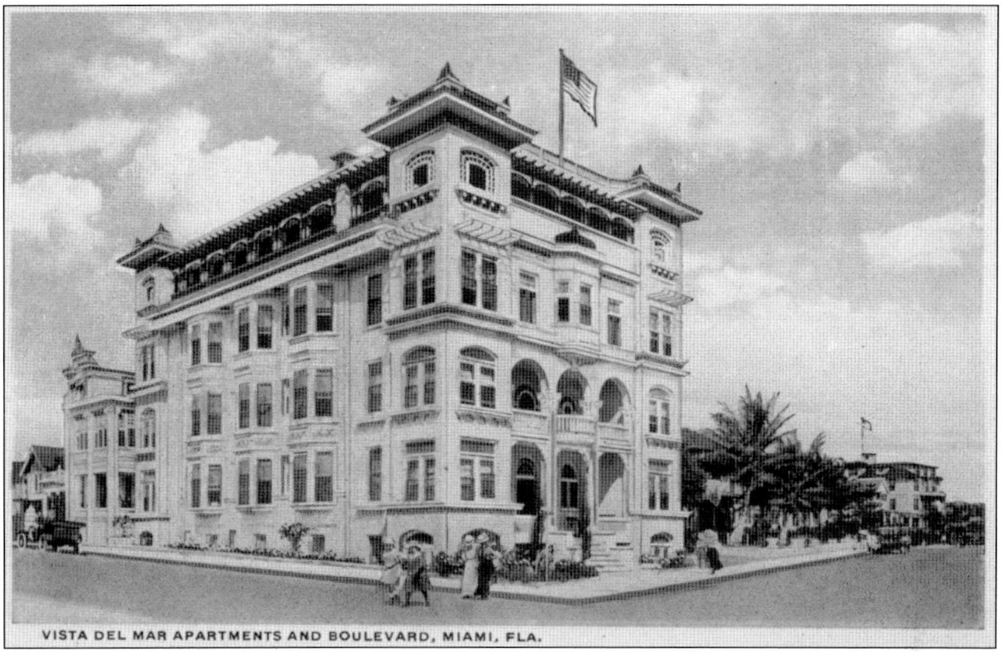

Residents enjoy a walk along the Boulevard in front of the Vista del Mar Apartments. (Published by H. & W.B. Drew Co.)

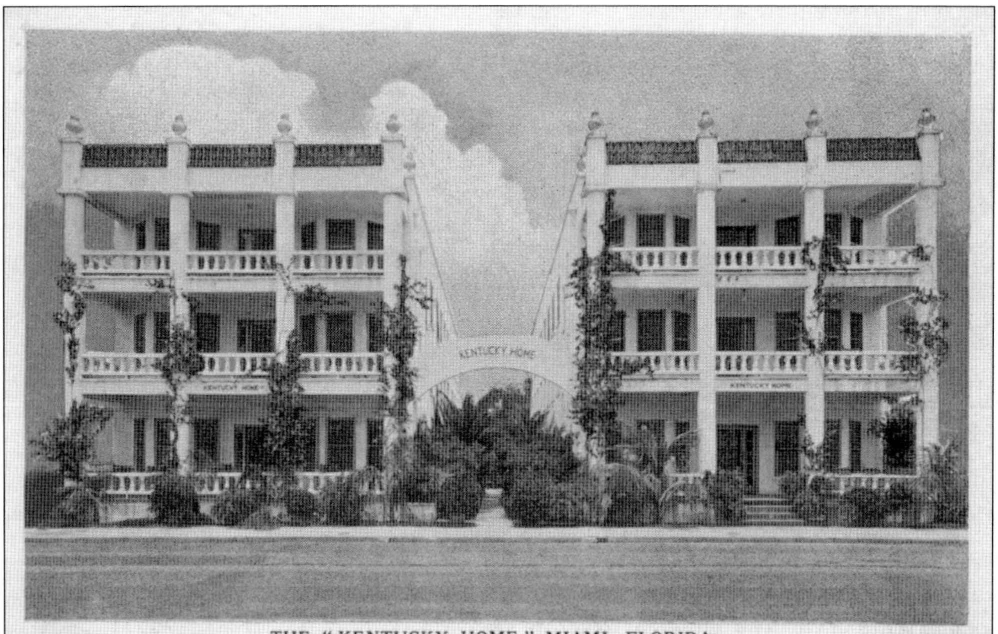

The Kentucky Home was located at Northeast First Avenue and Twelfth Street. This November 4, 1934 postcard carried a message on the back from manager W.R. Butler offering potential New York vacationers the seasonal rate of $11 per week for room and board—and a hint that rooms were filling fast.

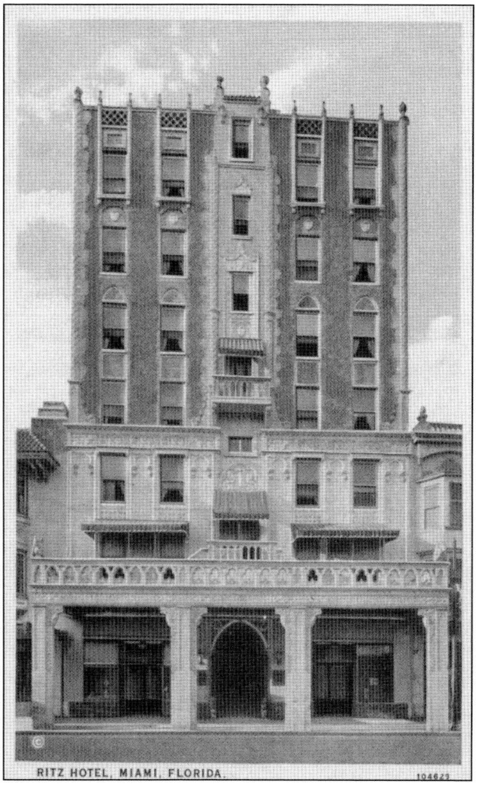

The charming Ritz Hotel, located on East Flagler Street, advertised itself as being located "in the heart of everything." (Published by J.N. Chamberlain.)

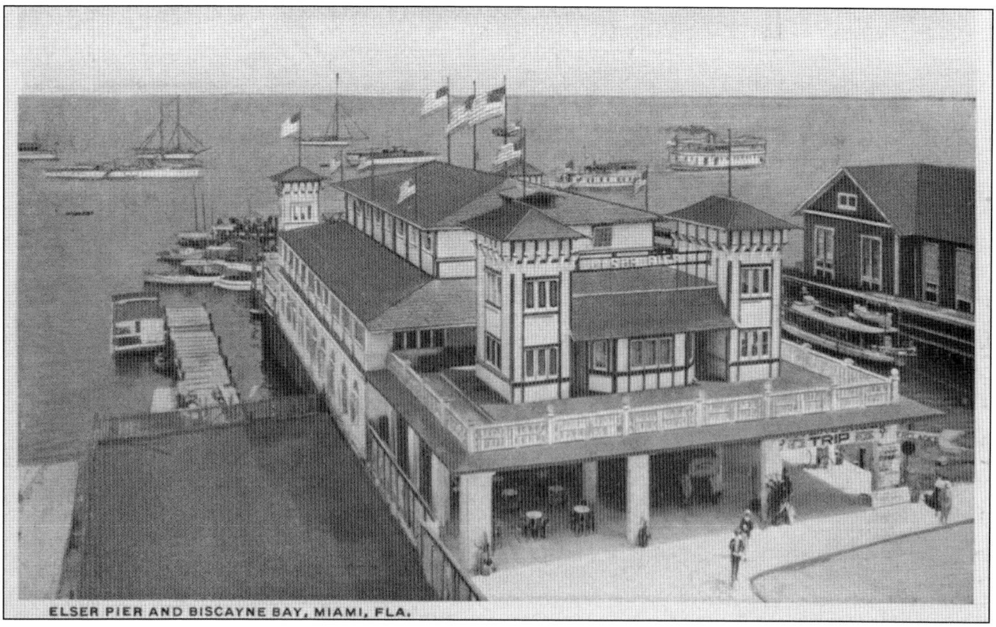

Elser Pier, located at the foot of Flagler Street, offered many fun-filled activities. The recreation center had a shooting gallery, refreshments, and a dance hall at night. The site was purchased in 1924 for $340,000 and filled in to create Bayfront Park. (Published by J.N. Chamberlain.)

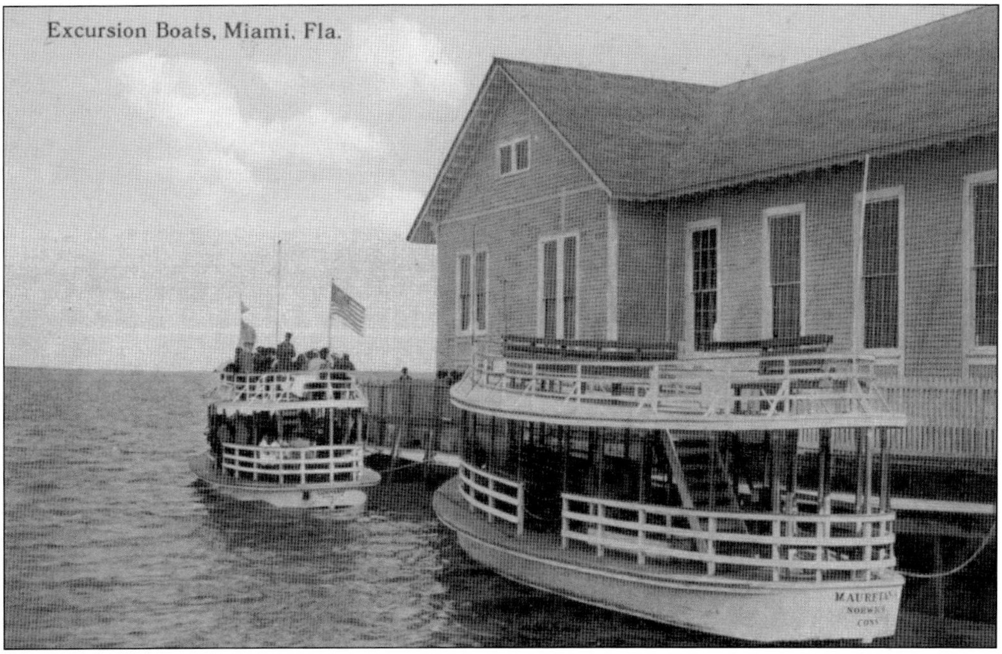

Excursion boats were popular for tours of the Biscayne Bay and the Everglades. Moored in the foreground is the *Mauretania* of Norwich, Connecticut, while the *Lusitania* is leaving the dock filled with passengers. (Published by J.N. Chamberlain.)

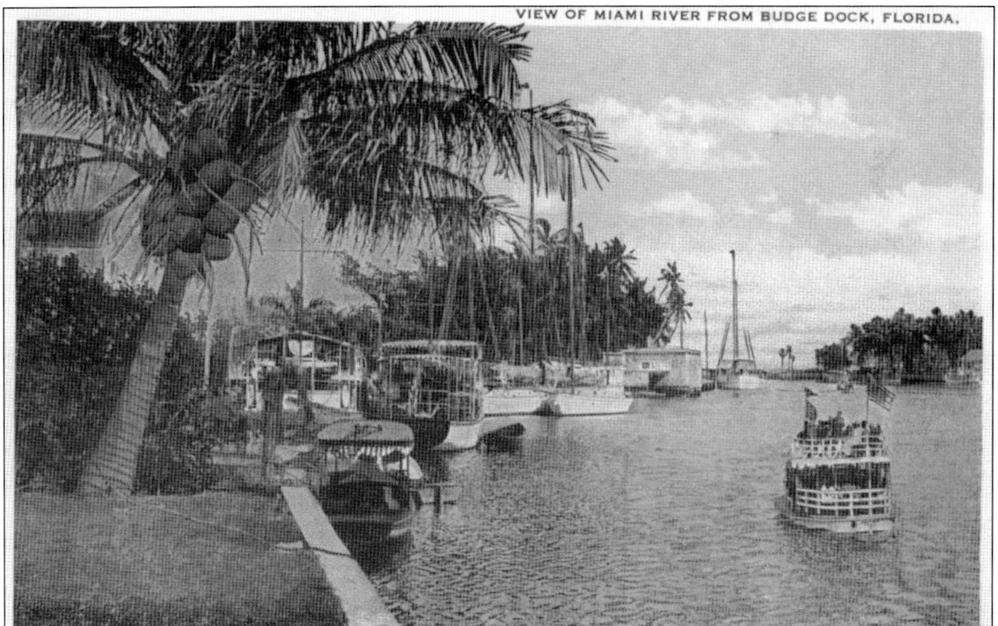

This view from Budge Dock shows the *Lusitania* carrying its passengers along the Miami River. The Budge family was known for establishing the city's first hardware store in 1896, which furnished supplies to Miami residents for the next 50 years. (Published by Curt Teich.)

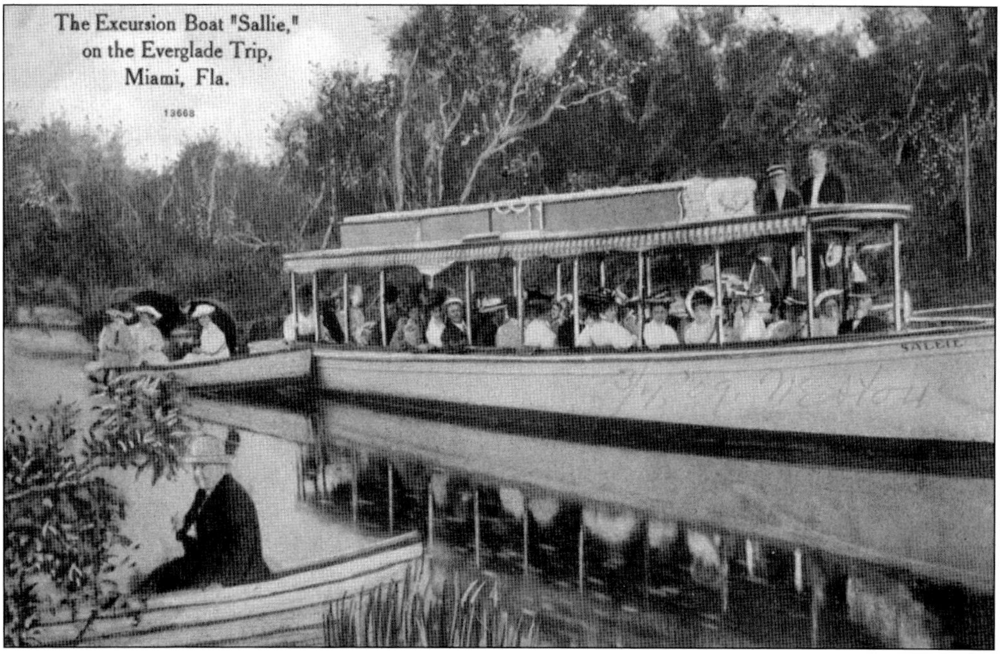

The excursion boat *Sallie* took guests for a 3-mile journey up the Miami River. Stops at the Musa Isle Indian Village and Alligator Joe's, an alligator-wrestling exhibit, were particular highlights of the tour. (Published by C.B. Pennock.)

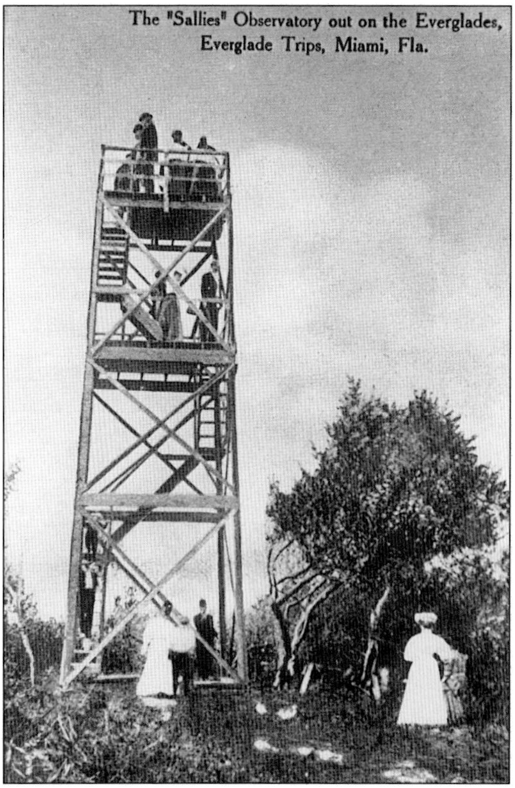

Passengers from the *Sallie* take in a view of the Everglades from the observation tower at Musa Isle. (Courtesy of Florida State Archives.)

Continued growth in tourism led to the development of numerous hotels, such as the Alta Vista Hotel shown here during the 1920s. (Courtesy of Florida State Archives.)

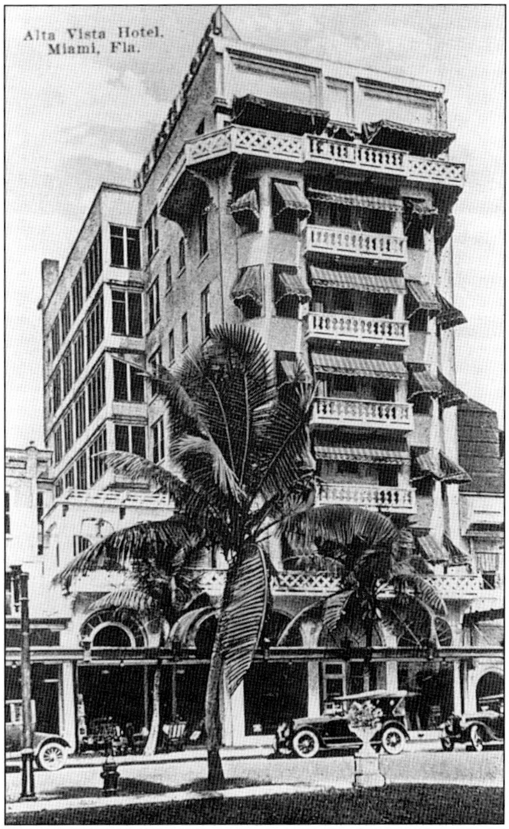

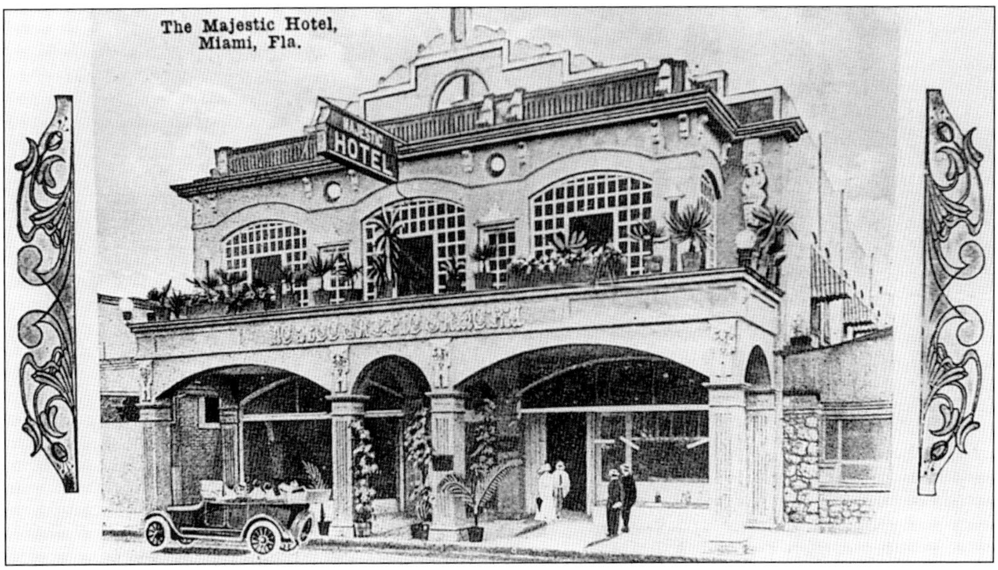

The Majestic Hotel building previously housed the Wee Tappie Tavern. W.H. Nichols, owner of the hotel, purchased the building in 1916 for $50,000, which was considered an extremely high price at that time. (Courtesy of Florida State Archives.)

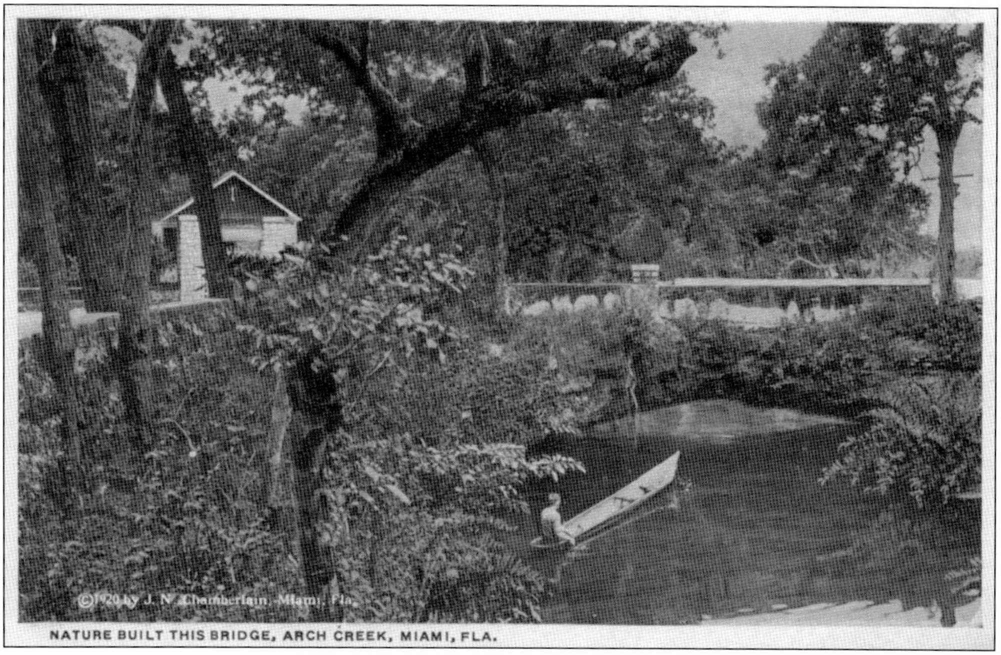

The natural rock bridge at Arch Creek was a popular attraction for both residents and tourists. Over thousands of years the creek eroded the porous limestone, creating the natural bridge. In 1974, the bridge collapsed just hours after the state of Florida purchased the site for preservation. The Arch Creek Park opened in 1982 and a replica of the bridge was built on the original site. (Published by J.N. Chamberlain.)

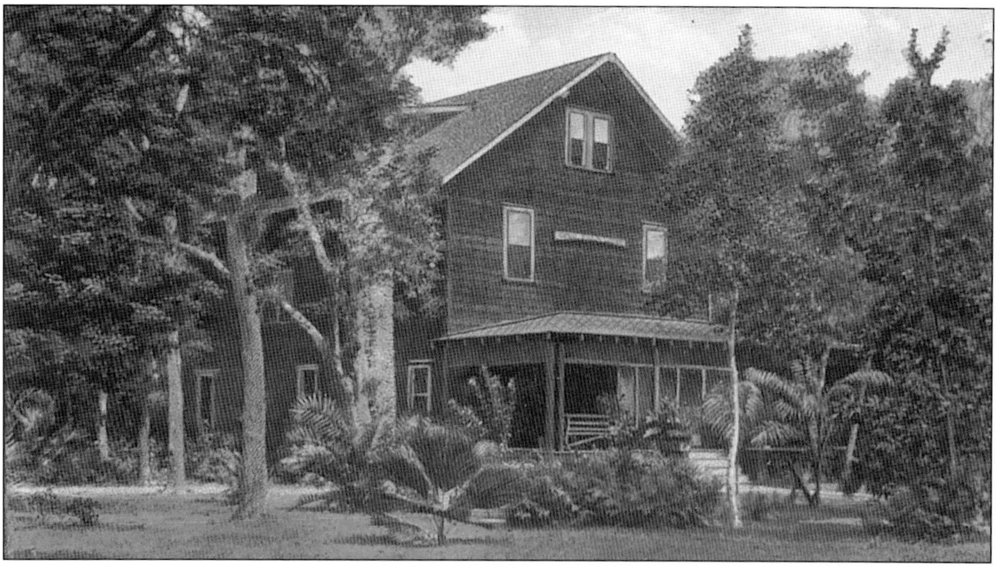

Nature-loving residents traveled south near Homestead, Florida, where the Royal Palm State Park opened in 1916. Shown here, the Royal Palm Lodge, built in 1918, welcomed visitors to the park. In 1925, more than 30,000 visitors signed the register at the lodge. The Everglades National Park, which opened in 1947, grew out of the Royal Palm State Park. (Courtesy of Florida State Archives.)

Three

A Day at the Beach

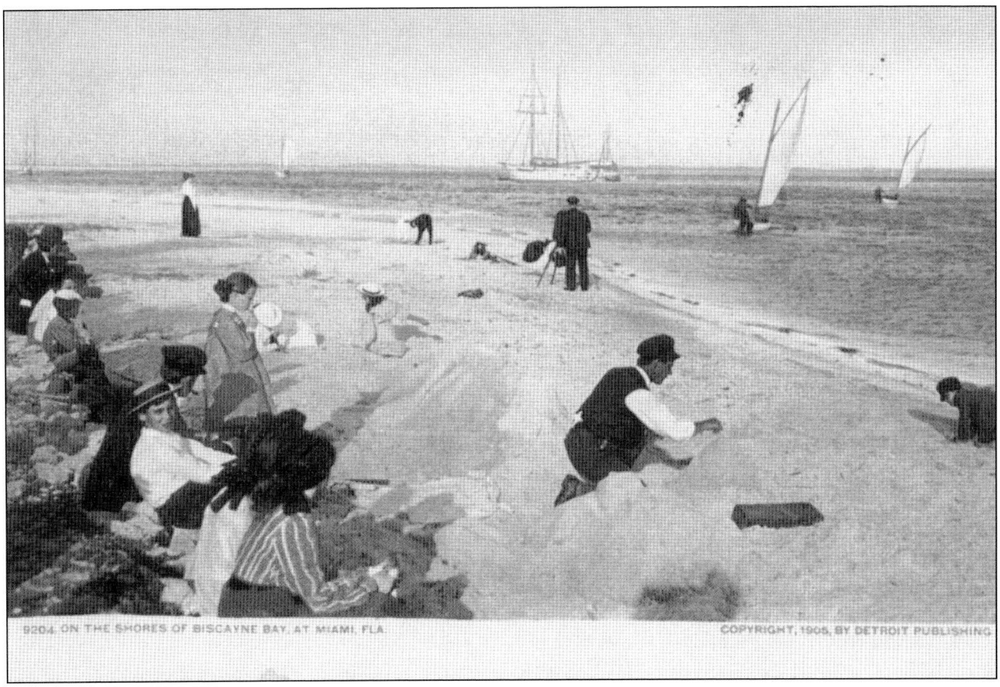

Visitors to the Miami area could choose, as they can today, from a variety of beaches along the Biscayne Bay or the Atlantic Ocean. Shown above, the sunny shores and warm tropical waters of the Biscayne Bay provided the perfect setting for an outing on this beautiful day in 1905. (Published by Detroit Publishing Co.)

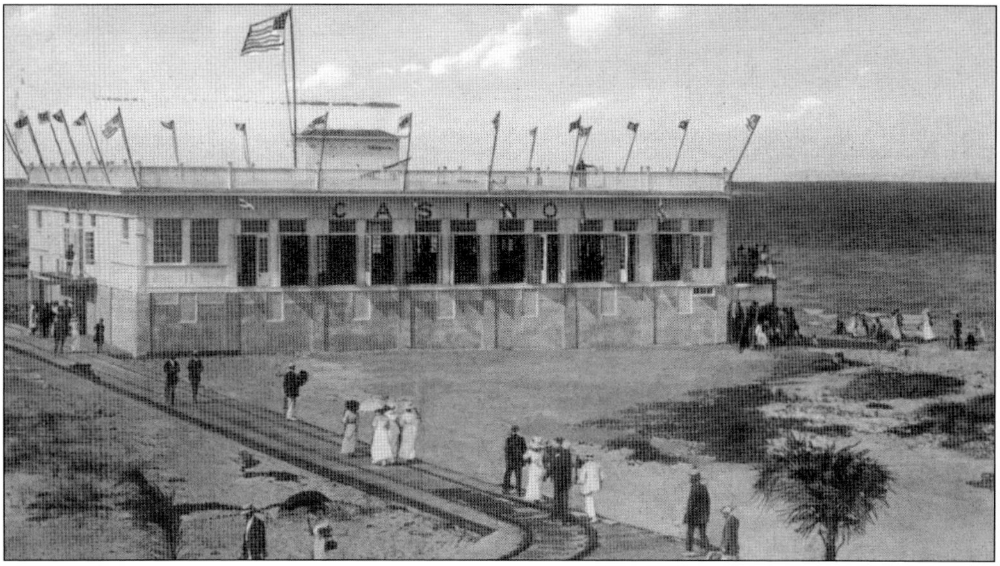

Before the opening of John Collins Bridge, Ocean Beach could be reached only by ferry or private boat. Located on the southern part of what is now the city of Miami Beach, the popular international resort city was incorporated in 1915. The beach visitors shown here are on their way to the Ocean Beach Casino. At the time, "casino" meant "bathing pavilion." Admission was a nickel and bathing suit rentals were a quarter. (Published by J.N. Chamberlain.)

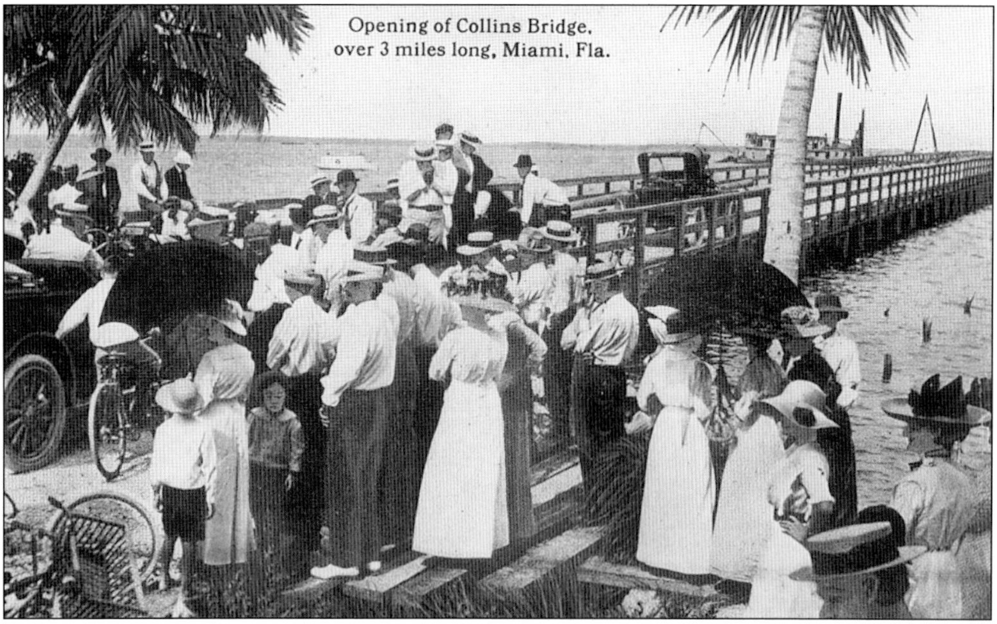

Crowds celebrate the opening of the Collins Bridge in 1913. Considered the world's longest wooden bridge at the time, it reached from the mainland to Bull Island (now Bell Island.) From there, visitors used a footbridge from the island to the beach. The Venetian Causeway replaced the Collins Bridge in 1925. (Courtesy of Florida State Archives.)

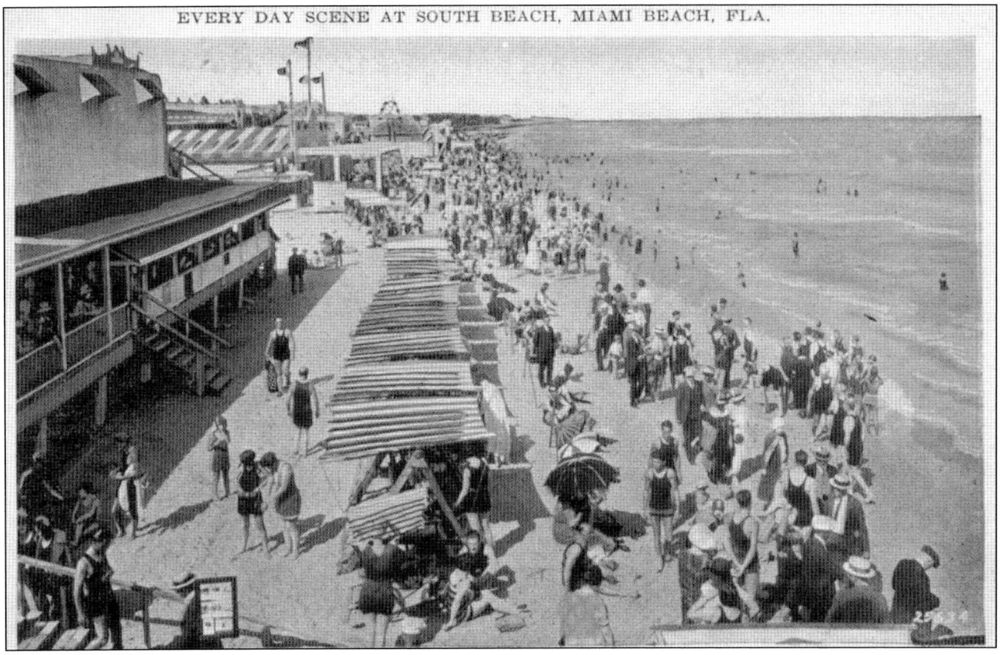

South Beach offered fun in the sun 85 years ago as it does now. Shown here, visitors at the Hardie and Smith Casinos enjoy a variety of activities, such as sunbathing, a picnic on the beach, and swimming. (Published by J.N. Chamberlain.)

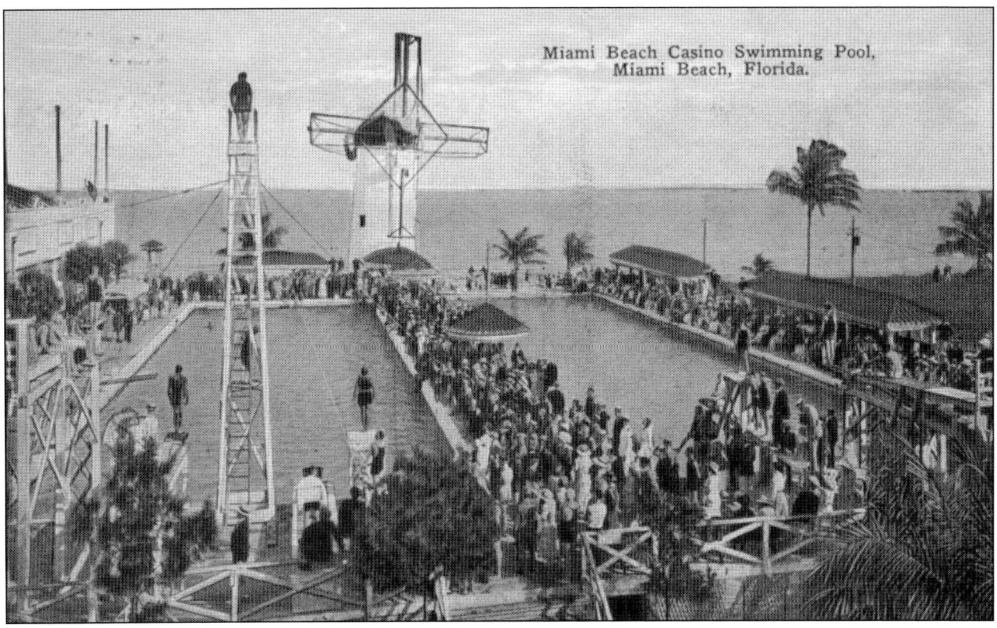

Once the Collins Bridge was completed, Carl Fisher opened the Miami Beach Casino in 1914 near Twenty-third Street. A windmill pumped salt water into two large swimming pools, where diving and swimming exhibitions drew large crowds. (Published E.C. Kropp Co.)

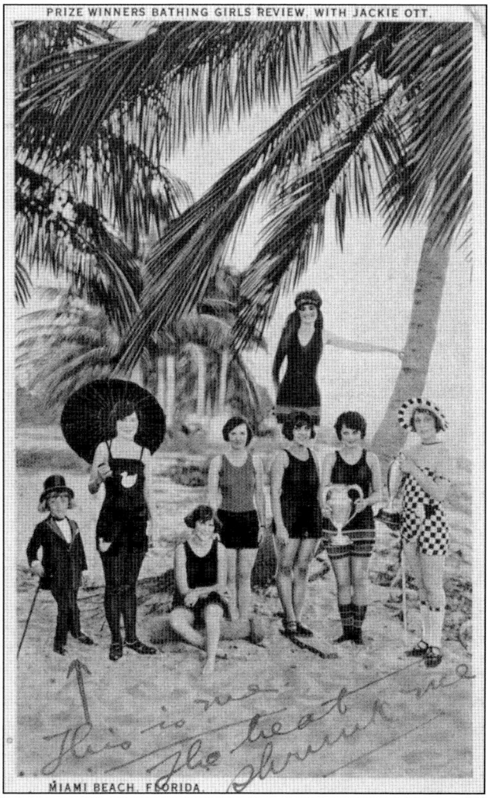

The prize-winners in a "Bathing Girls Review" posed with Jackie Ott in this *c.* 1920 postcard. The lovely winner holding the trophy is at the height of fashion with a bathing suit and matching socks. (Published by J.N. Chamberlain.)

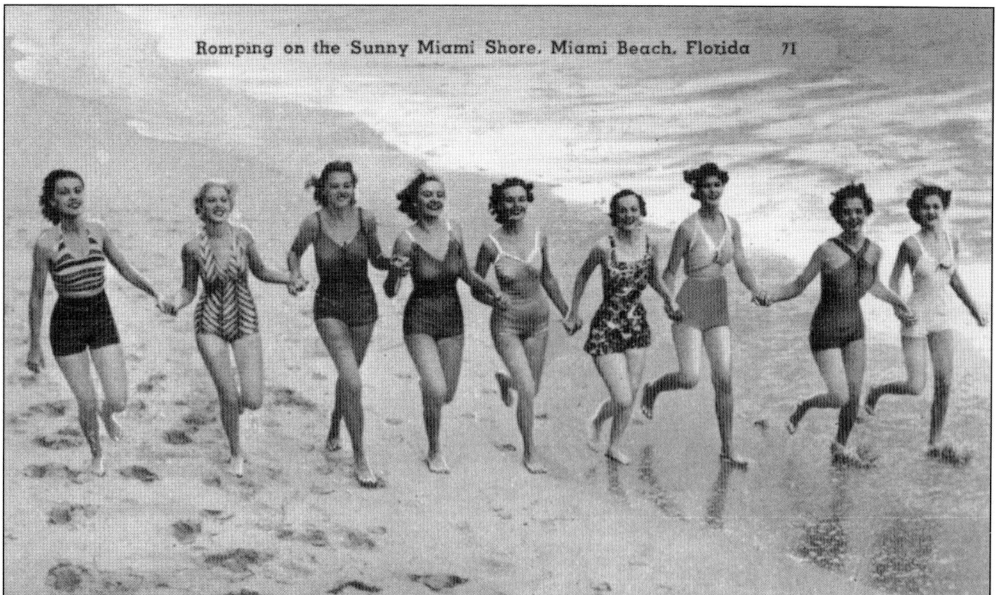

The more things change, the more they remain the same . . . the appeal of the beach and bathing beauties is timeless. Above, exuberant visitors run along the shore on Miami Beach in the late 1930s. (Published by Tichnor Bros.)

Vacationers enjoy the oceanfront swimming in front of the Miami Beach Hotel at Fifth Street. As the popularity of Miami Beach grew, the number of hotels, large and small, grew with it. By 1925, the city had 33 hotels, 80 apartment buildings, and hundreds of private homes. (Published by Curt Teich.)

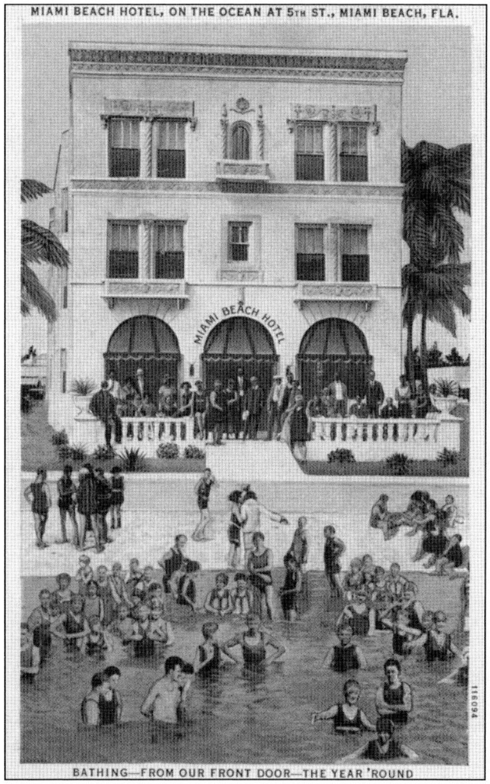

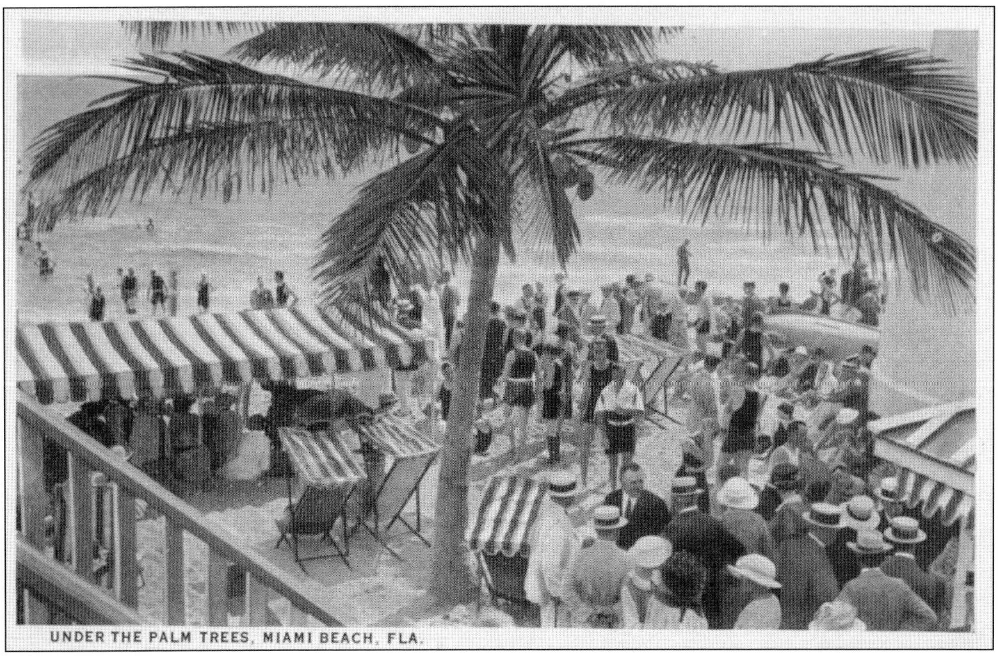

Sunshine, palm trees, and warm ocean waters symbolized Miami to those seeking escape from the rigors of Northern winters. Beach visitors enjoy the tropical surroundings at the Roman Pools in the early 1920s.

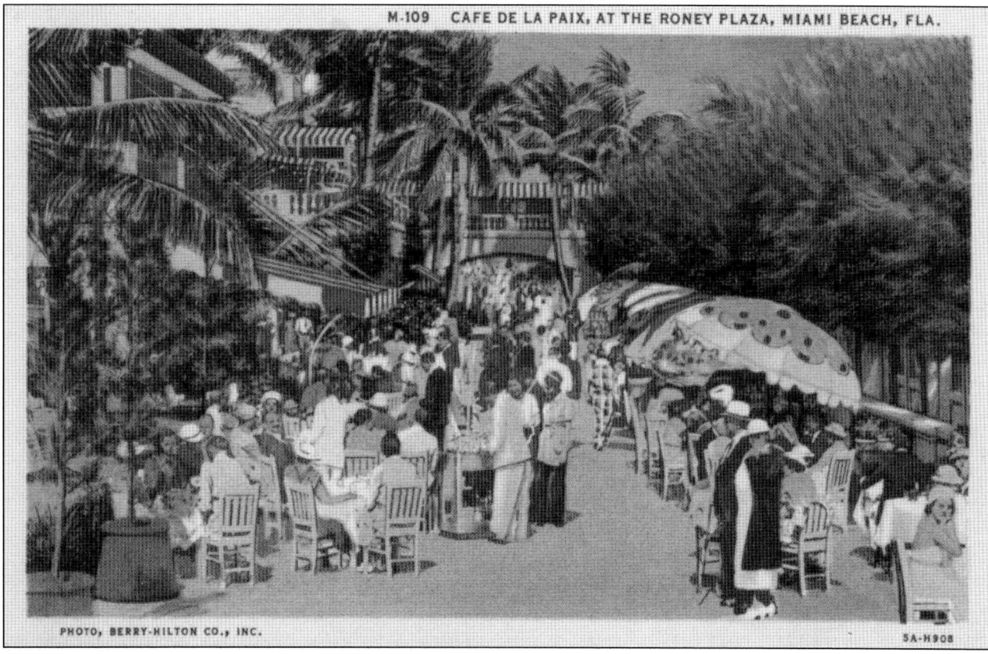

"People watching" from sidewalk cafes was as popular in the 1930s as it is today. Crowds fill the Café de la Paix at the Roney Plaza Hotel in this 1935 card. (Published by Curt Teich.)

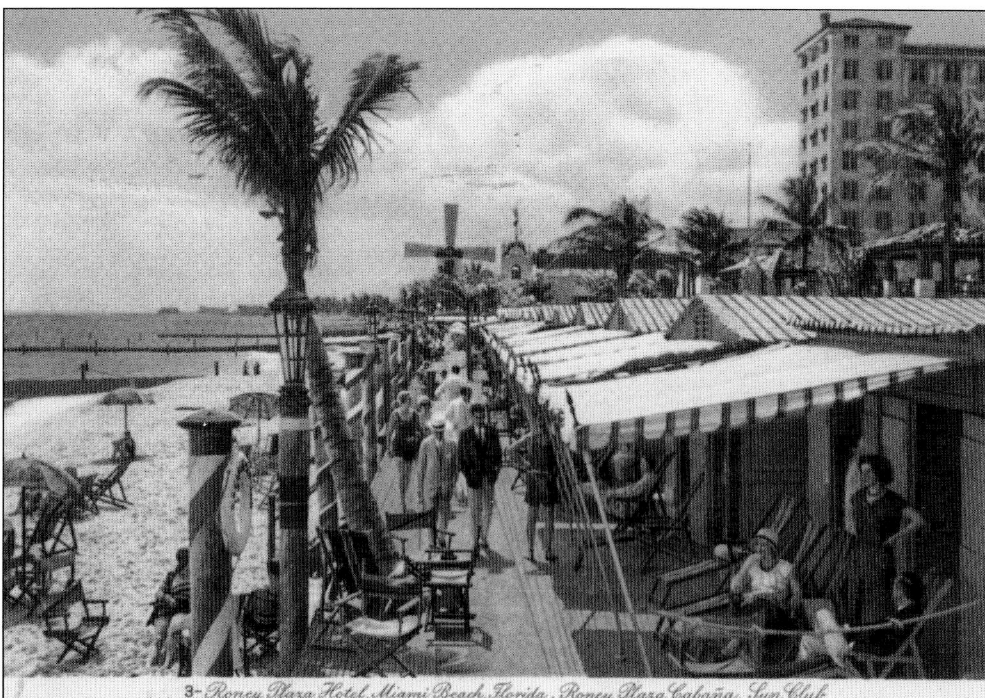

Guests at the Roney Plaza could enjoy their own cabanas and an unobstructed view of the ocean. (Published by K.S. Tanner.)

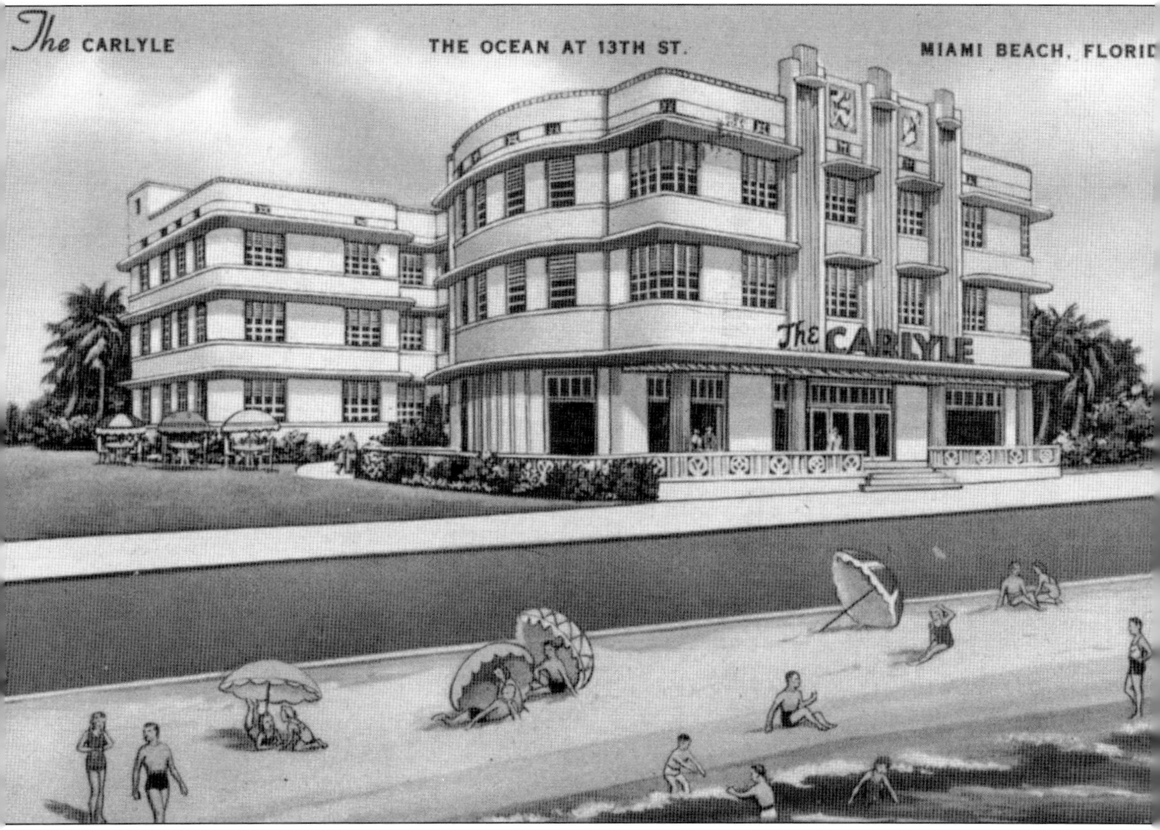

The 1930s and 1940s brought the creation of the Art Deco gems that today make up the Miami Beach Art Deco Historic District. Architects used motifs of the Art Deco style seen in Europe in the 1920s and characteristics of the streamlined shapes made popular by American industrial designers of the 1930s. At the time, the new image was simply called "Moderne." The term "Art Deco" would not be coined until the 1960s. Shown here, the Carlyle Hotel was designed by architects Kiehnel and Elliott in 1941. One of the finest examples of the streamline style, the Carlyle was used in the film *The Birdcage* in 1995. The neon Carlyle sign was replaced by a "Birdcage" sign. (Published by Colourpicture.)

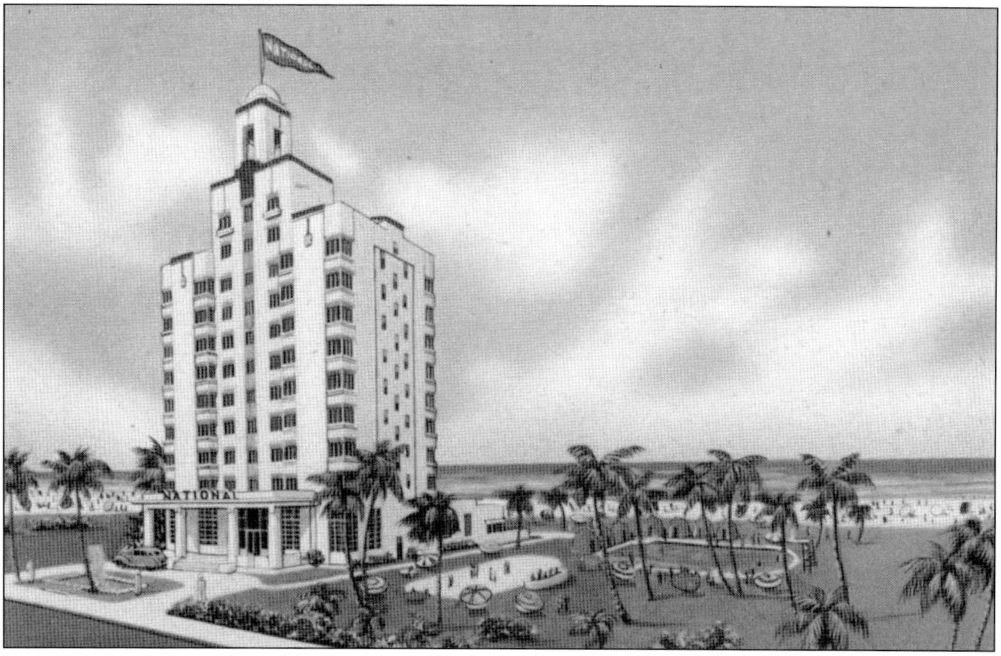

Roy F. France, a prominent Art Deco architect, designed the National Hotel at 1677 Collins Avenue. When it opened in 1940, the National was one of the most luxurious hotels on Miami Beach. The fashionable and popular hotel recently underwent an award-winning restoration. (Published by Colourpicture.)

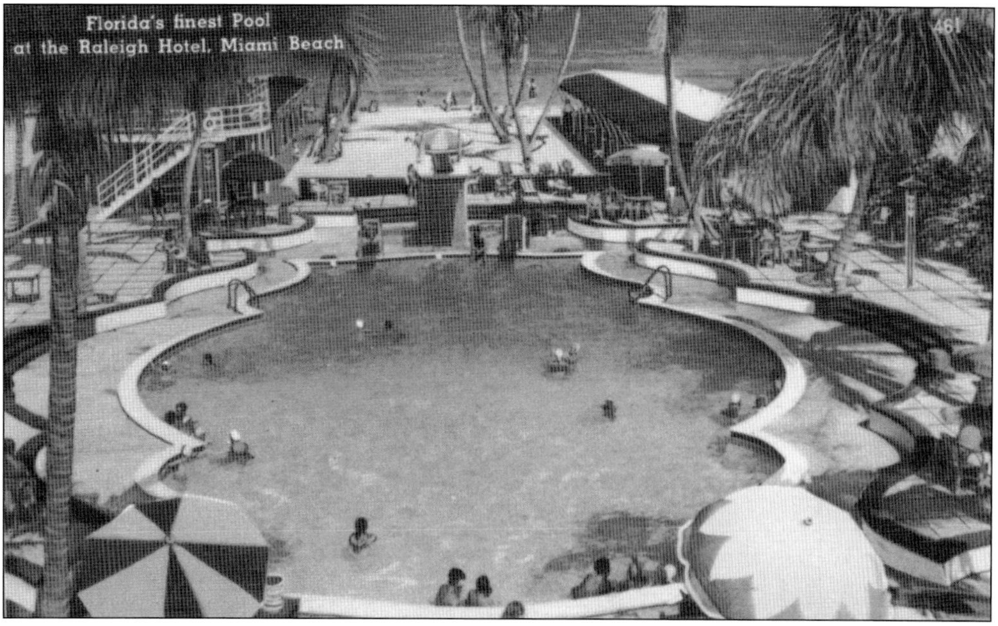

The Raleigh Hotel's Art Deco swimming pool, considered one of Florida's most beautiful, was featured on the cover of *Life* magazine in the 1940s. Actress Esther Williams filmed many of her most famous swim scenes at this site. (Published by Tichnor Bros.)

The Delano, with its unmistakable winged tower, was designed in 1945 by Robert Swartburg and was the tallest building in Miami Beach at that time. The Roosevelt family kept a penthouse at the Delano for many years. Beautifully refurbished, the Delano still maintains its prominent position on Miami Beach today. (Published by Colourpicture.)

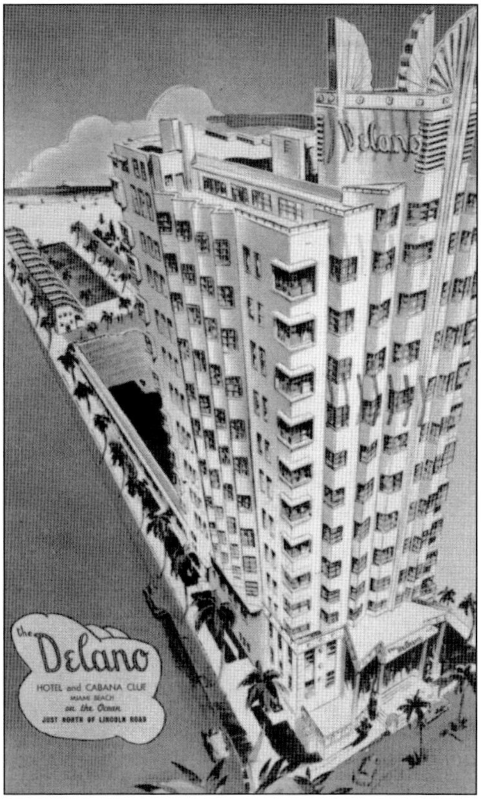

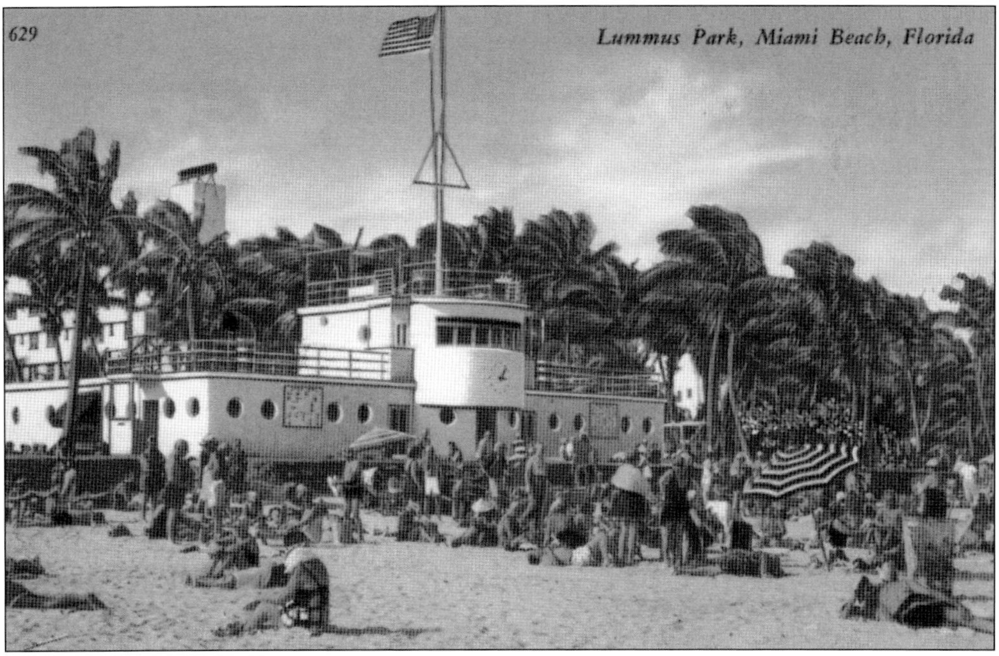

The nautical, Art Deco–style Beach Patrol Headquarters at Lummus Park was a popular site for socializing and basking under the Florida sun. (Published by Tichnor Bros.)

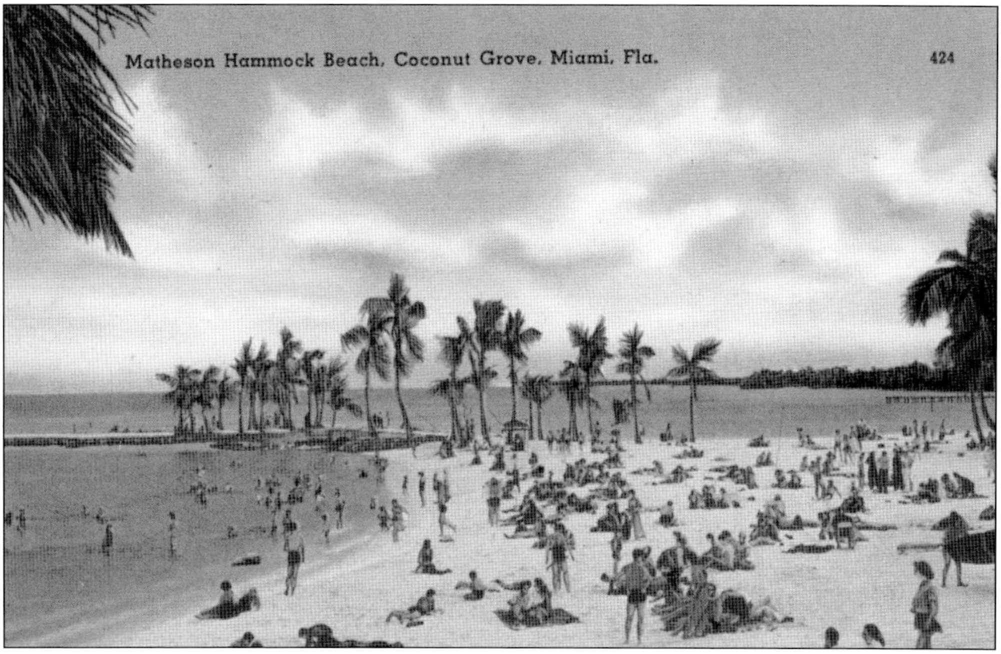

Swimmers and sunbathers enjoy Matheson Hammock Beach in Coconut Grove during the 1930s. The Matheson family donated land for the beach and park to the city. (Published by Tichnor Bros.)

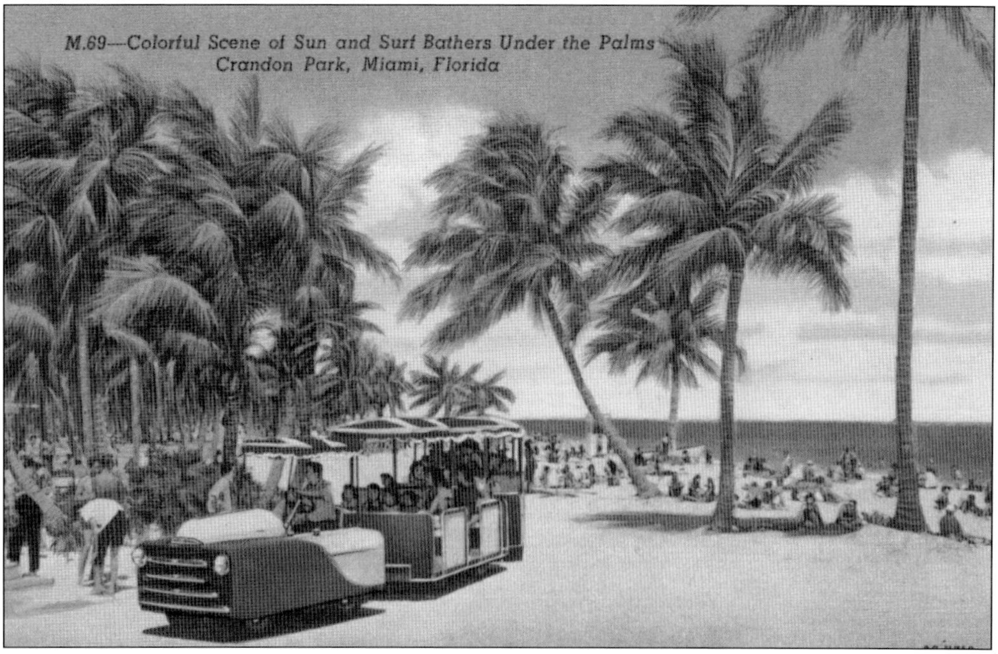

The Matheson family also donated Crandon Park on Key Biscayne. Many of the coconut palms on Key Biscayne today were originally planted as part of a coconut plantation developed by William Matheson. (Published by Curt Teich.)

Four

PEOPLE AND PLACES

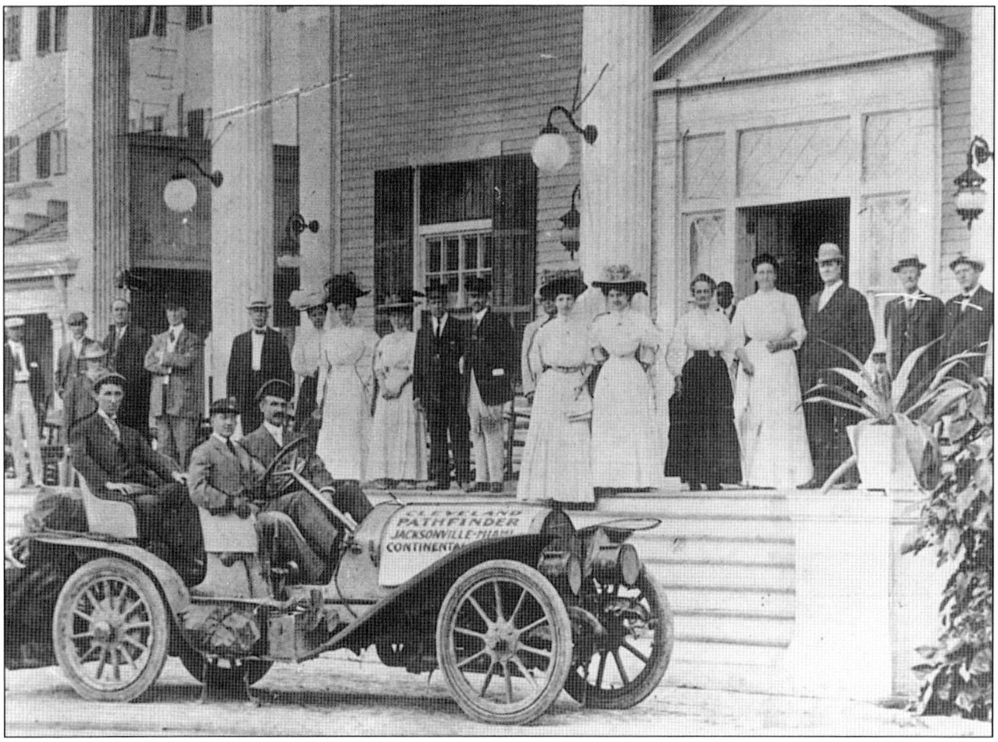

By 1911, it was possible to drive all the way from Jacksonville to Miami on Carl Fisher's Dixie Highway. The first car to complete that journey is shown arriving at the entrance to the Royal Palm Hotel in January 1911. (Courtesy of the Romer Collection, Miami-Dade Public Library.)

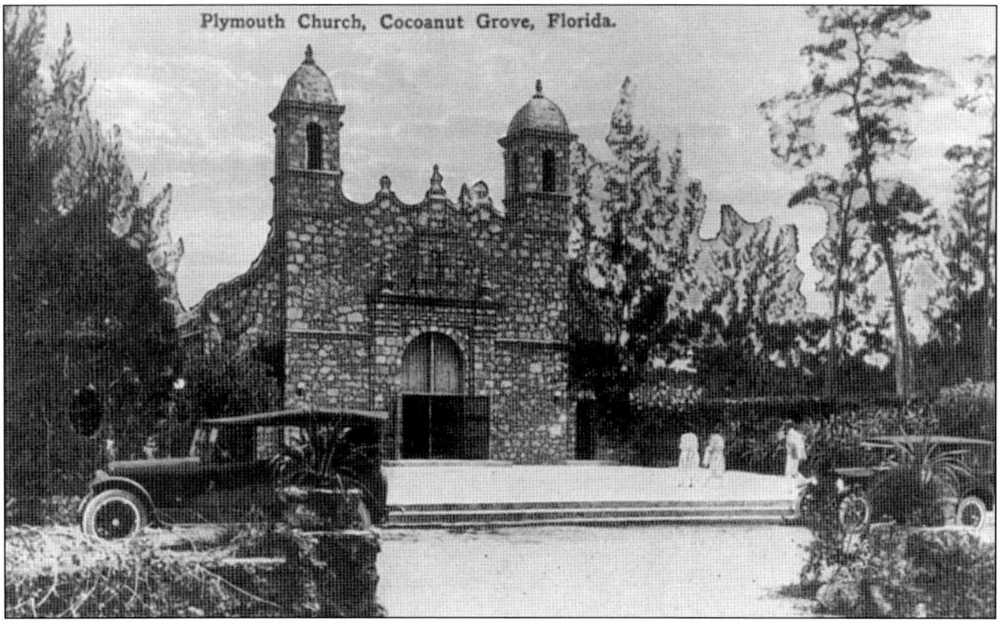

In 1891 Ralph Munroe donated the land for the nondenominational Union Chapel, which evolved into the Union Congregational Church. Union Congregational became the Plymouth Congregational Church, which still exists in Coconut Grove. (Courtesy of Historical Museum of Southern Florida.)

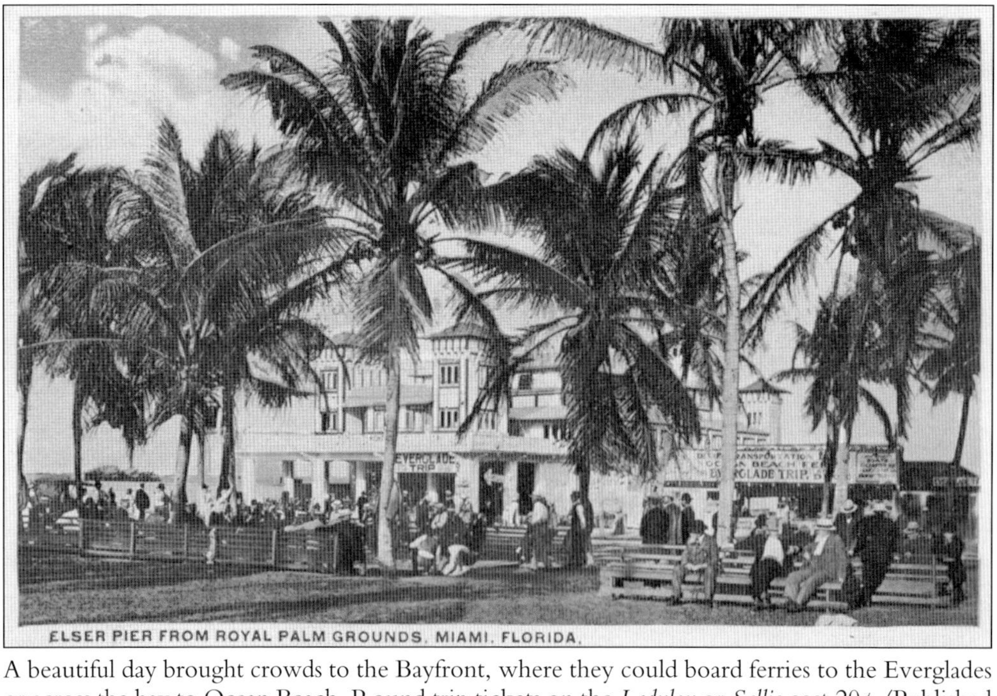

A beautiful day brought crowds to the Bayfront, where they could board ferries to the Everglades or across the bay to Ocean Beach. Round trip tickets on the *Ladylou* or *Sallie* cost 20¢. (Published by Crandon-Hunter Co.)

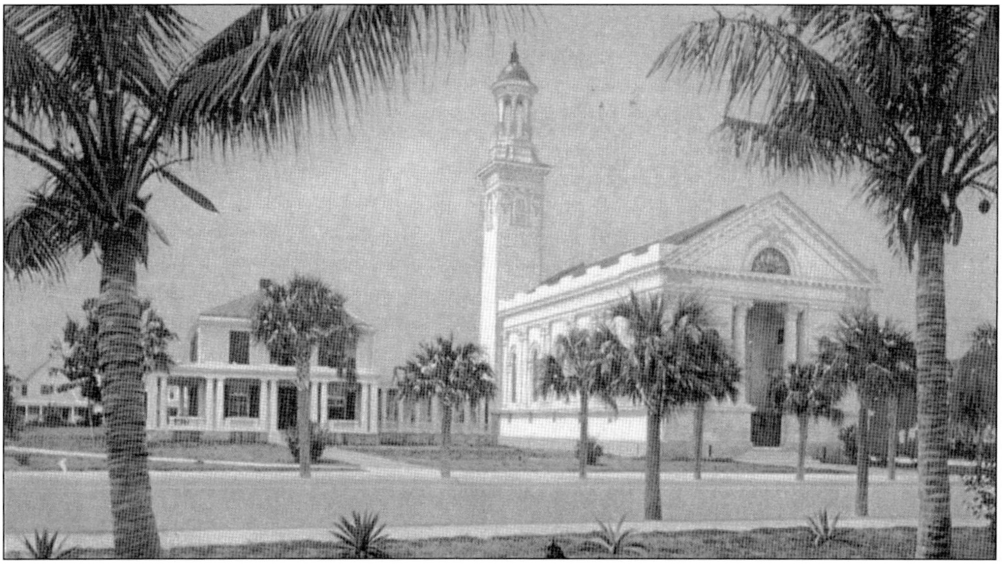

The First Presbyterian Church was built in 1899, and designed by Hastings and Carrere of Ponce de Leon Hotel fame. Located at today's East Flagler Street and Southeast Third Avenue, the church was a gift from Henry Flagler. In the 1940s the congregation moved to a new church at 609 Brickell Avenue, and this beautiful church was torn down. The message on the back of this postcard, addressed to an Indiana clergyman, mentions that parishioner William Jennings Bryan had 80 students in his Bible class. (Published by Detroit Publishing Co.)

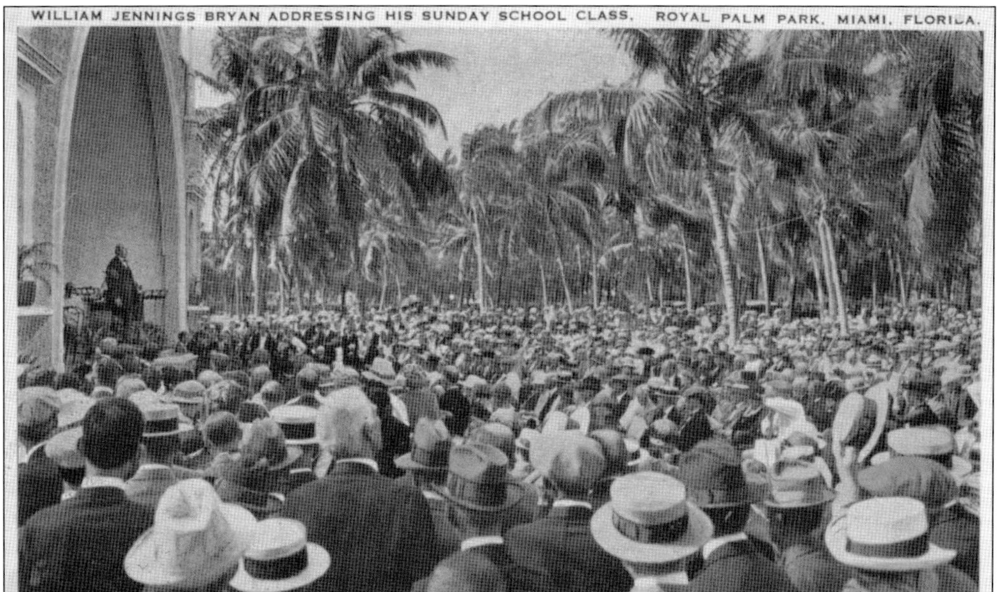

William Jennings Bryan's Sunday school class became so popular that the attendance surpassed the capacity of the church. The classes were moved into Royal Palm Park, where Mr. Bryan is shown addressing his class from the park's bandshell. (Published by Tichnor Bros.)

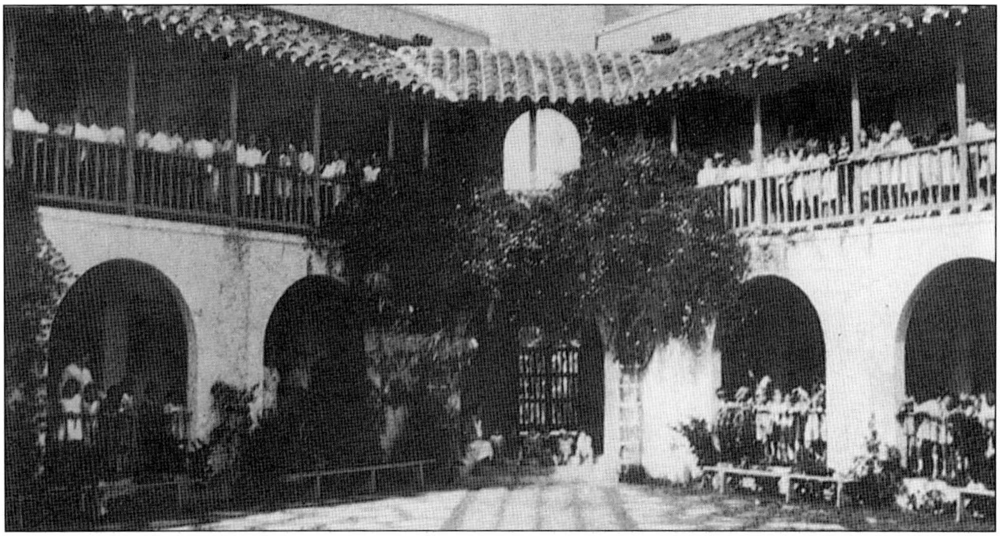

When Laura Cushman opened the Cushman School in 1924, the first brochure stated the school's philosophy . . . "A school seeks to develop the child mentally, physically and in character growth. To do this the child must be placed in happy surroundings, be properly adjusted to his work, and have wholesome participation in living experiences. The creation of such a school life is our aim." During her 70 years in the field, Miss Laura practiced this philosophy, as her school does to this day. The early photograph above shows students and teachers in the building that became the school's new location at Northeast Sixtieth Street in 1926.

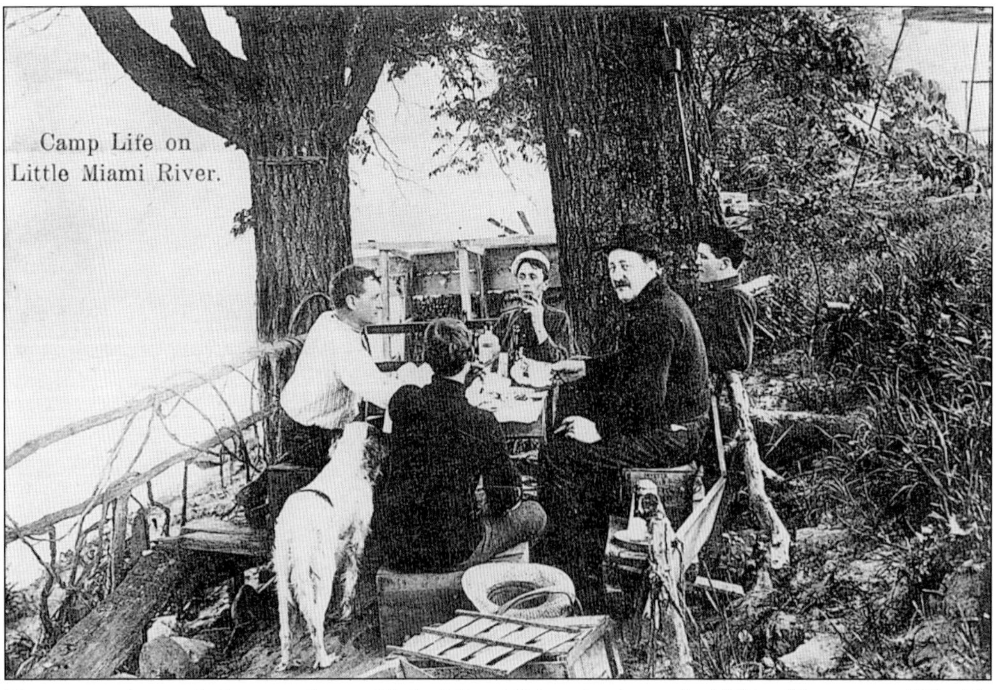

Five men relax at their campsite on Little Miami River in the early 1900s. (Courtesy of Florida State Archives.)

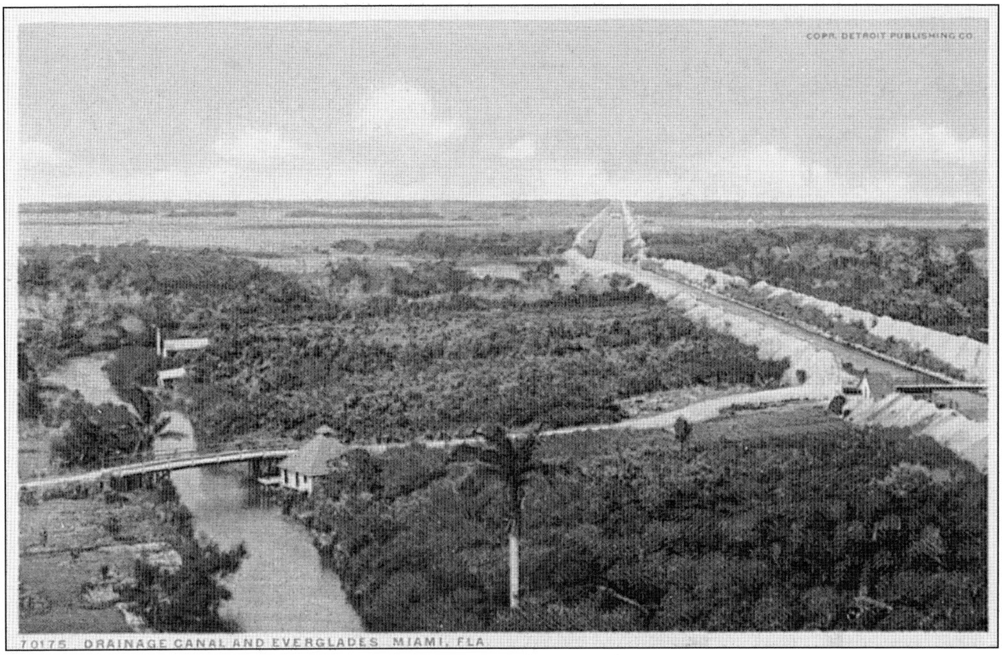

This postcard, made from a photograph taken on January 29, 1912, shows a bridge crossing the Miami River at what is now Twenty-seventh Avenue. The drainage canal on the right was part of the Everglades drainage project begun in 1909 by the State of Florida. By 1913, the flow of the Miami River was made slower by the dynamiting of the river's falls. (Published by Detroit Publishing Co.)

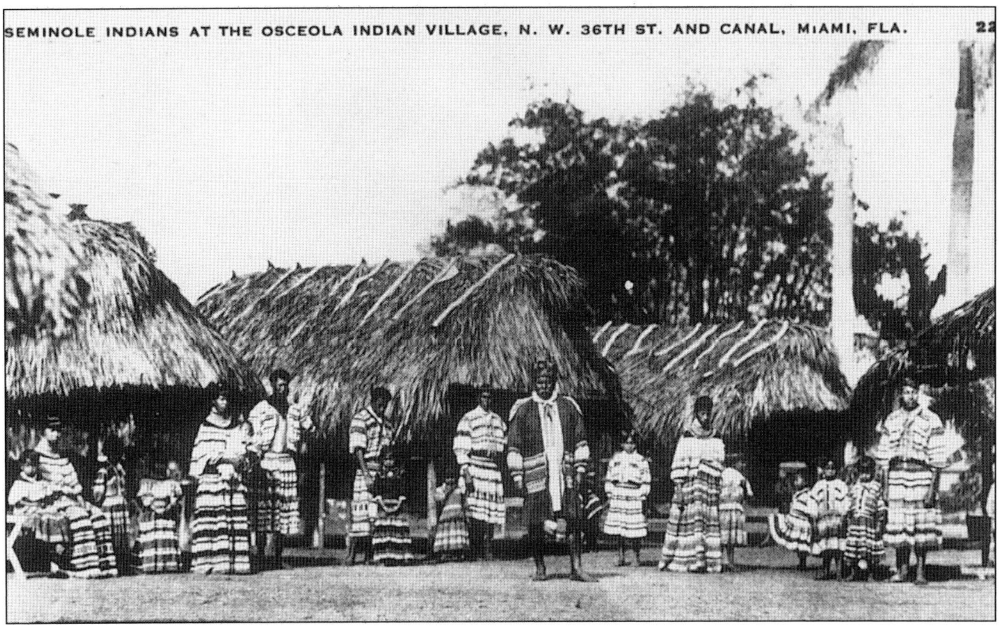

Seminole Indian families pose for this early photograph at the Osceola Indian Village. The village was located at Northwest Thirty-sixth Street at the Everglades Canal. (Courtesy of Florida State Archives.)

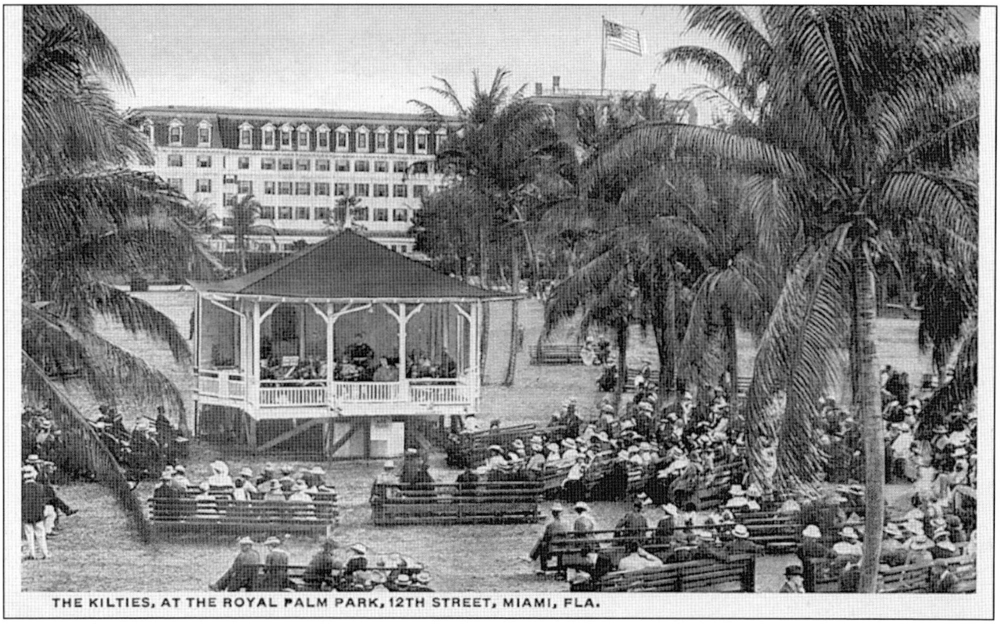

Royal Palm Park was the site of many popular gatherings, such as this outdoor performance by the Kilties. Today the park site is the location of the Southeast Bank Building. The Kilties, a well-known local Scottish band, performed regularly at the Royal Palm. (Published by J.N. Chamberlain.)

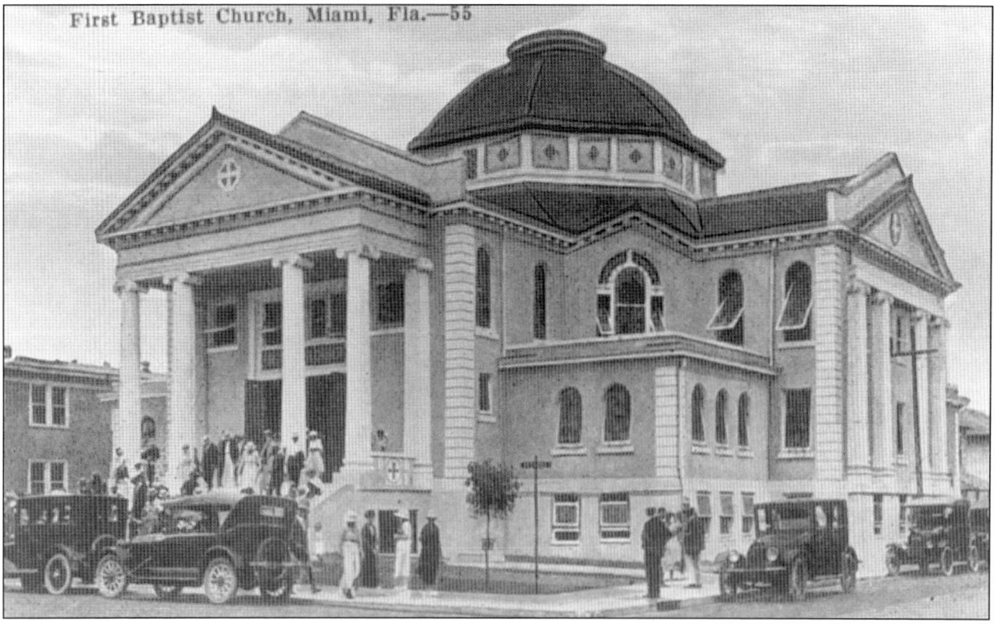

John Sewell was largely responsible for the organization of the Baptist Church, which began with 16 members in 1896. Three decades later, Sewell wielded the shovel at the groundbreaking ceremony for the new church shown above. This building, at Northeast First Avenue and Fifth Street, is now Central Baptist Church. (Courtesy of Historical Museum of Southern Florida.)

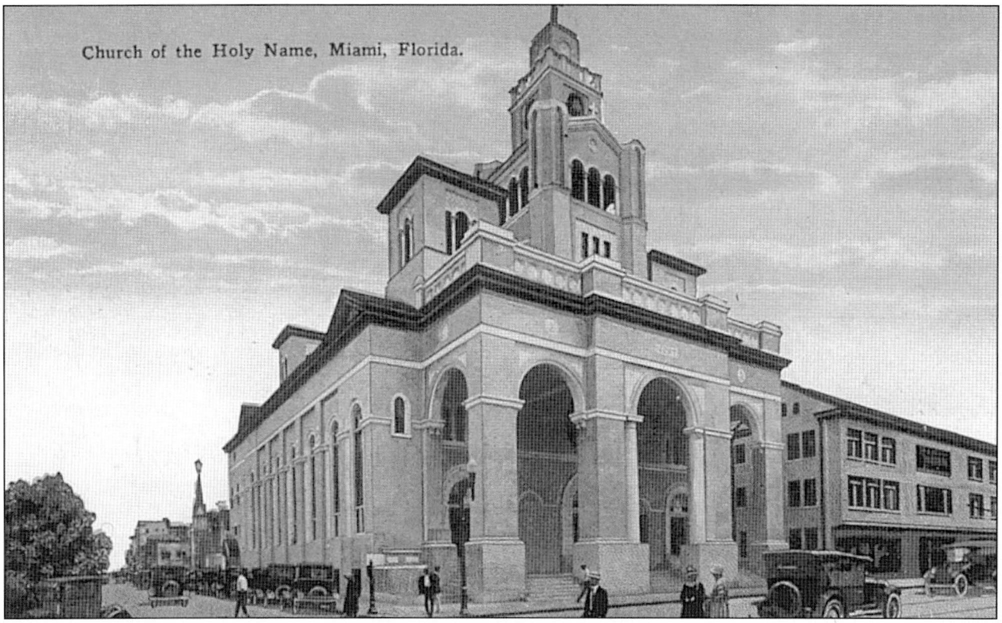

The Church of the Holy Name, the first Catholic congregation in Miami, was formed in 1896. The church and convent shown above were built on land donated by Henry Flagler. In 1925, the church building became Gesu Catholic Church. (Published by E.C. Kropp Co.)

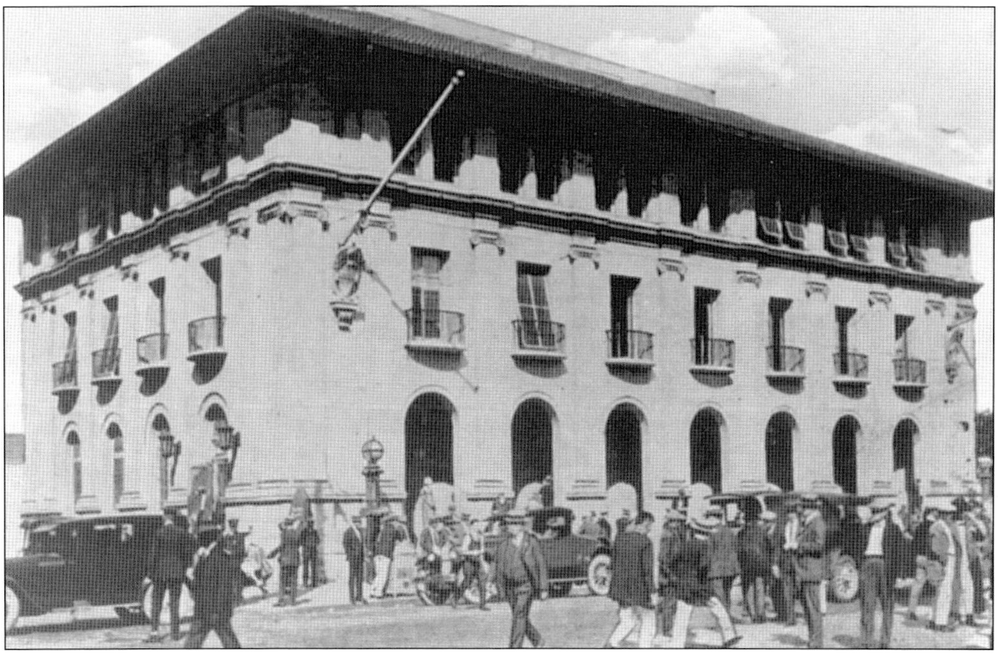

By the 1920s, Miami's bustling economy required an impressive central post office building. In contrast to today, note that many of the pedestrians are wearing vested suits, almost all are wearing hats, and there is not a woman in the picture. (Courtesy of Historical Museum of Southern Florida.)

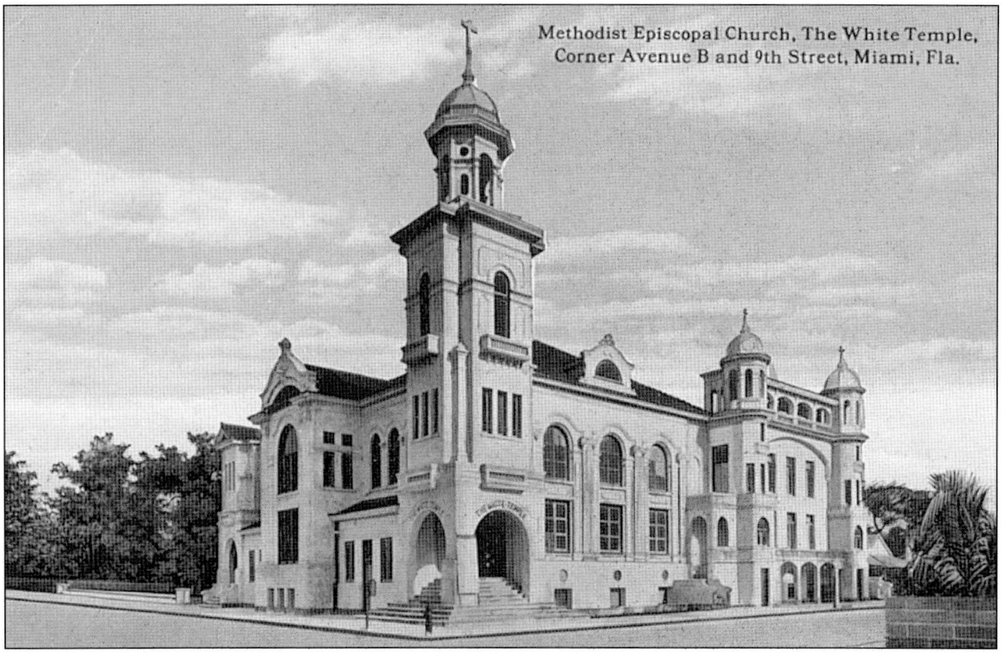

Rev. E.V. Blackman came to Miami in 1896 and organized the First Methodist Episcopal Church. Henry Flagler donated land at the corner of First Street and Northeast First Avenue. The church later sold that property and built the White Temple, shown above, at the corner of Avenue B and Ninth Street. The White Temple was demolished to make room for the Wolfson Campus of Miami-Dade Community College. (Published by H. & W.B. Drew Co.)

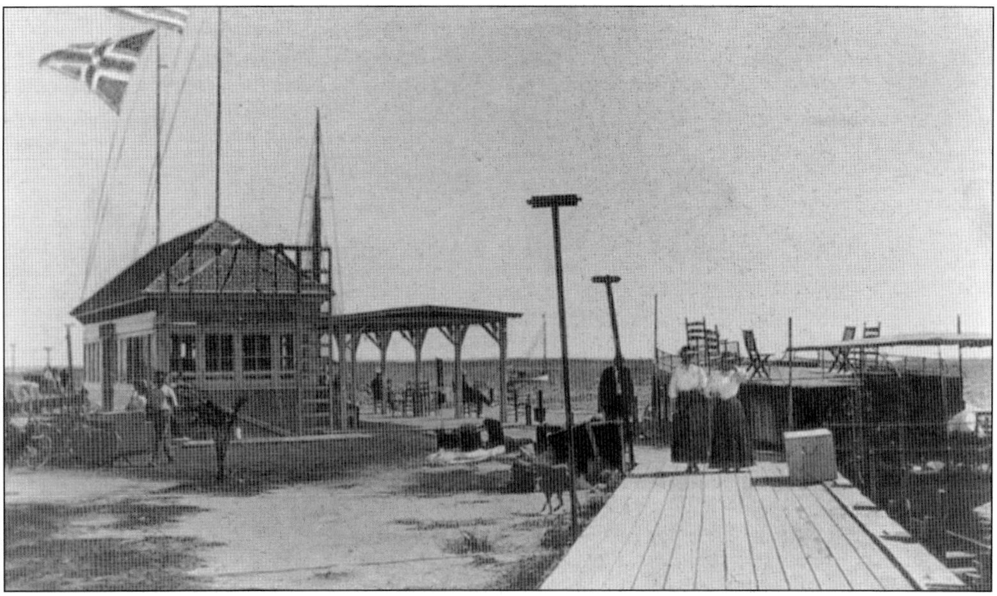

Visitors stroll past a houseboat tied up alongside the Royal Palm Dock, while others sit and enjoy the breathtaking view of Biscayne Bay. (Courtesy of Historical Museum of Southern Florida.)

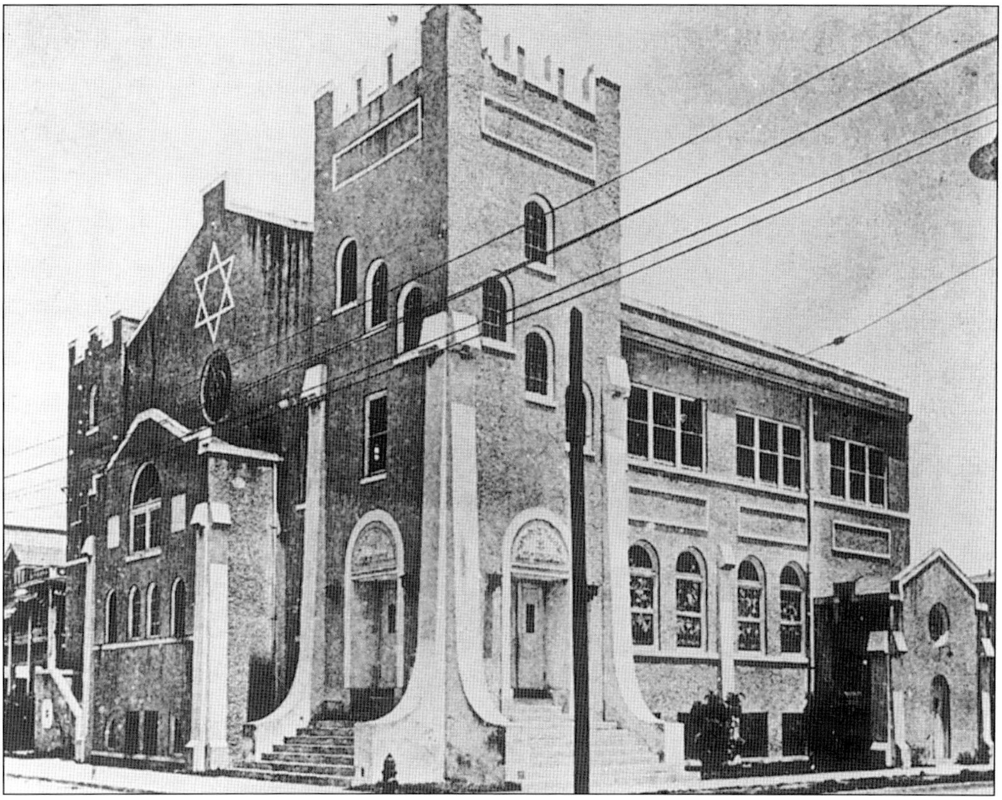

Beth David, Miami's first synagogue, was founded in 1912. Originally named Beth Zion, the congregation was re-incorporated in 1917 as Beth David, in honor of David Afremow. Three years later, Beth David purchased the former building of the First Christian Church. This building, shown above, was Beth David's spiritual home from 1920 until 1929, when the congregation moved to its present home at 2625 Southwest Third Avenue. The synagogue holds the Lawrence Museum of Judaica, which contains over 150 religious artifacts and works of art. (Courtesy of Jewish Museum of Florida.)

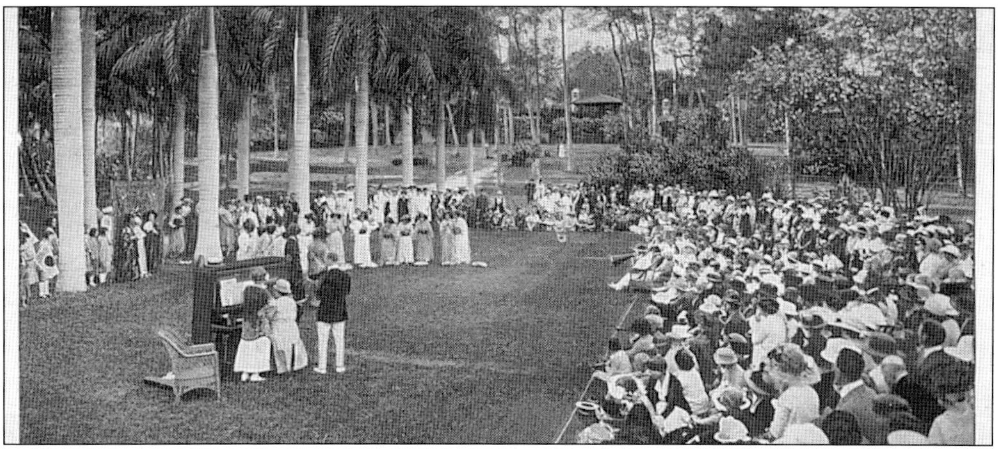

Outdoor music concerts were extremely popular and well attended. The scene above shows a concert held at the James Estate in Coconut Grove. (Published by E.C. Kropp Co.)

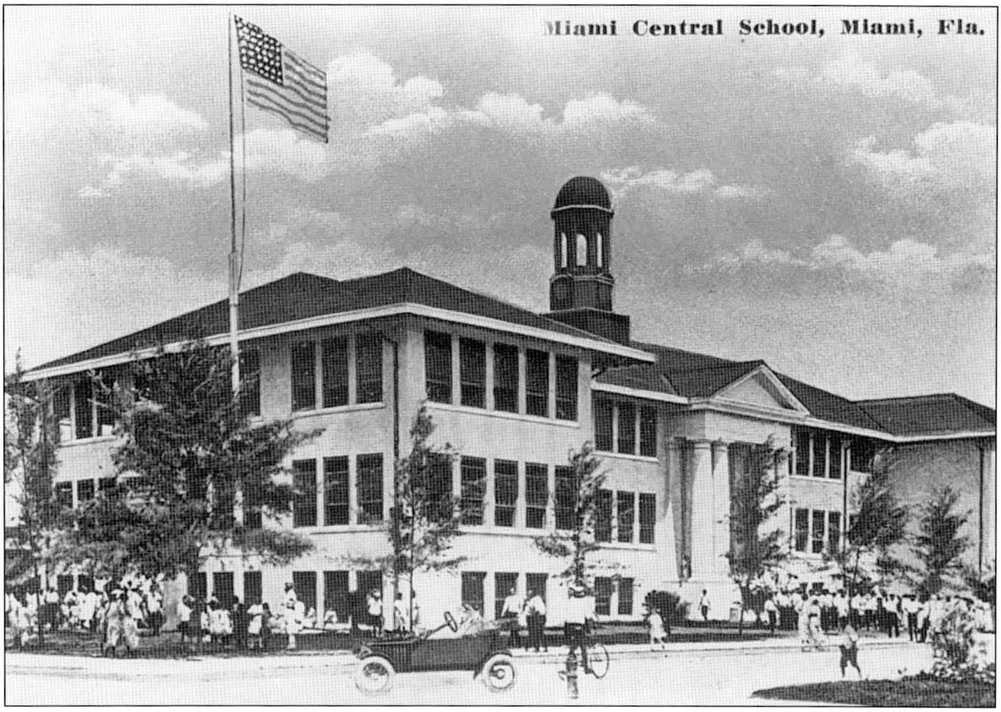

Miami Central School was built in 1909, and that same year the school produced its first yearbook. The three-story, fireproof building included all 12 grades. (Courtesy of Florida State Archives.)

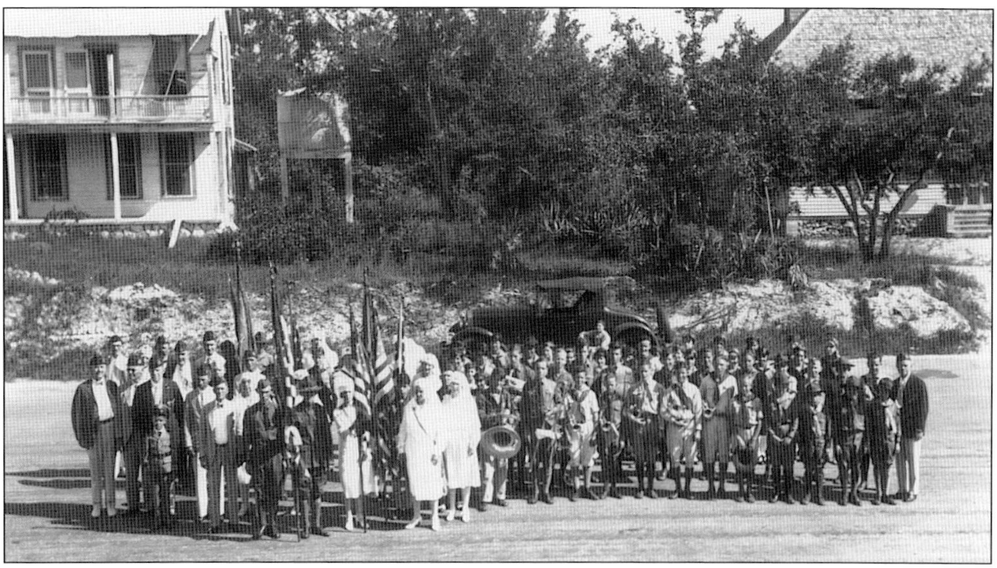

November 11th was known as Armistice Day, celebrating the end of World War I. After World War II, this date became known as Veterans Day to honor veterans of all United States wars. Shown above, a group of paraders pose in front of St. Stephens Church in Coconut Grove on Armistice Day, 1928. (Courtesy of the Romer Collection, Miami-Dade Public Library.)

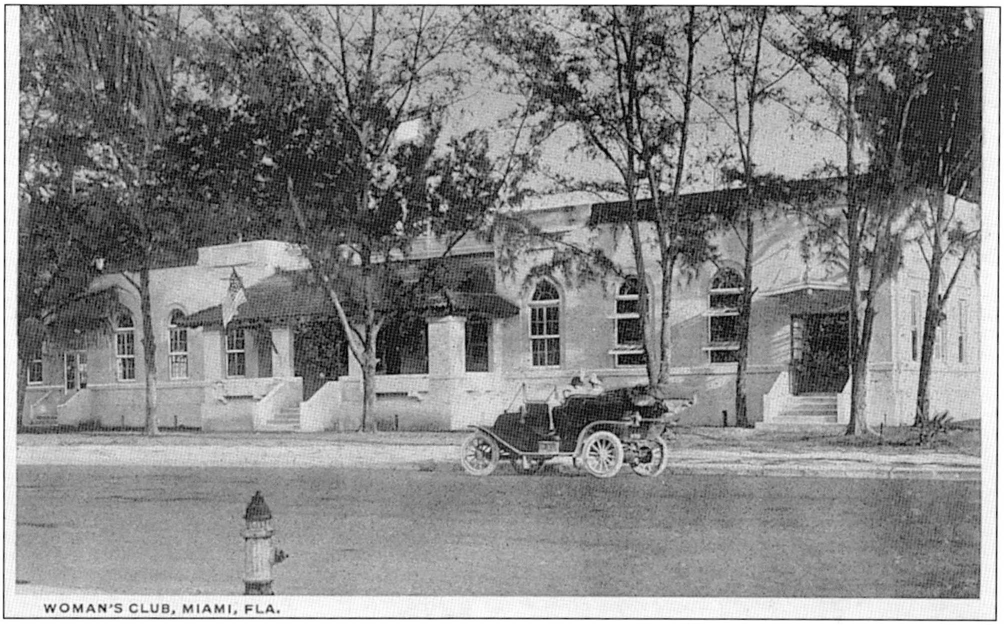

The Miami Women's Club, founded by Mrs. James M. Jackson, was located on Southeast Third Avenue. Once again, Henry Flagler donated land for the club, which became very valuable during the building boom in the 1920s. The Women's Club sold the land and built a new clubhouse and library at 1737 Northeast Bayshore Drive. The Women's Club had previously maintained the city's first library at the Fair Building. (Published by H. & W.B. Drew Co.)

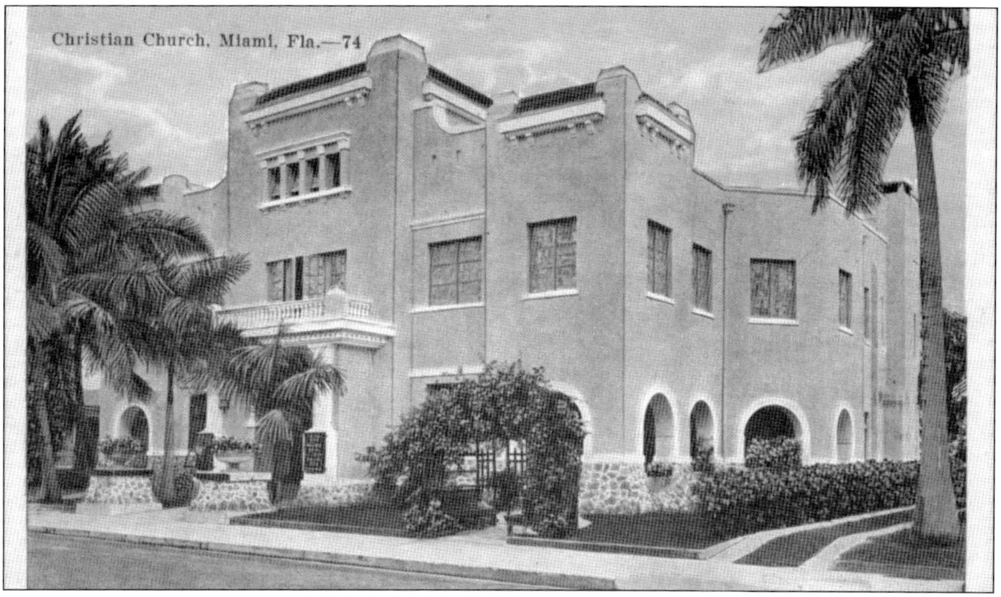

When the First Christian Church was begun in 1905, the congregation met in the Fair Building. The building shown above was constructed in 1919 on Northeast Fourth Street, a half-block from Biscayne Bay. The church provided facilities for rest as well as a rooftop gymnasium. (Published by E.C. Kropp Co.)

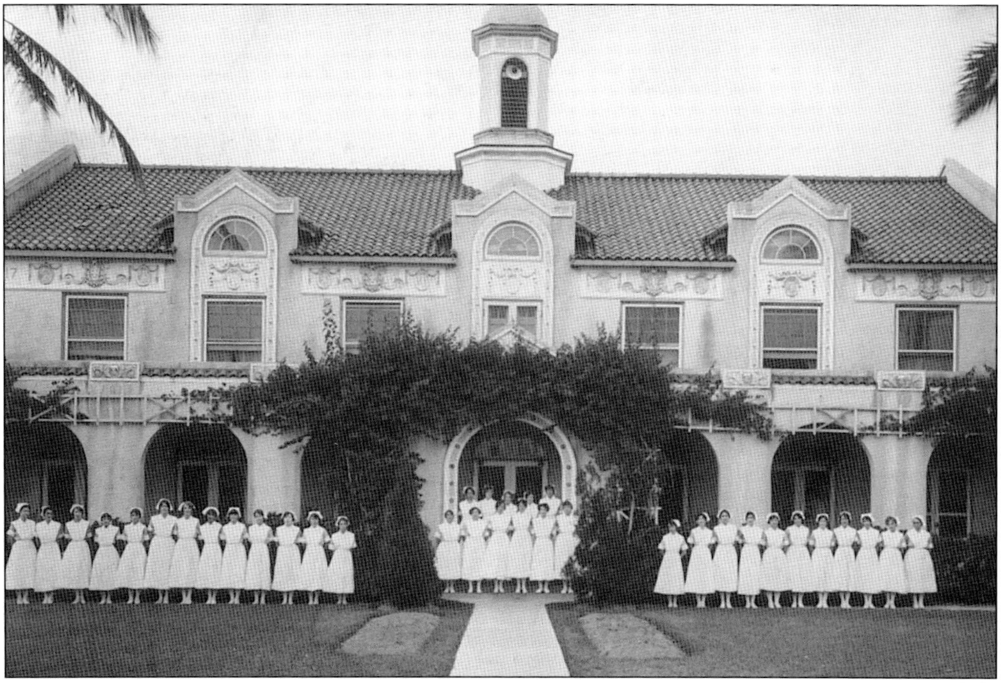

The Miami City Hospital, designed by August Geiger, opened in 1918 under the direction of Dr. James M. Jackson. The hospital was renamed in honor of Dr. Jackson after his death in 1924. The original building, shown here, was nicknamed "The Alamo" and is now used as a visitors center and medical museum at the Jackson Memorial Hospital Complex. A group of proud 1929 nursing school graduates pose in front of the early hospital. (Courtesy of the Romer Collection, Miami-Dade Public Library.)

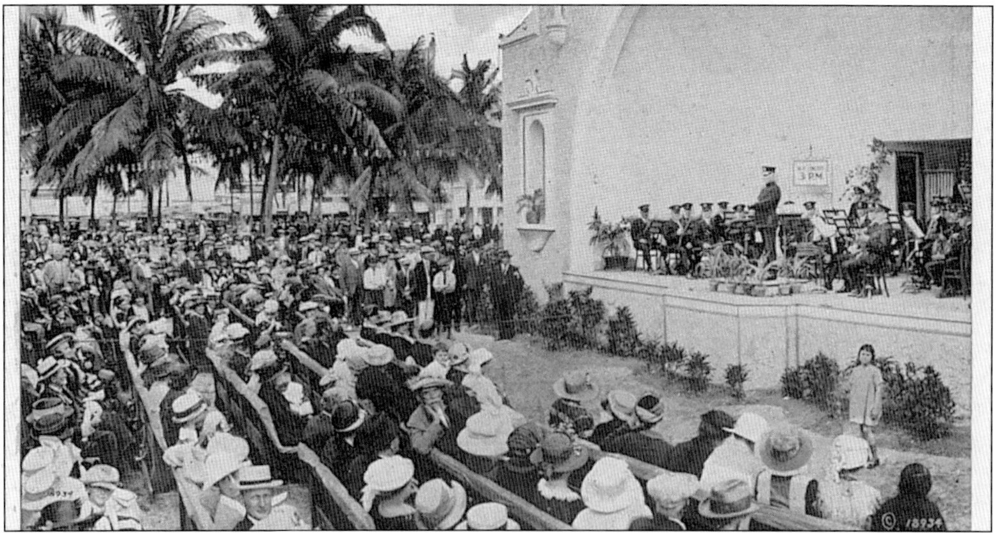

It was "standing room only" at the concert by the Pryor's Band, a popular local band, held in Royal Palm Park on this beautiful South Florida day. Outdoor concerts were always well attended. The sign on the stage lists concert times at 3 p.m. daily, and 3 p.m. and 7 p.m. on Sundays. (Published by J.N. Chamberlain.)

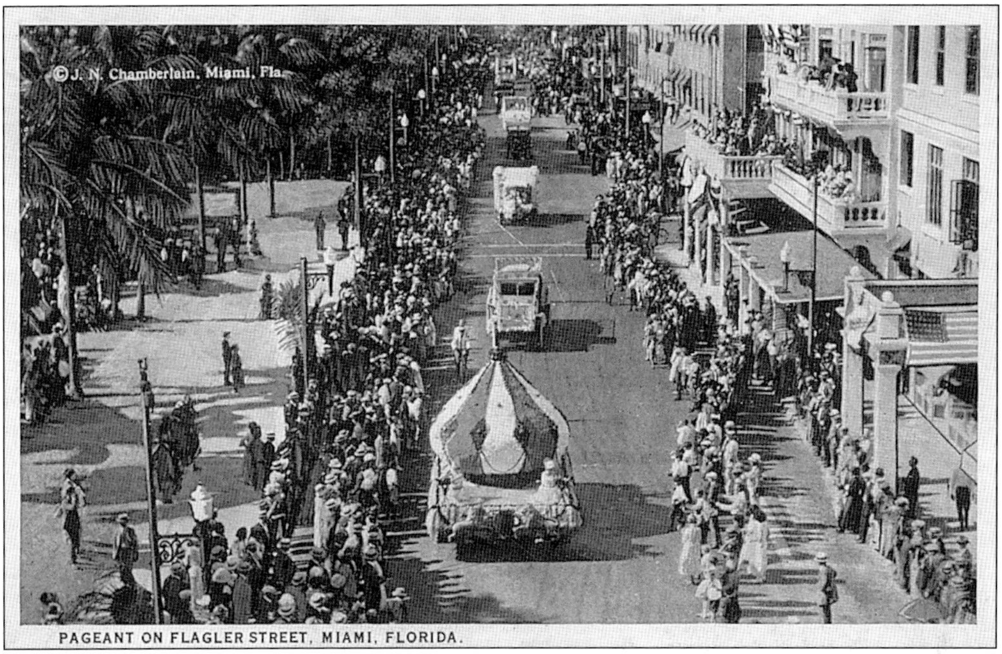

Crowds watch the pageantry as floats proceed down Flagler Street during a celebration in the 1920s. (Published by J.N. Chamberlain.)

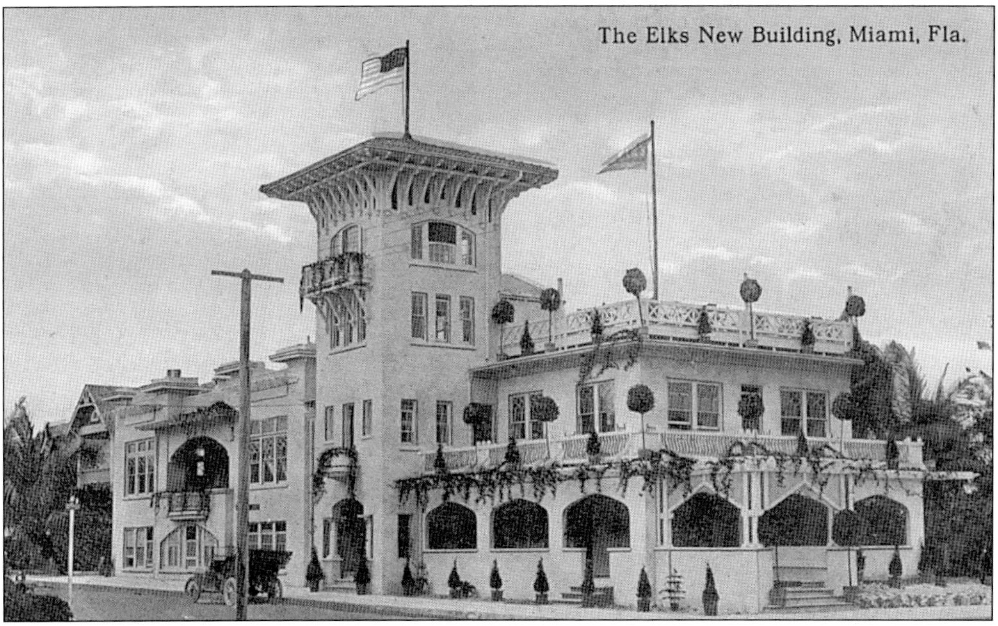

The Miami Elks Lodge was founded in 1905 and originally met in the Townley Building. In 1910, the Lodge acquired the building shown above, located at the corner of Flagler Street and Southeast Third Avenue. The building was extensively remodeled in the 1920s and remained the home for the Elks until the downtown area became too crowded. At that time a new lodge was opened on Brickell Avenue. (Published by J.N. Chamberlain.)

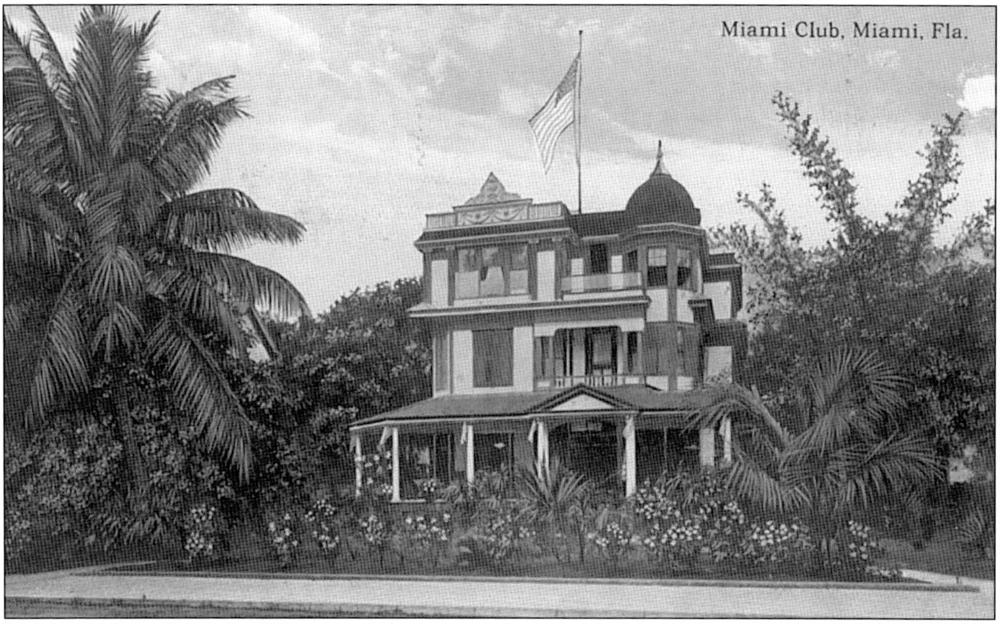

The Miami Club, a business and social club for men, opened in 1909 in the former residence of Charles Garthside. The house was located on Avenue B facing Royal Palm Park. (Published by H. & W.B. Drew Co.)

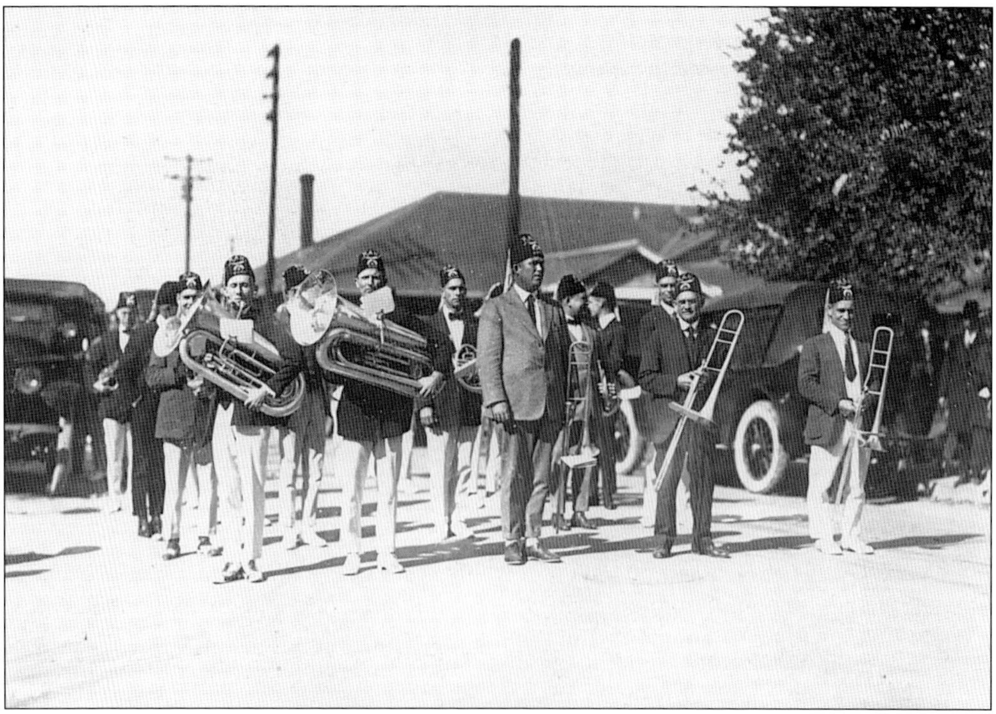

Members of the Shriners Band parade past the FEC Railway Station in downtown Miami in this *c.* 1920 photo. (Courtesy of Florida State Archives.)

George Merrick donated the land for and built the Coral Gables Congregational Church. It was the first church in Coral Gables and was dedicated by Merrick in memory of his father, who had been a Congregationalist minister. Designed in 1925 by architects Kiehnel and Elliott, the church exhibits obvious influences of Mediterranean design. Today the church hosts an excellent chamber concert series each summer. (Published by Curt Teich.)

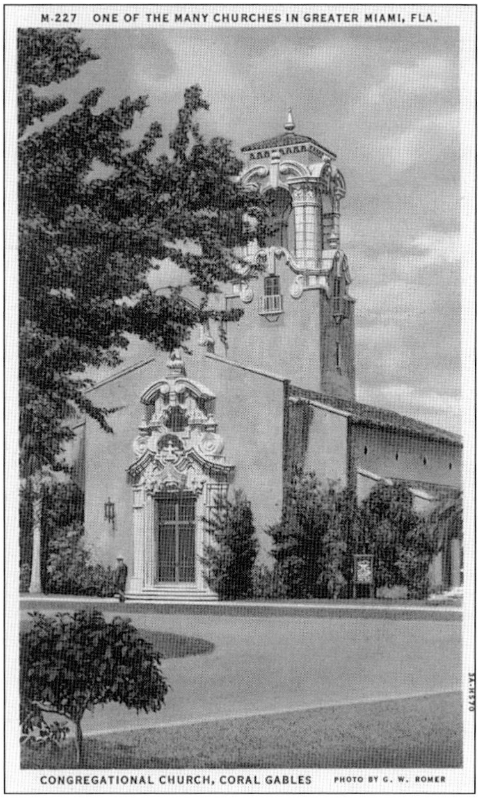

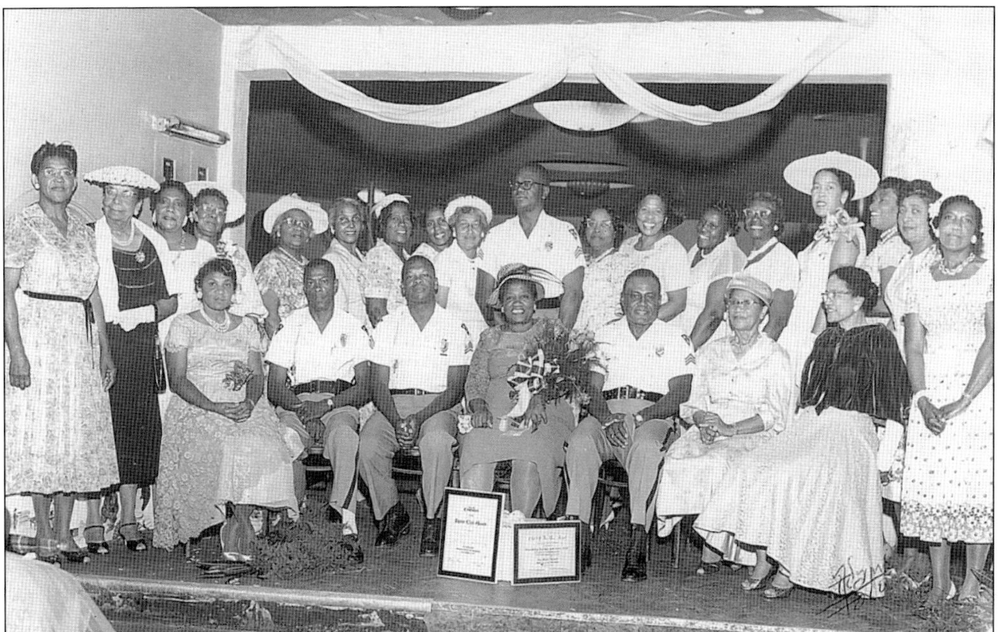

Four Overtown police officers receive an award from the Friendship Garden and Civic Club in this 1940s photograph. (Courtesy of Black Archives Foundation.)

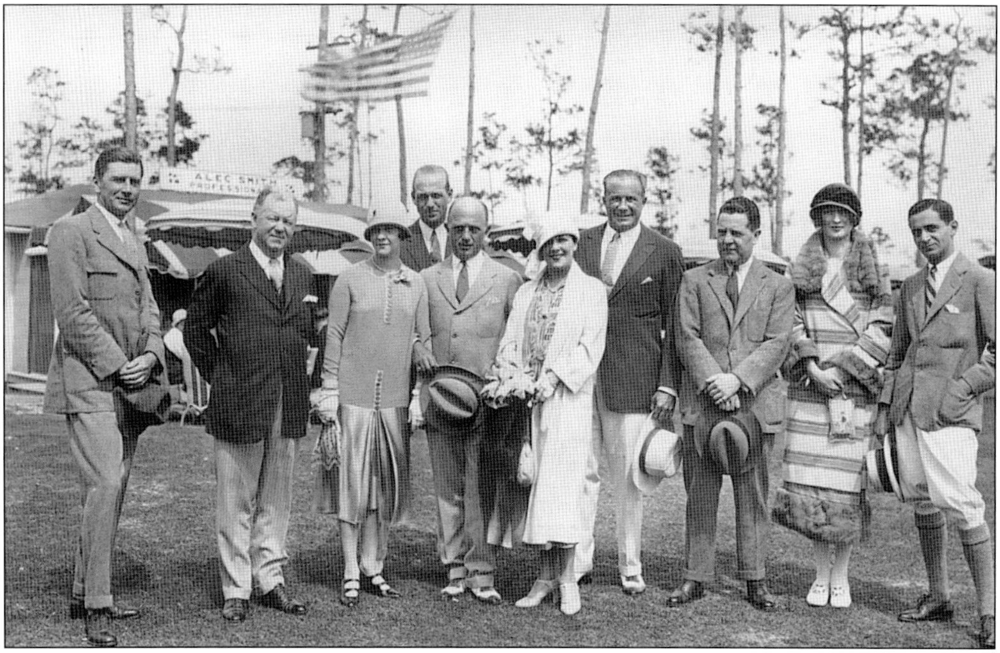

A group poses in front of the Miami Biltmore Country Club in this 1925 photo. Pictured in the center, clad in a white coat and holding a bouquet, is Mrs. George Merrick, wife of the founder of Coral Gables. (Courtesy of Florida State Archives.)

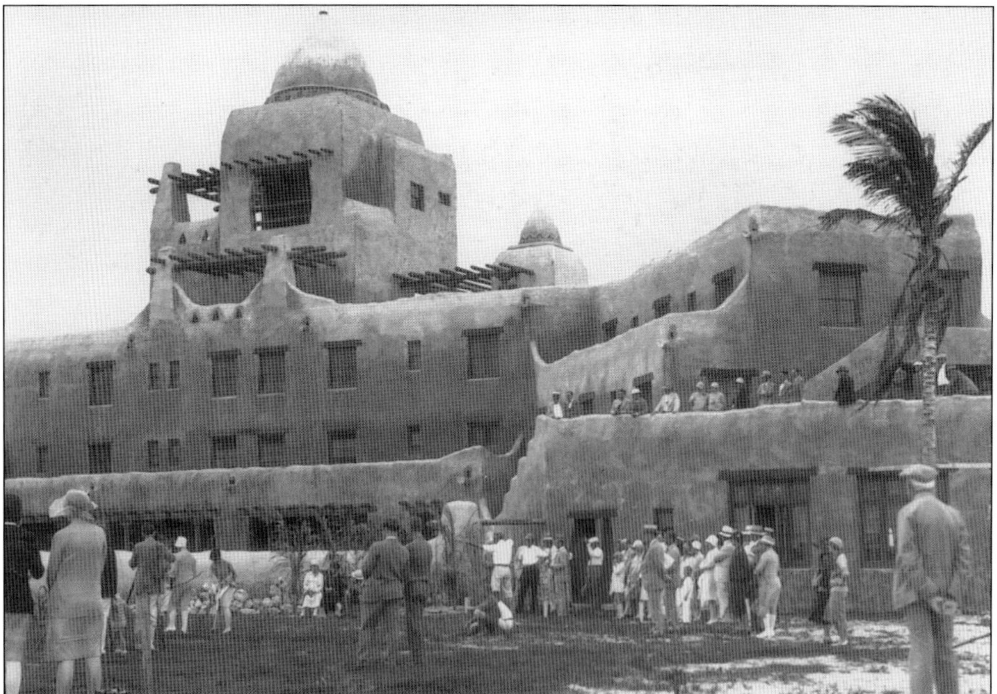

Spectators gather to watch an archery exhibit at the Pueblo Hotel in Miami Springs in February of 1928. (Courtesy of the Romer Collection, Miami-Dade Public Library.)

Five

The Building Boom, Bust, and Recovery

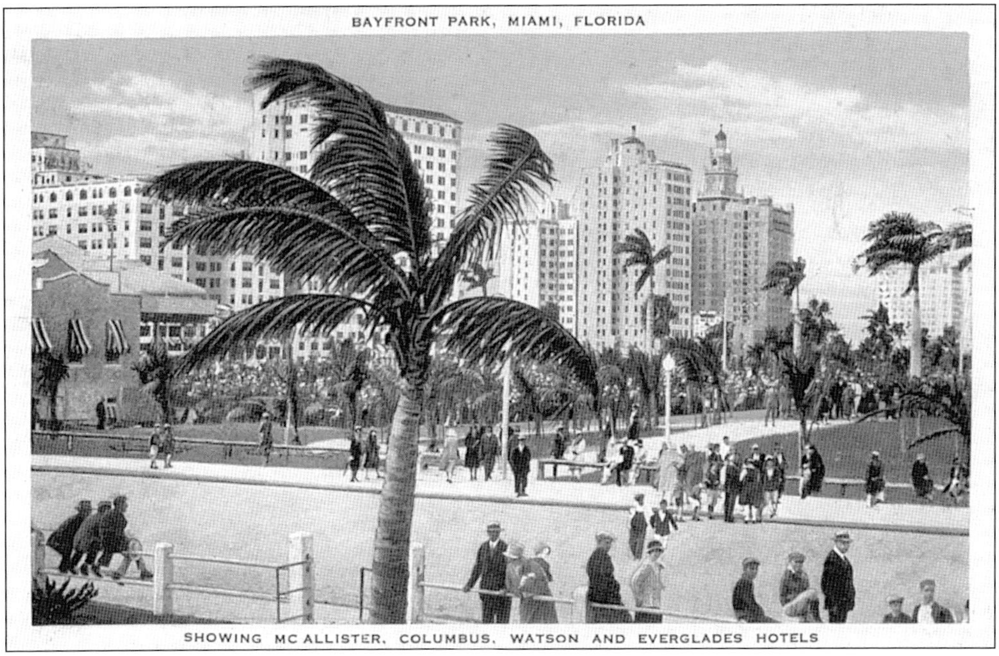

By the late 1920s, the building boom had dramatically changed the skyline of downtown Miami. Bayfront Park, in the foreground, was created from landfill from Biscayne Bay. The McAllister, Columbus, Watson, and Everglades Hotels can be seen in the distance. (Published by Pictorial Centre.)

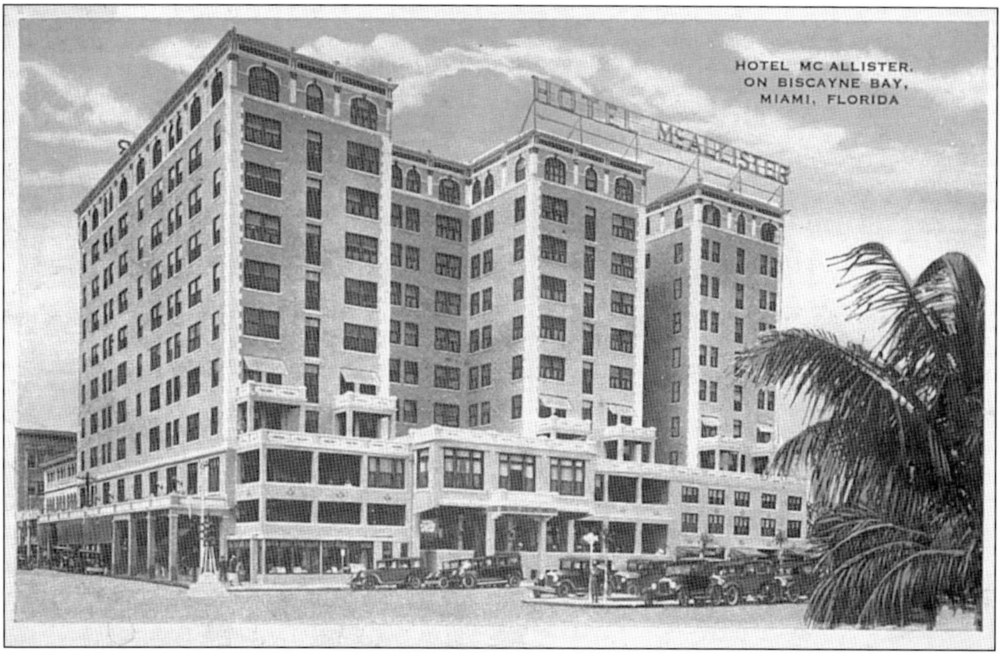

The McAllister Hotel, at ten stories, was the tallest building in Miami when just opened in 1924. Located at Flagler Street and Biscayne Boulevard, the hotel faced directly onto Biscayne Bay. (Published by E.C. Kropp Co.)

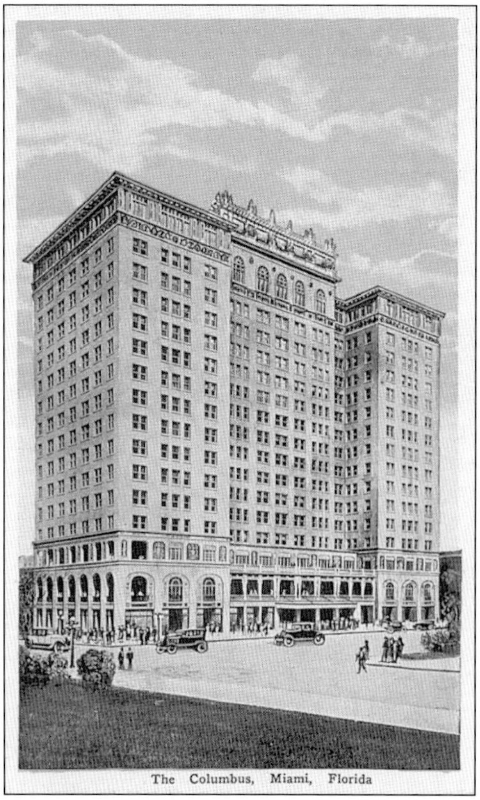

The 600-room Columbus Hotel was typical of the large, modern hotels built along the bayfront in downtown Miami. (Published by E.C. Kropp Co.)

The Miami News Tower, known today as the Freedom Tower, was built in 1925. The architects on the project were Schultze and Weaver, the firm responsible for New York's Grand Central Station, the Waldorf-Astoria, Miami Beach's Roney Plaza, and the Coral Gables' Biltmore. The pair used the Giralda Tower in Seville, Spain, as inspiration for the News Tower. The *Miami News* occupied the building until 1957. The tower was used for many years as the Cuban Refugee Processing Center, earning it the name "Freedom Tower." (Published by E.C. Kropp Co.)

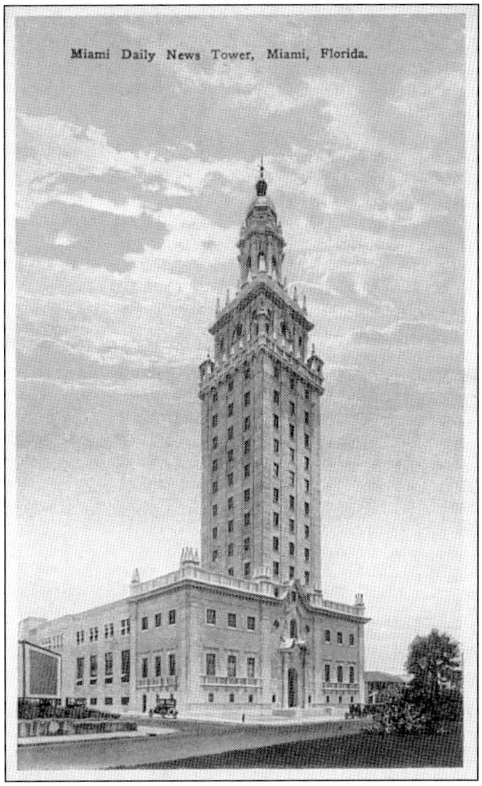

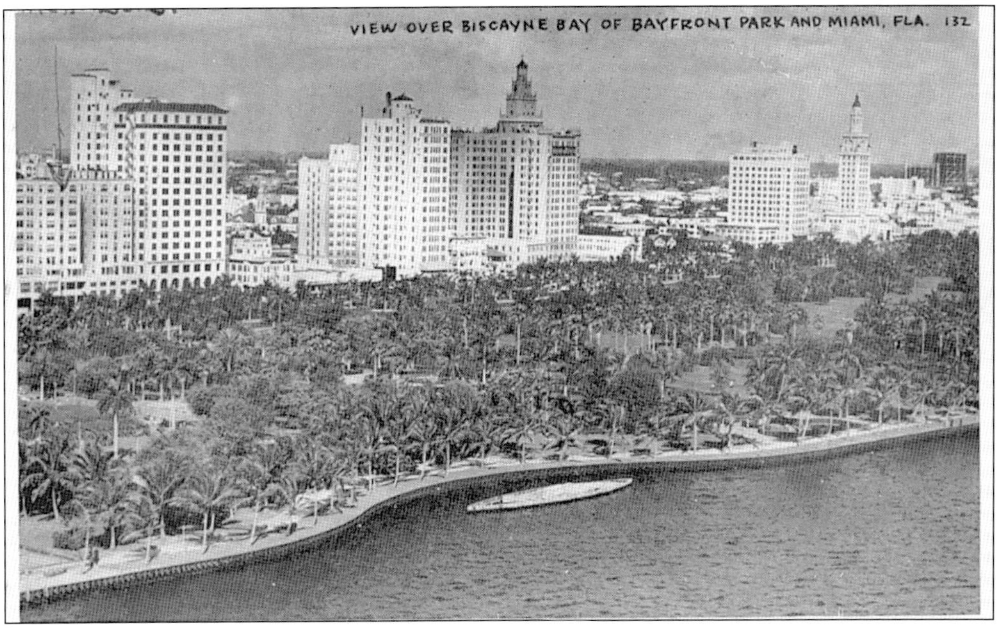

This aerial view from the early 1930s shows the completed Bayfront Park with the Everglades Hotel in the center of the photo, easily identified by the tower on the roof. The other tower to the far right is that of the Miami News Tower. (Published by Kromekote.)

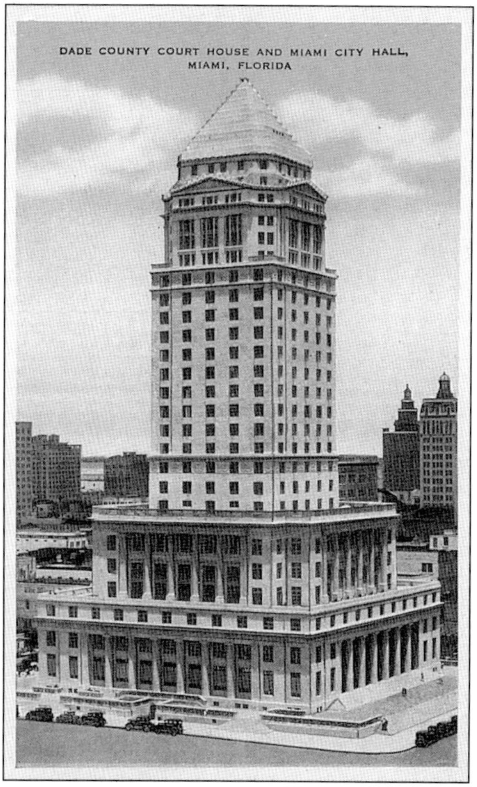

The new 27-story Dade County Courthouse was built between 1925 and 1929 at a cost of $4 million. The building was also used as City Hall, with the top 11 floors used as a jail. The courthouse was literally built around the 1904 courthouse shown on page 22. (Published by Pictorial Centre.)

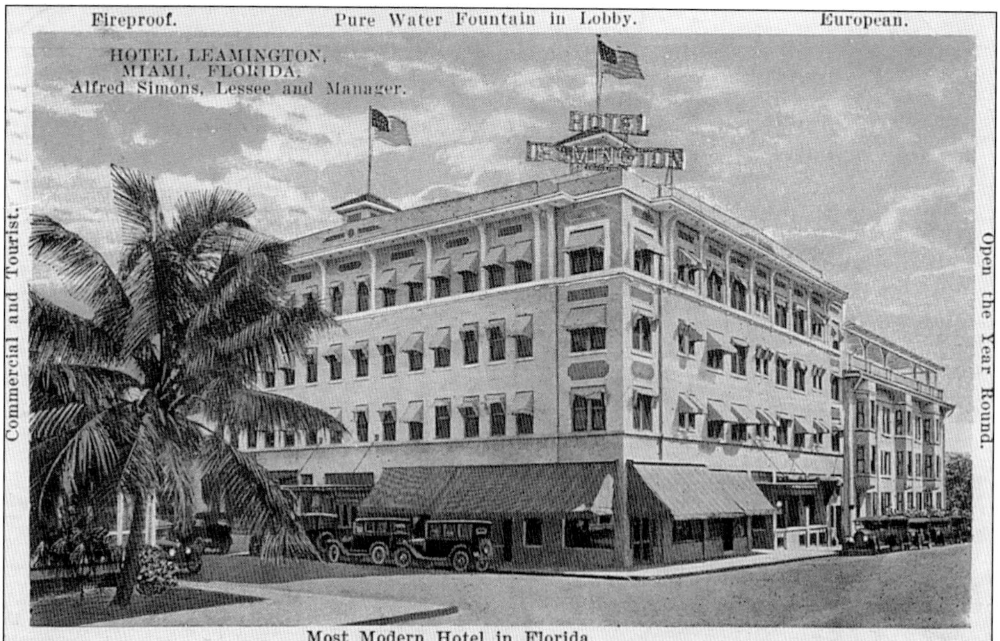

The Hotel Leamington catered to both business travelers and tourists. The hotel offered rooms for $3 to $5 for a single, $5 to $8 for a double, and could accommodate 150 guests. (Published by E.C. Kropp Co.)

The Everglades Hotel, as seen through the palm trees of the newly created Bayfront Park, stands majestically along the downtown bayfront. (Published by Pictorial Centre.)

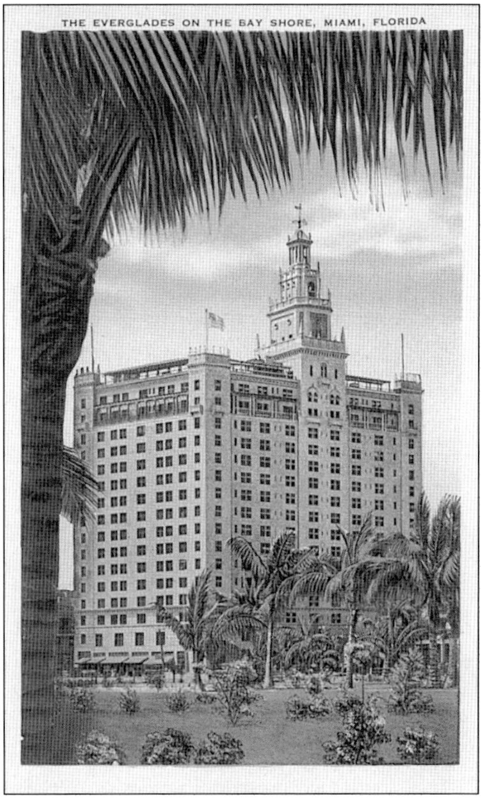

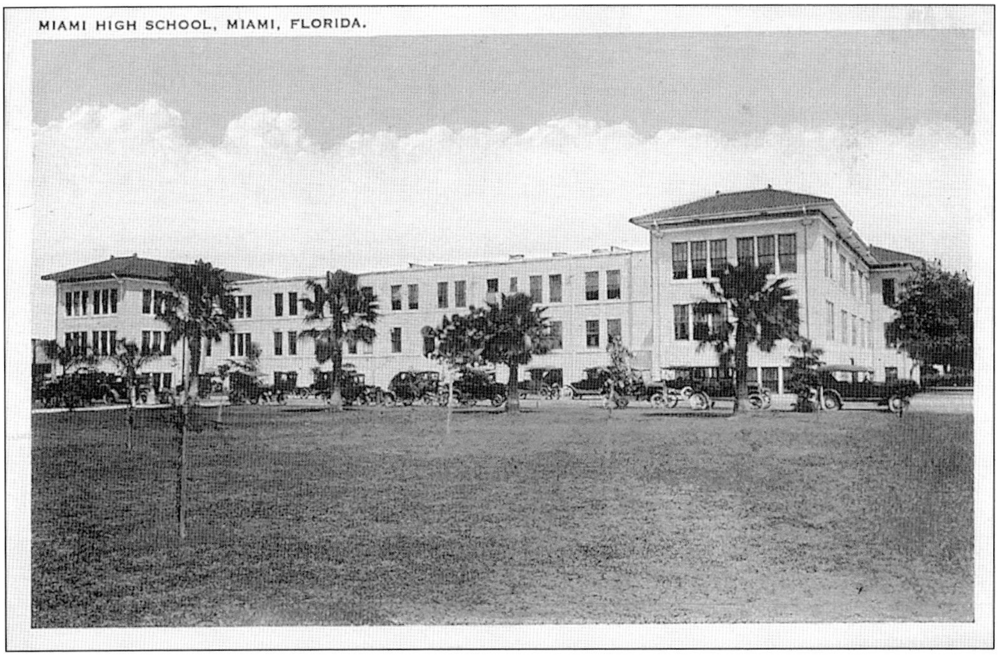

The student population of Miami was obviously growing at a rapid rate as can be seen from this *c.* 1920 postcard of Miami High School. (Published by Pictorial Centre.)

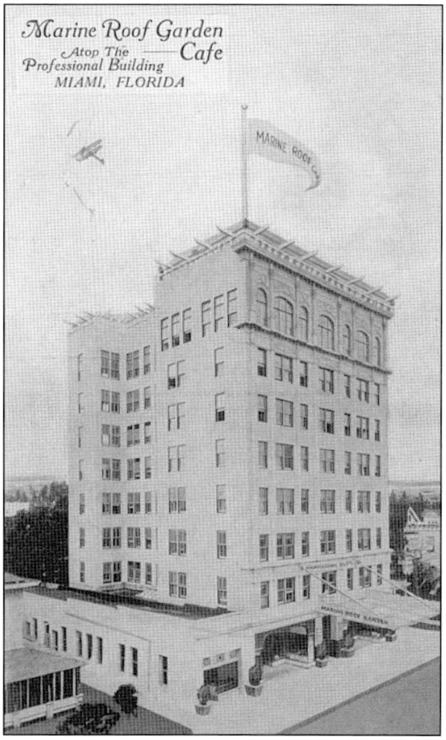

The Marine Roof Garden Café was located on the top of the Professional Building. This *c.* 1925 postcard invites the public to visit the Garden Café "after the races" at the new Miami Jockey Club. (Published by Lumitone.)

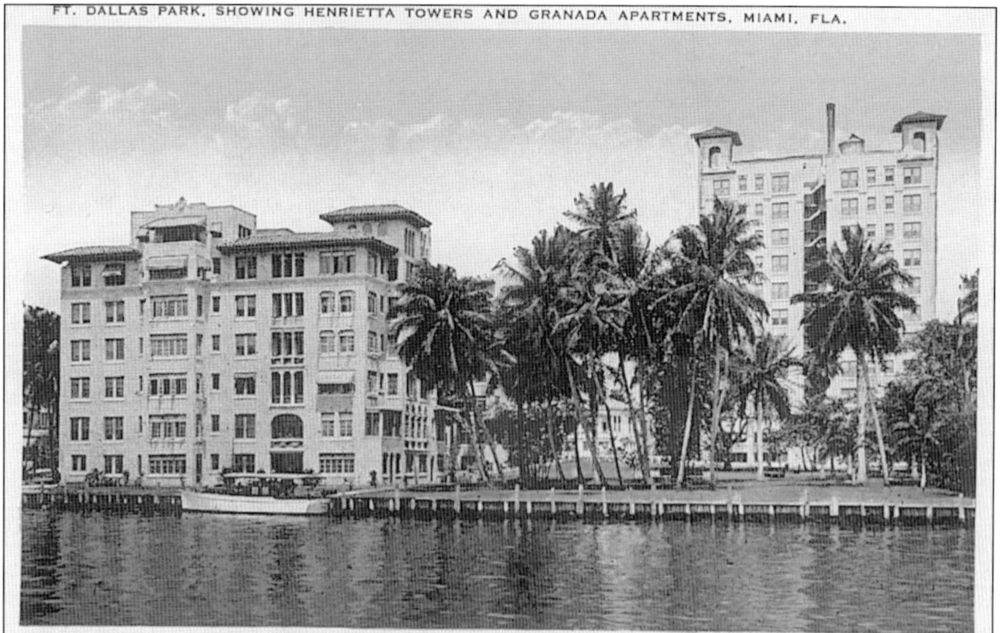

Julia Tuttle's son utilized the family land at the mouth of the Miami River to create Fort Dallas Park. The Granada Apartments, shown on the left, were Miami's first apartments. The building was eventually demolished and today the Hyatt Hotel occupies the site. (Published by Pictorial Centre.)

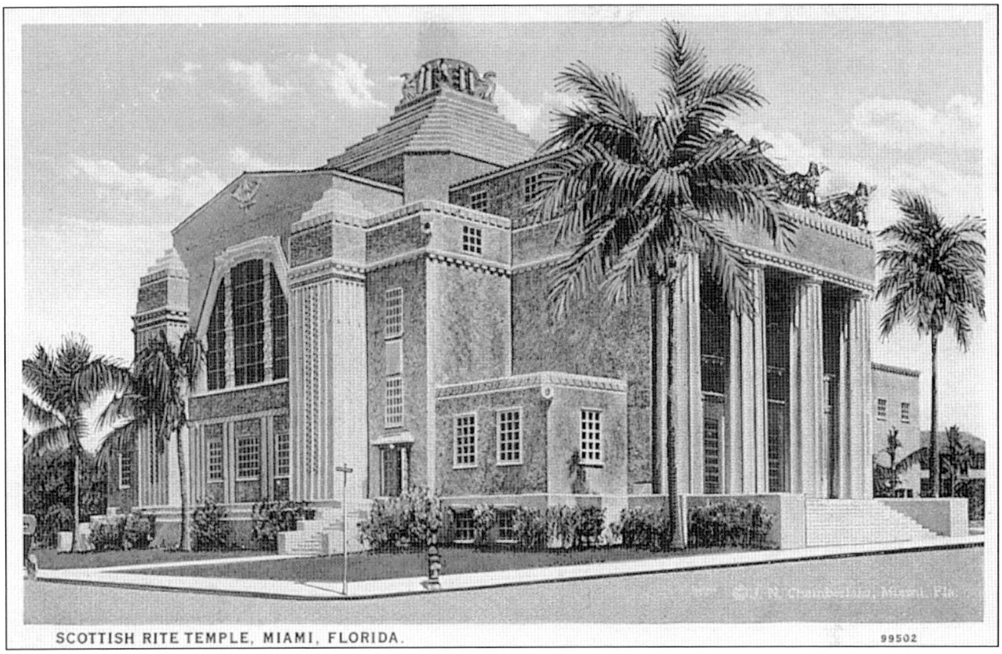

The Scottish Rite Temple, designed by architects Kiehnel and Elliott, is one of the earliest examples of Art Deco architecture in the United States. Built in 1922 at 471 Northwest Third Street, the building predates the Art Deco District in Miami Beach. (Published by J.N. Chamberlain.)

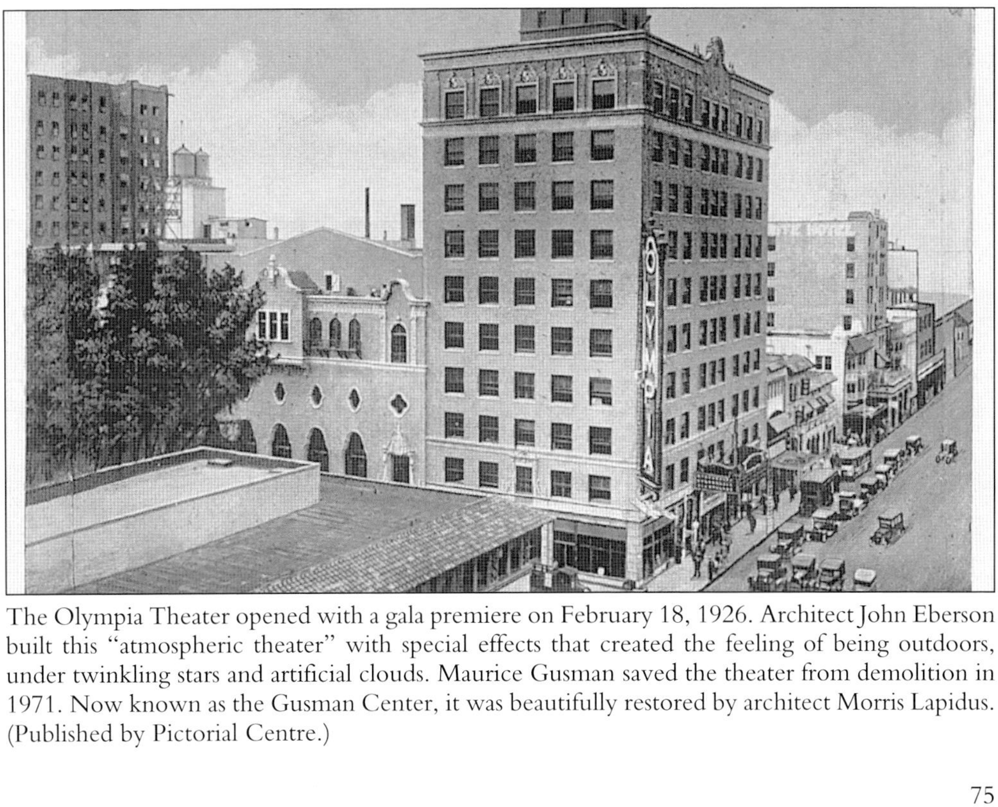

The Olympia Theater opened with a gala premiere on February 18, 1926. Architect John Eberson built this "atmospheric theater" with special effects that created the feeling of being outdoors, under twinkling stars and artificial clouds. Maurice Gusman saved the theater from demolition in 1971. Now known as the Gusman Center, it was beautifully restored by architect Morris Lapidus. (Published by Pictorial Centre.)

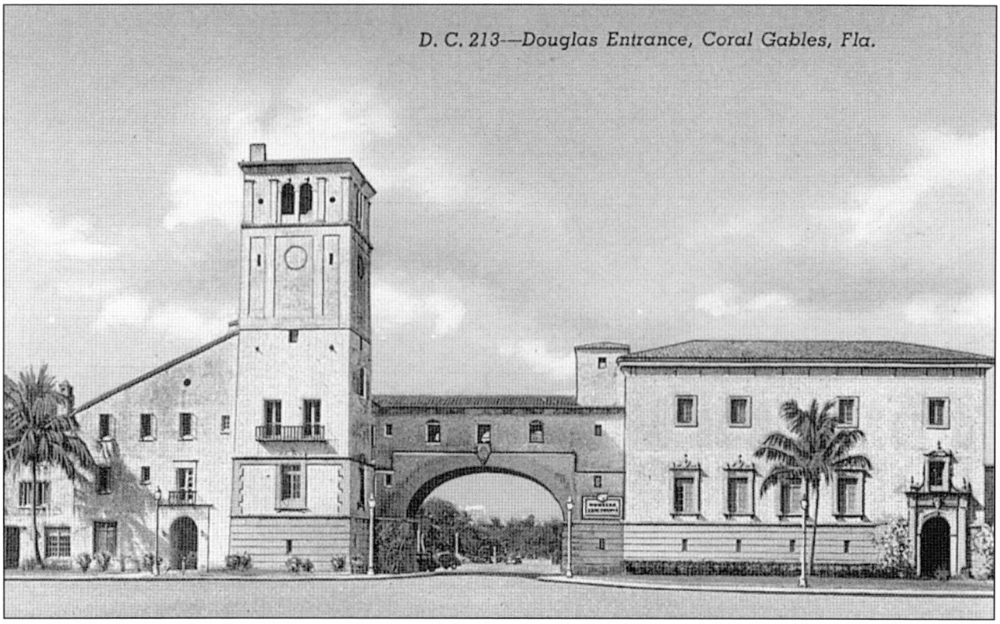

In 1921 George Merrick began planning his "City Beautiful" on his family's land. He named it Coral Gables after the name of their home. Shown above is the Douglas Entrance to the city, "La Puerta De Sol," located at the Tamiami Trail and Douglas Road. Although eight entrances to the city had been planned, the Douglas Entrance was the fourth and last one to be built. (Published by Curt Teich.)

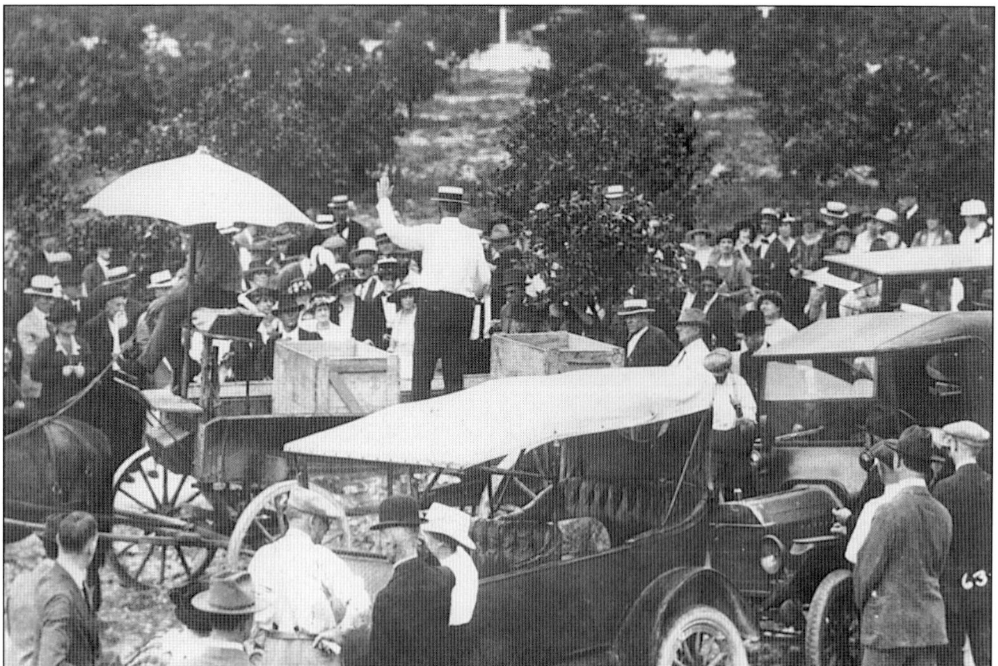

Speculation in Florida land grew to a fevered pitch during the 1920s. Pictured above is an auctioneer selling off lots to eager buyers. (Courtesy of Florida State Archives.)

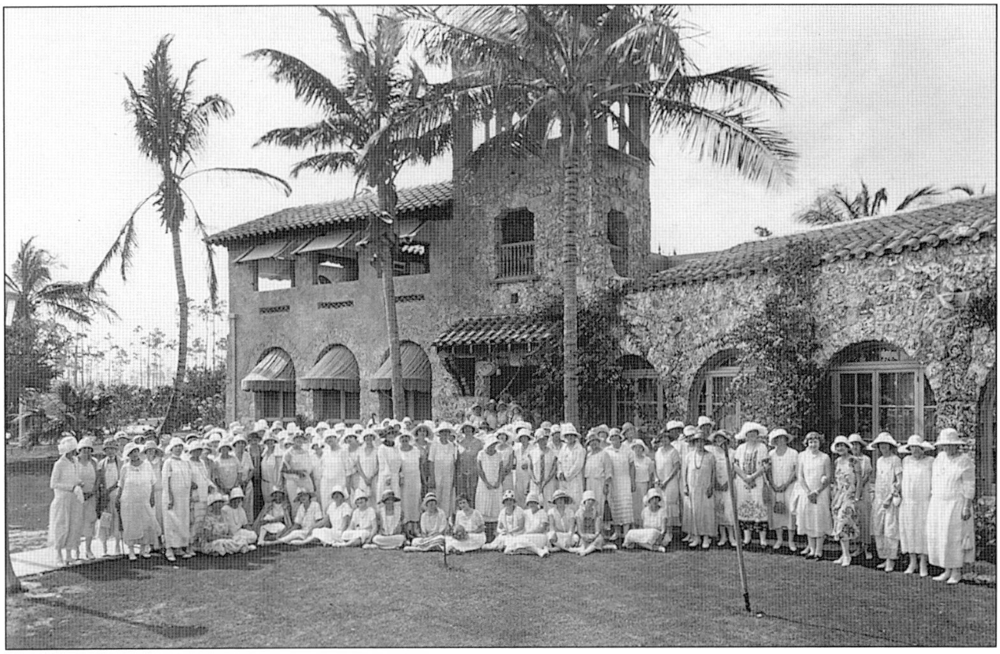

The Coral Gables Country Club was the setting for this ladies social gathering in 1926. (Courtesy of Florida State Archives.)

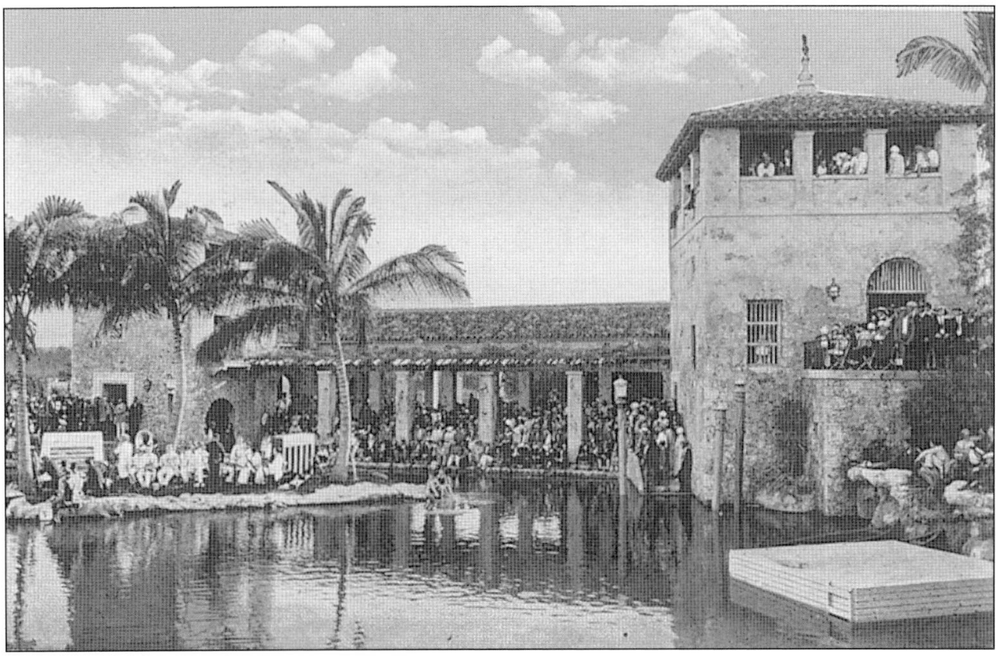

An orchestra (wearing white) performs for an appreciative audience at the Venetian Pool in Coral Gables. The pool, which opened in 1924, was carved out of a limestone quarry. William Jennings Bryan often stood on the square island to the right extolling the virtues of investing in Coral Gables property, and for this he was paid $50,000 per year and an equal amount of land. (Published by Pictorial Centre.)

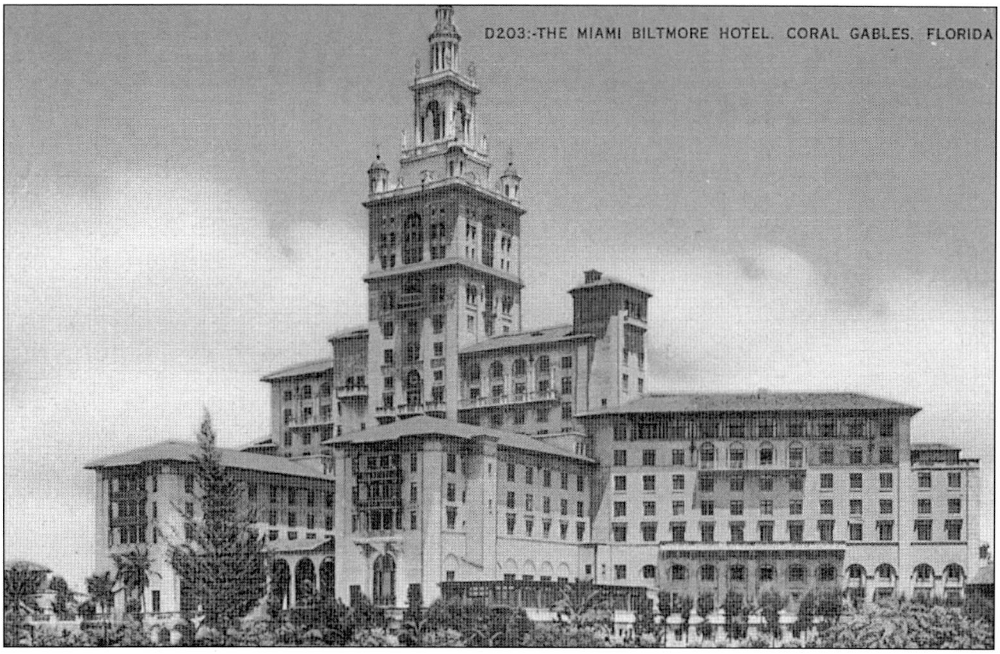

George Merrick and John McEntee Bowman teamed up to build the Miami Biltmore Hotel, which opened on January 15, 1926, with great fanfare. People were brought from the north on special trains marked "Miami Biltmore Specials." Guests could ride in a gondola through the waterways to Tahiti Beach. The elegant hotel attracted royalty and celebrities. Today the magnificently restored hotel is one of Miami's premiere destinations. (Published by Metropolitan.)

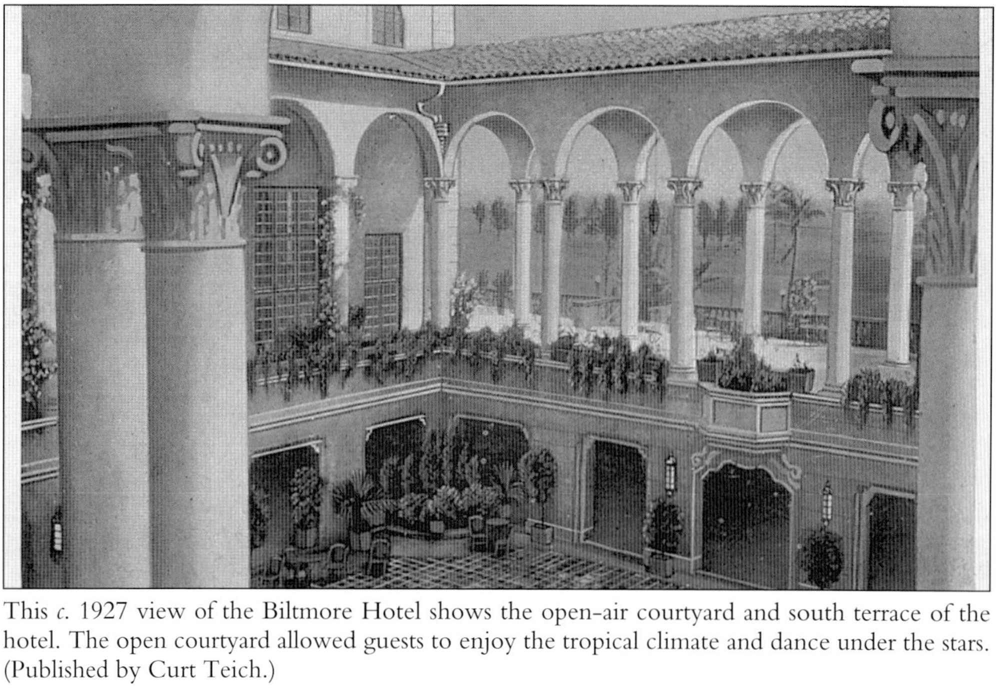

This *c.* 1927 view of the Biltmore Hotel shows the open-air courtyard and south terrace of the hotel. The open courtyard allowed guests to enjoy the tropical climate and dance under the stars. (Published by Curt Teich.)

This lovely 1924 home on Granada Boulevard is an example of the successful use of Mediterranean detail by architect H. George Fink. (Published by J.N. Chamberlain.)

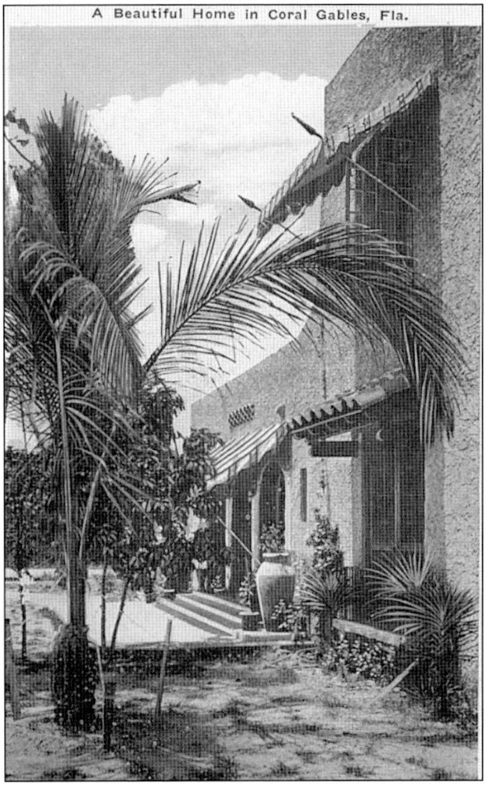

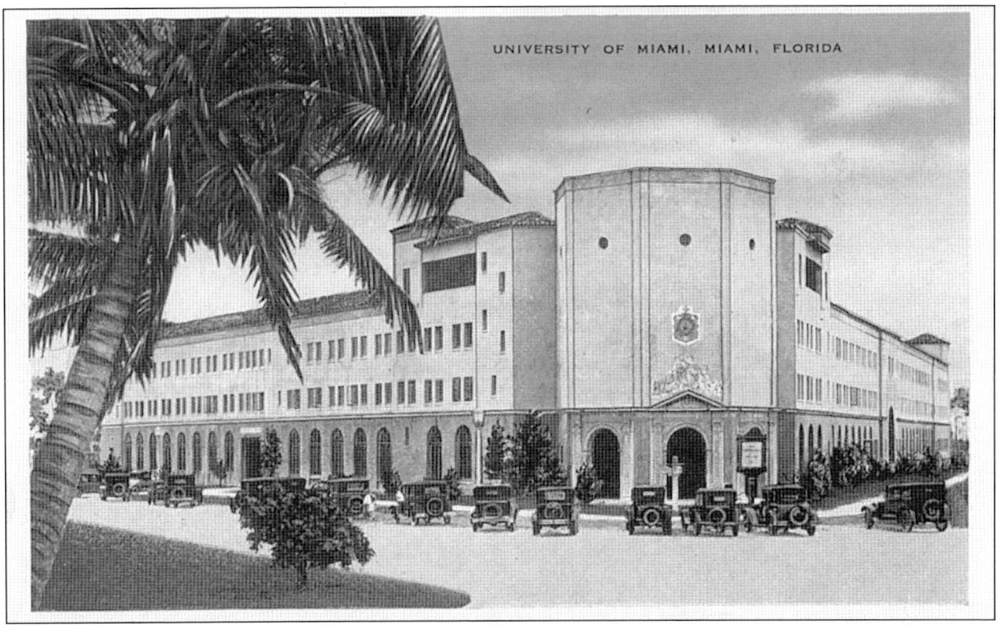

Architect H. George Fink also designed this building, which was meant to be the Anastasia Hotel. However, when the University of Miami facilities were not ready for the school term beginning in the fall of 1926, the University leased and eventually purchased the building for classroom use. (Published by E.C. Kropp Co.)

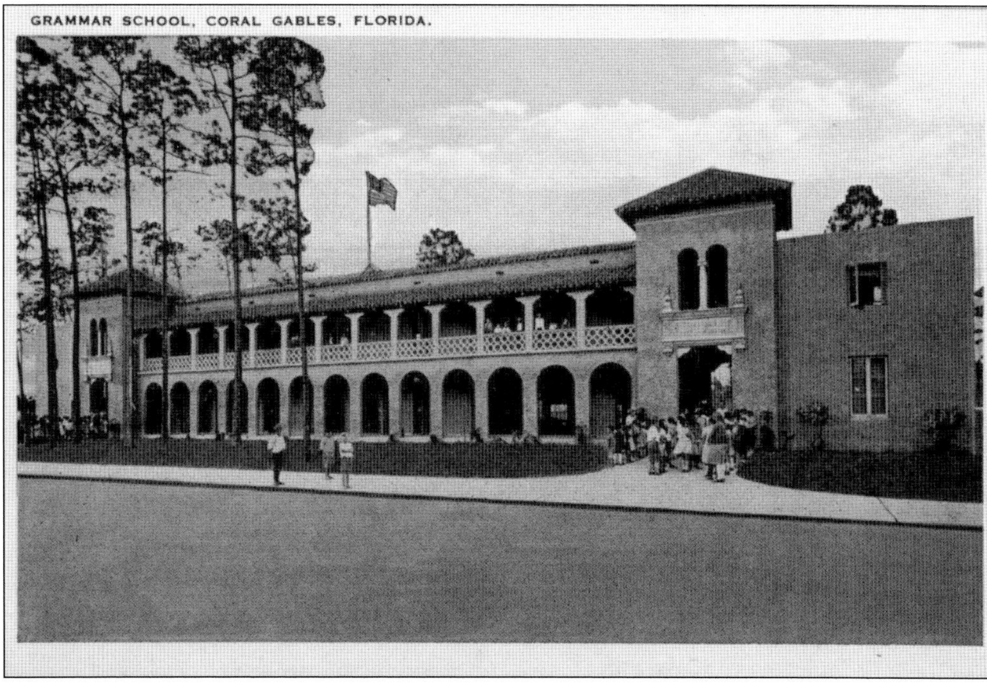

The Coral Gables Grammar school, located at 105 Minorca Avenue, was designed by architect Richard Kiehnel. The Mediterranean Revival–style school was built between 1923 and 1926. (Published by Pictorial Centre.)

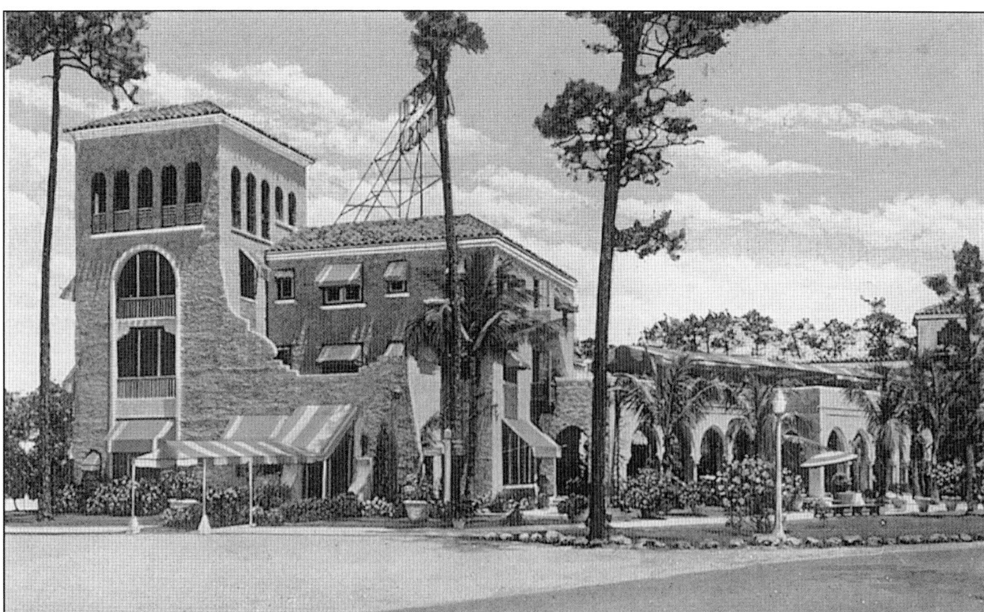

The Antilla Hotel, located on Ponce de Leon Boulevard, opened in January 1925. The hotel offered outdoor patio dining, dancing, and lovely surroundings. The Antilla was demolished in 1960 to make room for the new Chateaubleu Motel. (Published by Curt Teich.)

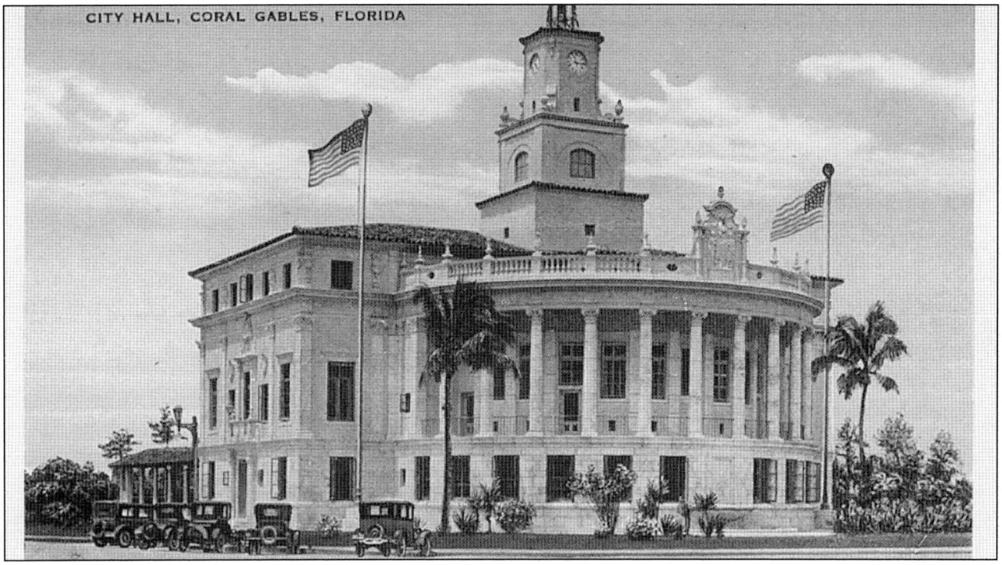

Coral Gables City Hall was constructed in only four months during 1928 at a total cost of $200,000. The Spanish Renaissance building was located at 405 Biltmore Way and designed by Phineas Paist, supervising architect for the city, and Harold Steward. The building is now the American Legion Post. (Published by Pictorial Centre.)

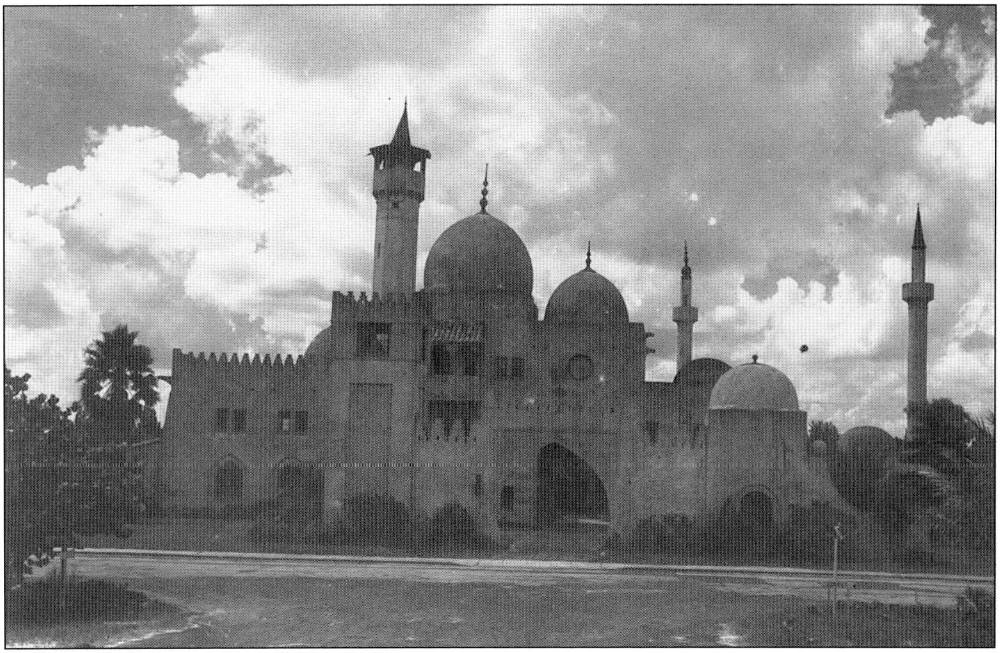

After developing Hialeah and Miami Springs with James Bright, famous aviator Glenn Curtiss went solo and created Opa-locka using an Arabian theme. Architect Bernhardt Muller wove the fantasies from *The One Thousand and One Tales from the Arabian Nights* into his designs. The Opa-locka City Hall, shown above, is one of the best examples. It was fully restored in 1988 and serves as the perfect backdrop for the yearly Arabian Nights Festival. (Courtesy of the Romer Collection, Miami-Dade Public Library.)

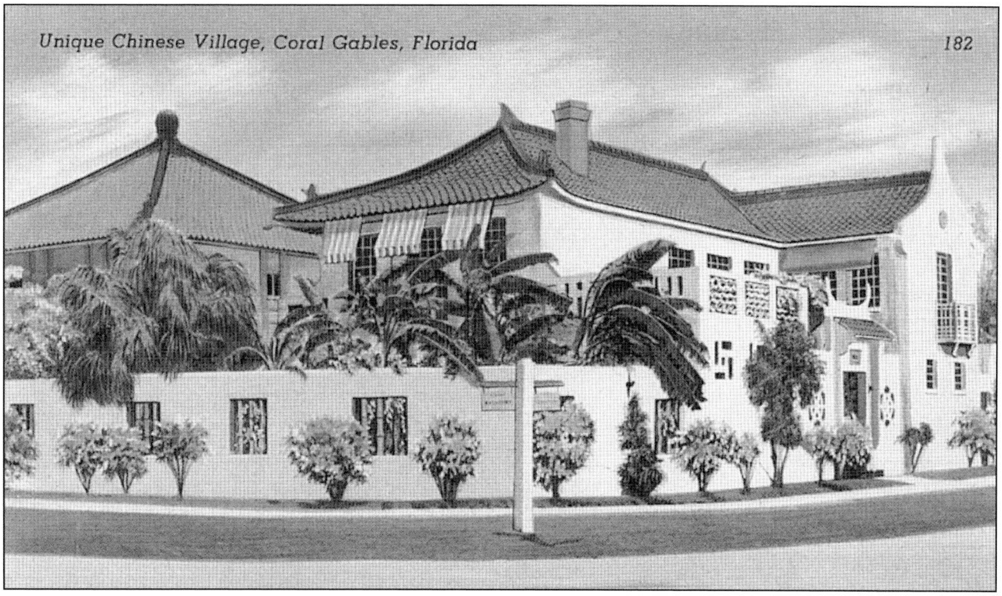

George Merrick's vision of Coral Gables was one predominantly inspired by Mediterranean architecture. "Foreign" villages, such as the Chinese Village pictured above, were also included to provide a variety of neighborhoods. The Chinese Village was designed by Henry Killan Murphy and built in 1926. Merrick originally planned 11 such villages, but the decline in the land boom brought construction to a halt. (Published by Colourpicture.)

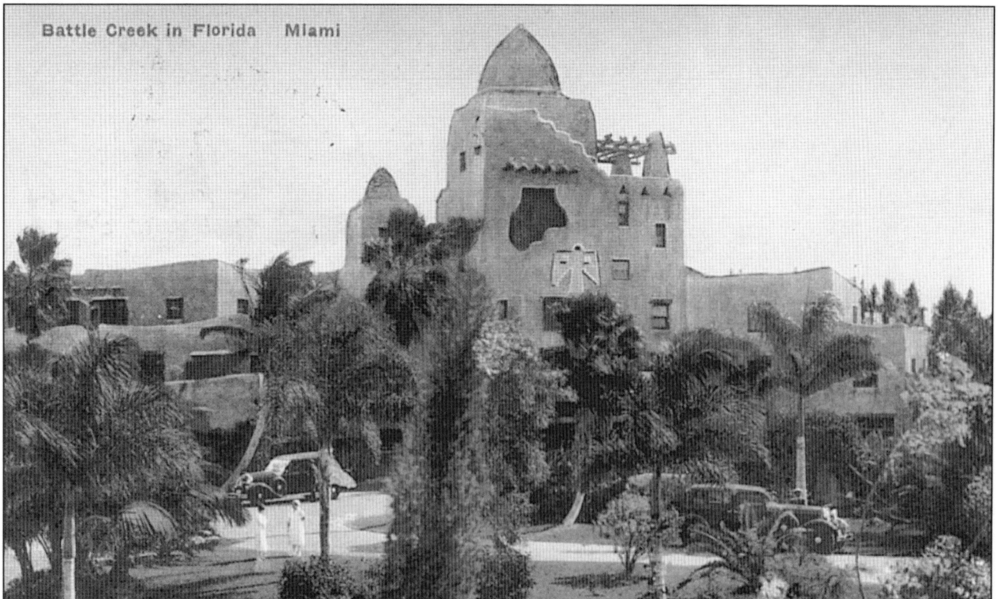

Breakfast cereal mogul John Harvey Kellogg purchased the former Pueblo Hotel (built in 1926) in 1929. Kellogg converted the hotel into the Miami Battle Creek Sanitarium. The building later served as a rest facility for soldiers during World War II, as a health spa, and then a retirement home. (Published by Albertype.)

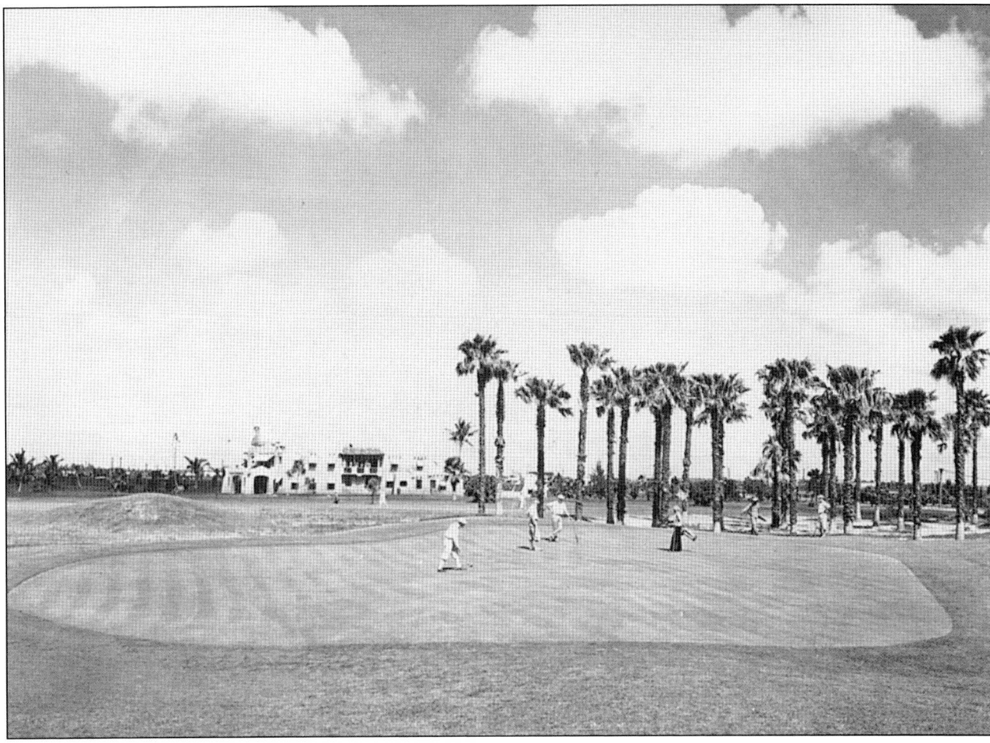

This 1926 photograph shows golfers enjoying a round of golf at Country Club Estates in Miami Springs. (Courtesy of Florida State Archives.)

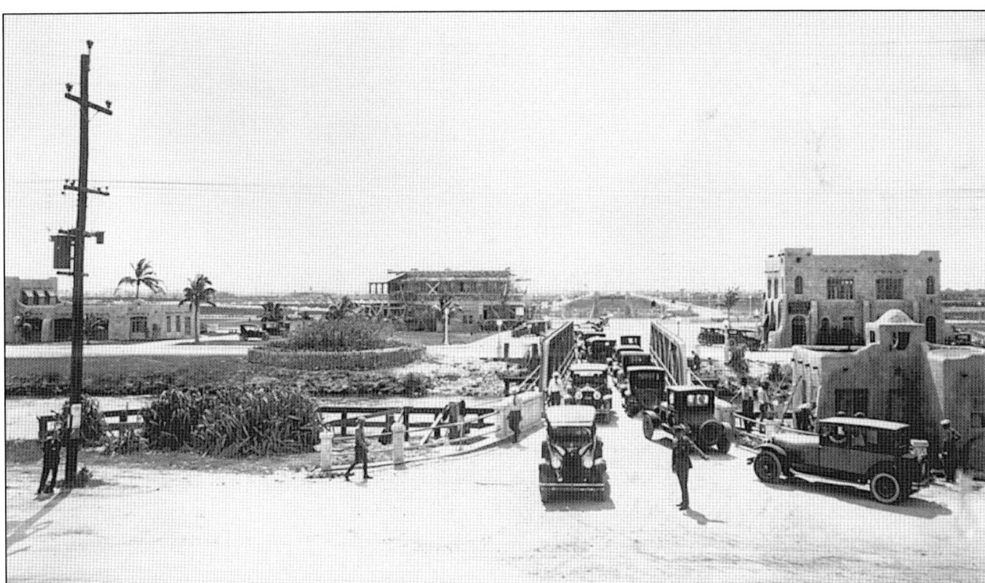

The main entrance to Country Club Estates was a flurry of activity in 1926, as was the entire city, before the devastating hurricane struck in September. The hurricane brought an end to the construction and the land boom. (Courtesy of Florida State Archives.)

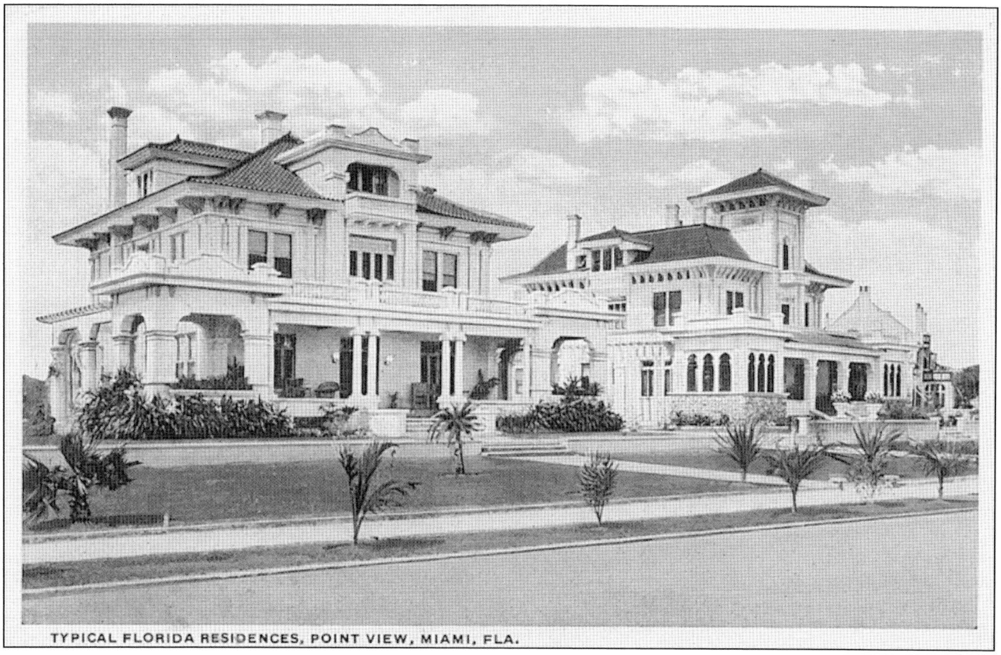

L.T. Highleyman created the exclusive Point View subdivision, just east of Brickell Avenue, by dredging the Biscayne Bay and filling in the bayfront north of today's Southeast Fifteenth Road. The lavish homes built in Point View made up Miami's first "Millionaire's Row." (Published by H. & W.B. Drew Co.)

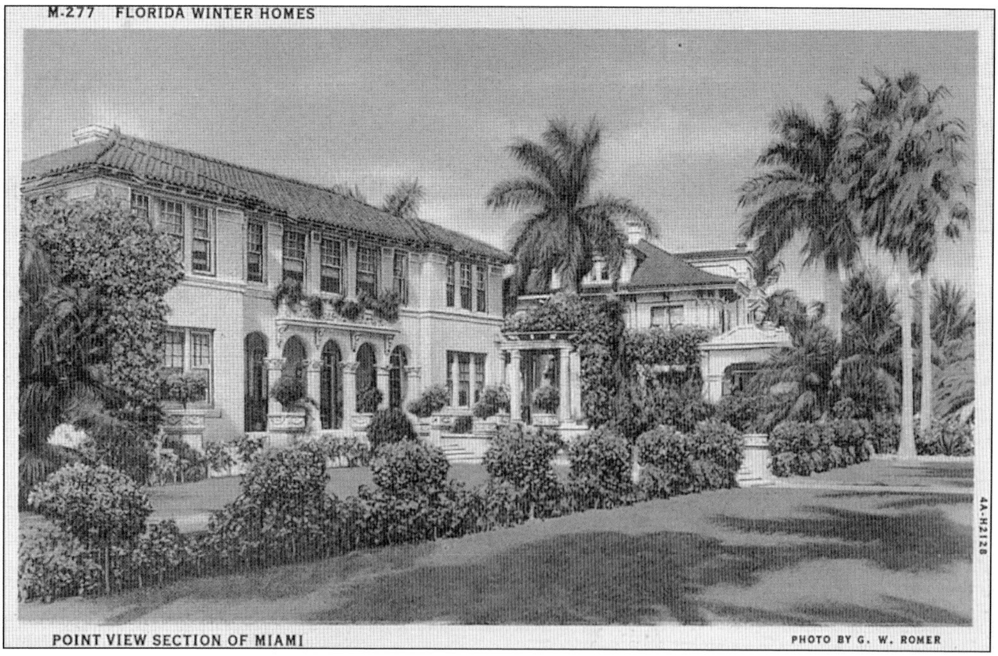

The Point View area offered magnificent waterfront views of Biscayne Bay. The views are now enjoyed by the residents of the highrise condominiums that have replaced the spacious, elegant homes shown in this 1934 postcard. (Published by Curt Teich.)

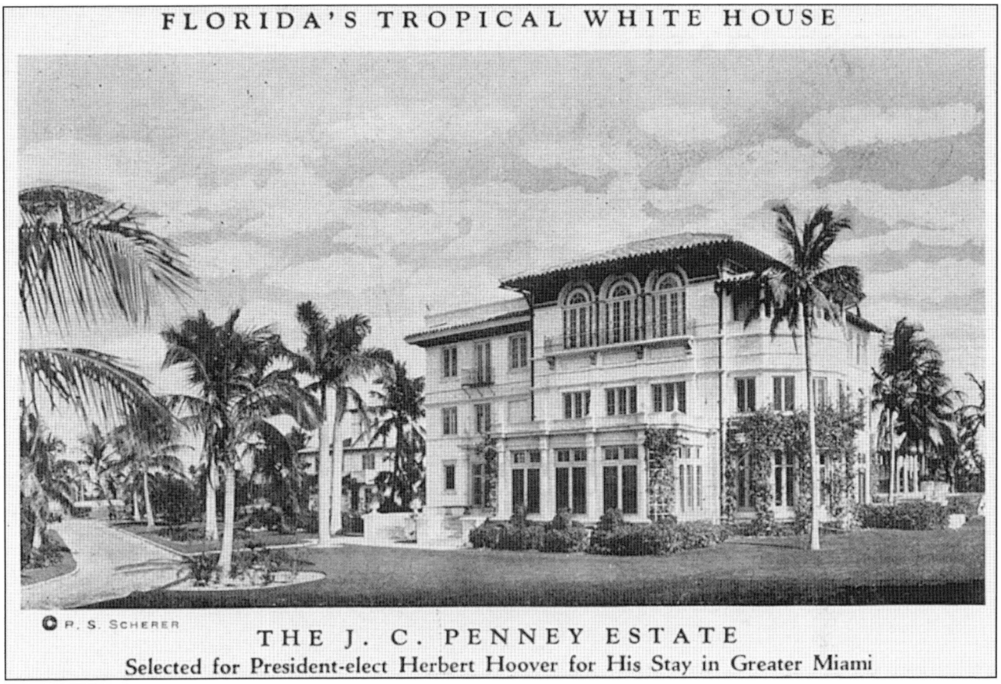

Winter estates and grand hotels were also being built across the bay in Miami Beach. By the 1920s, Carl Fisher had successfully promoted the new city as a "sportsman's paradise" and popular resort destination for the rich and famous. The J.C. Penney Estate, shown above, was selected for President-elect Herbert Hoover's residence during his visit to the Miami area. (Published by Tyler.)

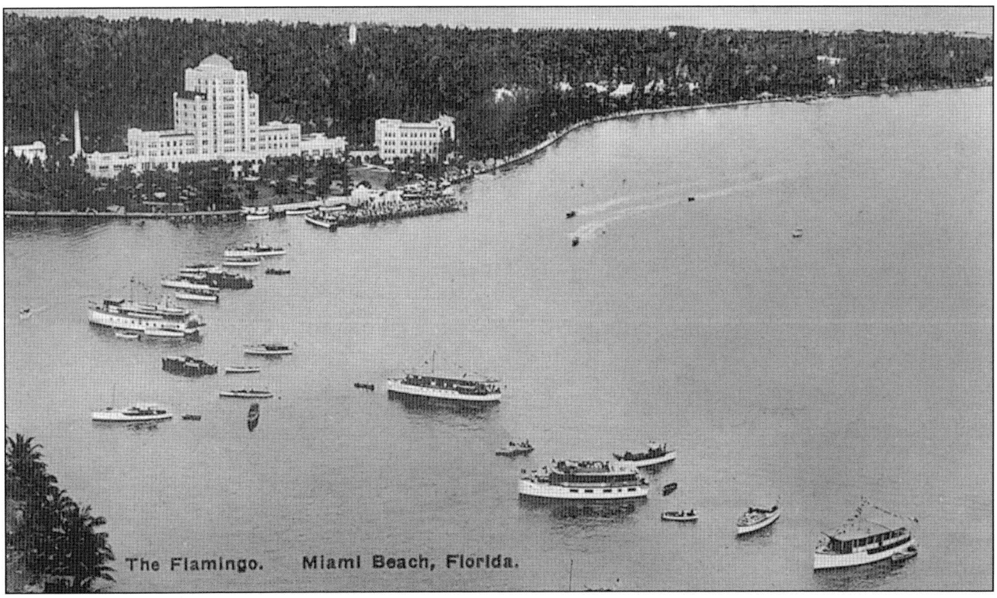

Carl Fisher's 150-room Flamingo Hotel opened on New Years Day 1921, at a cost of $2 million. Built on the Biscayne Bay, it was Miami Beach's first grand hotel and an instant hit with the public. (Published by Albertype.)

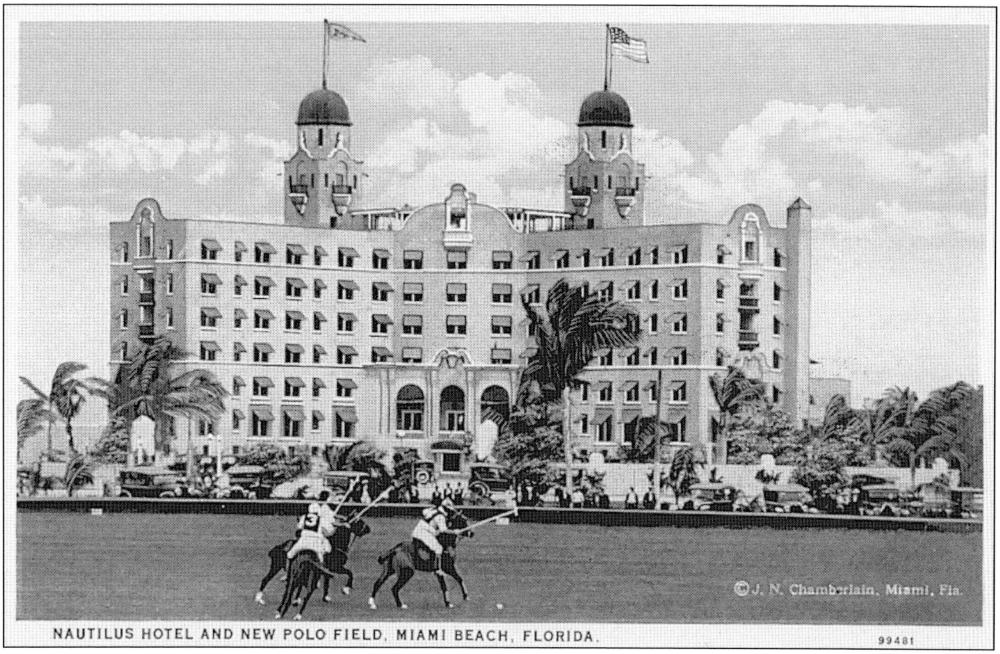

Players try out the new polo field at the Nautilus, another grand hotel built by Carl Fisher. It opened in 1923. (Published by J.N. Chamberlain.)

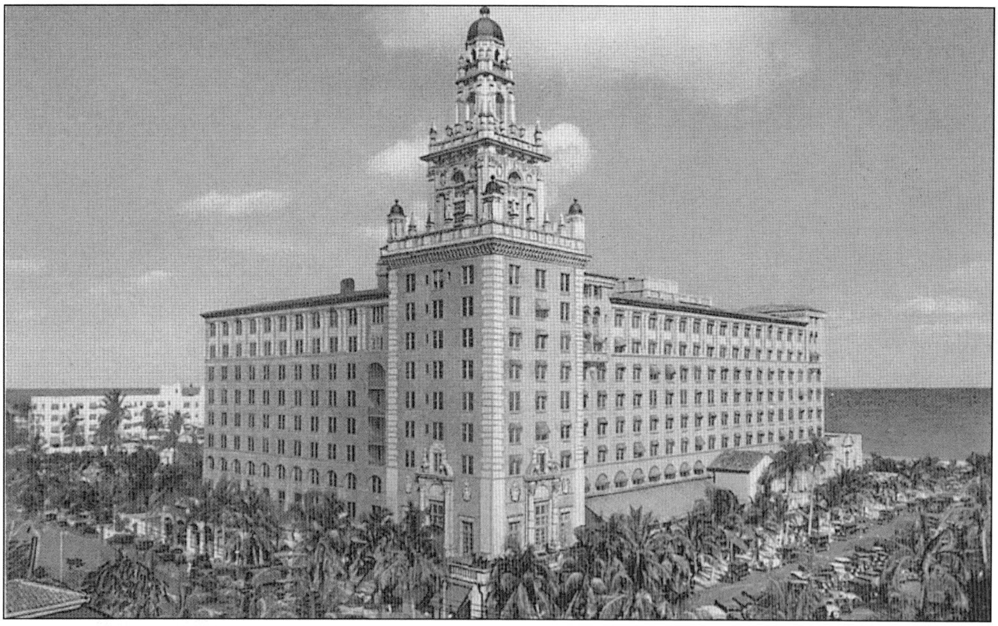

Carl Fisher once offered this site at no cost to any developer who would build a major hotel on it. No one was interested at that time, and his offer became a joke. Just over a decade later, N.B.T. Roney paid $2.5 million for the site, on which he built his Roney Plaza Hotel. The hotel opened in 1926, and included 15 acres of formal gardens, 1,500 feet of ocean frontage, cabanas, and restaurants for its guests. The Roney Plaza closed in 1968 and was torn down. (Published by K.S. Tanner Jr.)

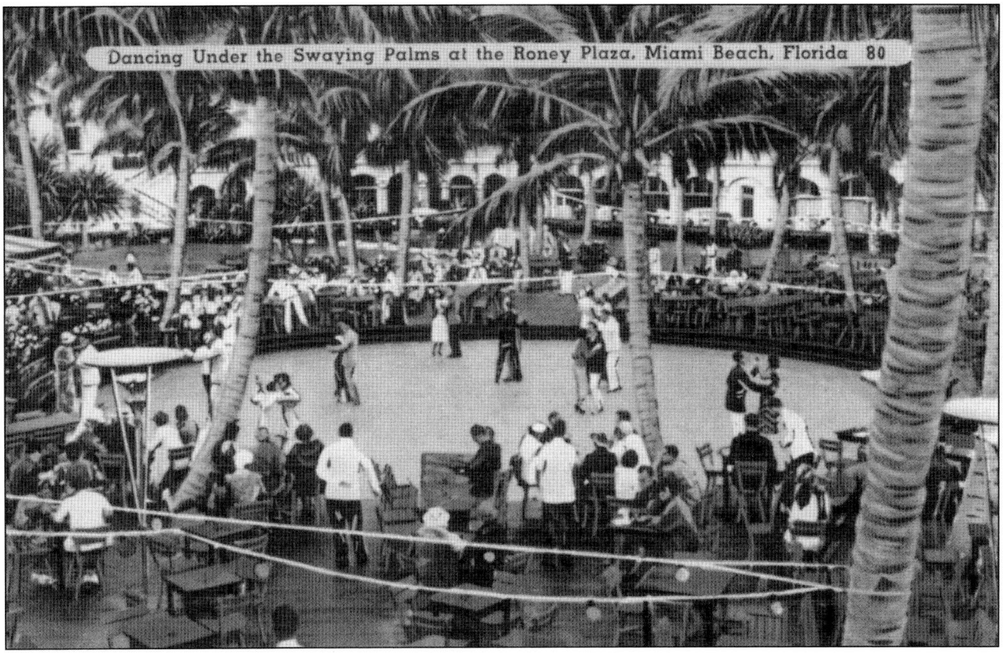

Guests at the Roney Plaza Hotel dance to "Moon over Miami" under the swaying palms, taking advantage of the tropical climate. (Published by Tichnor Bros.)

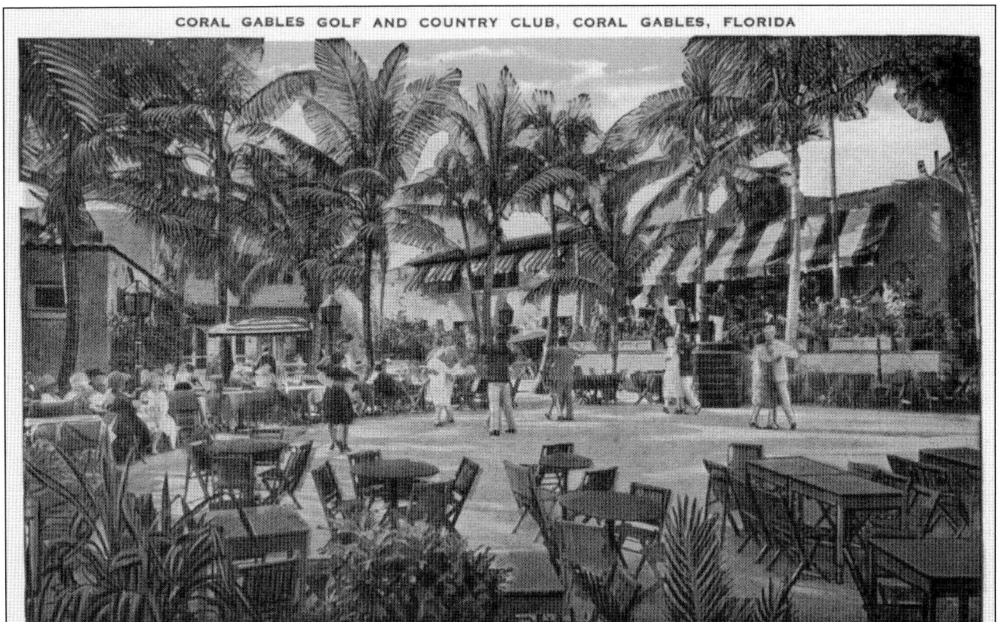

Couples danced to "When the Moon Shines in Coral Gables," often performed by renowned orchestras led by Jan Garber or Paul Whiteman at the Coral Gables Country Club. (Published by Pictorial Centre.)

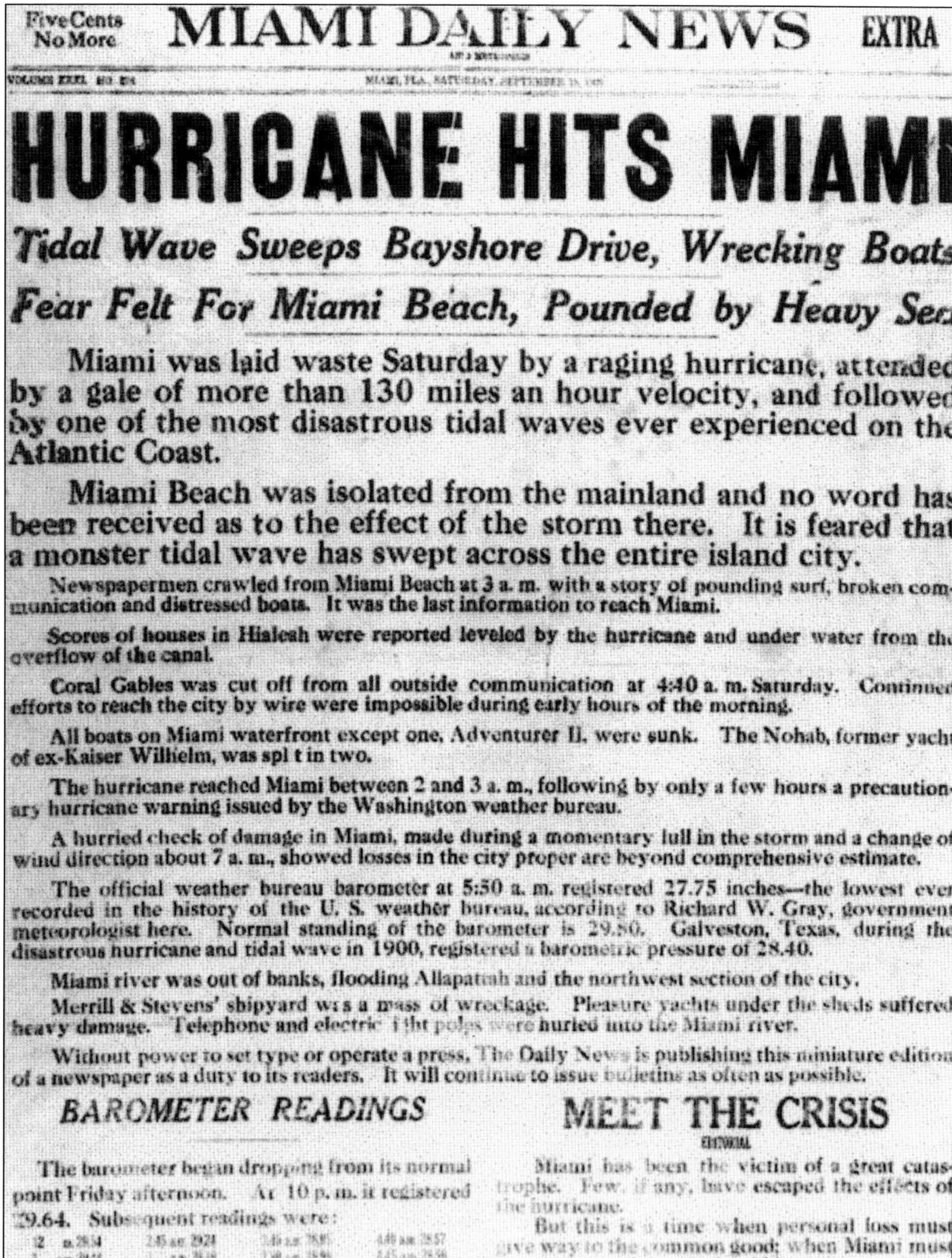
Five Cents No More

MIAMI DAILY NEWS

EXTRA

HURRICANE HITS MIAMI

Tidal Wave Sweeps Bayshore Drive, Wrecking Boats

Fear Felt For Miami Beach, Pounded by Heavy Seas

Miami was laid waste Saturday by a raging hurricane, attended by a gale of more than 130 miles an hour velocity, and followed by one of the most disastrous tidal waves ever experienced on the Atlantic Coast.

Miami Beach was isolated from the mainland and no word has been received as to the effect of the storm there. It is feared that a monster tidal wave has swept across the entire island city.

Newspapermen crawled from Miami Beach at 3 a. m. with a story of pounding surf, broken communication and distressed boats. It was the last information to reach Miami.

Scores of houses in Hialeah were reported leveled by the hurricane and under water from the overflow of the canal.

Coral Gables was cut off from all outside communication at 4:40 a. m. Saturday. Continued efforts to reach the city by wire were impossible during early hours of the morning.

All boats on Miami waterfront except one, Adventurer II, were sunk. The Nohab, former yacht of ex-Kaiser Wilhelm, was spl t in two.

The hurricane reached Miami between 2 and 3 a. m., following by only a few hours a precautionary hurricane warning issued by the Washington weather bureau.

A hurried check of damage in Miami, made during a momentary lull in the storm and a change of wind direction about 7 a. m., showed losses in the city proper are beyond comprehensive estimate.

The official weather bureau barometer at 5:50 a. m. registered 27.75 inches—the lowest ever recorded in the history of the U. S. weather bureau, according to Richard W. Gray, government meteorologist here. Normal standing of the barometer is 29.80. Galveston, Texas, during the disastrous hurricane and tidal wave in 1900, registered a barometric pressure of 28.40.

Miami river was out of banks, flooding Allapattah and the northwest section of the city.

Merrill & Stevens' shipyard was a mass of wreckage. Pleasure yachts under the sheds suffered heavy damage. Telephone and electric light poles were hurled into the Miami river.

Without power to set type or operate a press, The Daily News is publishing this miniature edition of a newspaper as a duty to its readers. It will continue to issue bulletins as often as possible.

BAROMETER READINGS

The barometer began dropping from its normal point Friday afternoon. At 10 p. m. it registered 29.64. Subsequent readings were:

MEET THE CRISIS

EDITORIAL

Miami has been the victim of a great catastrophe. Few, if any, have escaped the effects of the hurricane.

But this is a time when personal loss must give way to the common good; when Miami must meet the situation as it should be met.

The booming economy and happy life were struck a devastating blow with the arrival of the great hurricane of 1926. In the middle of the night on September 17–18, the hurricane struck the Miami area with winds of 125 miles per hour. Unaware that the temporary calm was the eye of the storm passing over, residents came out to view the damage, only to be hit with the second half of the storm. Hundreds of people were killed, homes and businesses were destroyed, and the building boom ended. (Courtesy of Florida State Archives.)

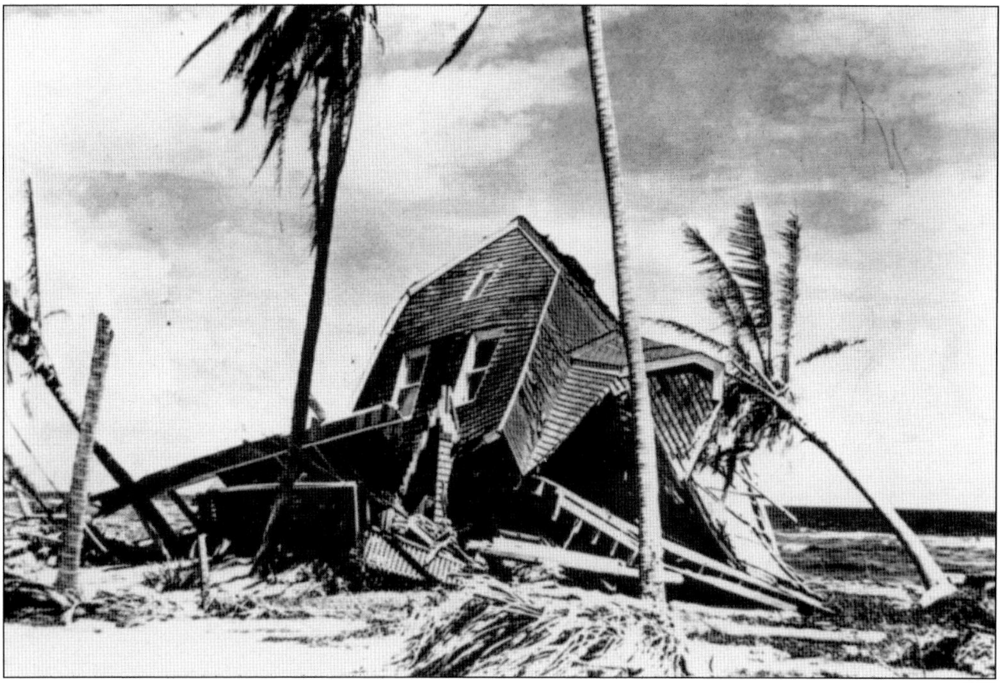

This house, located on the oceanfront near Twenty-eighth Street in Miami Beach, was no match for the destructive power of the hurricane.(Courtesy of Florida State Archives.)

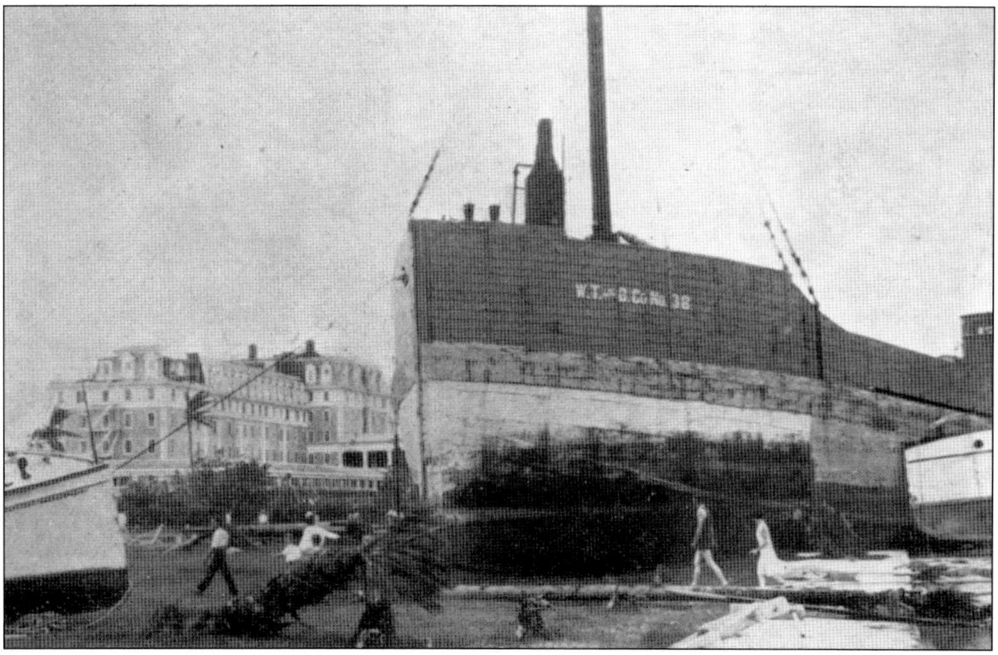

Freighter Number 38 from W.T. and O. Company was driven onto the land at Royal Palm Park. The badly damaged Royal Palm Hotel can be seen in the background. (Courtesy of Florida State Archives.)

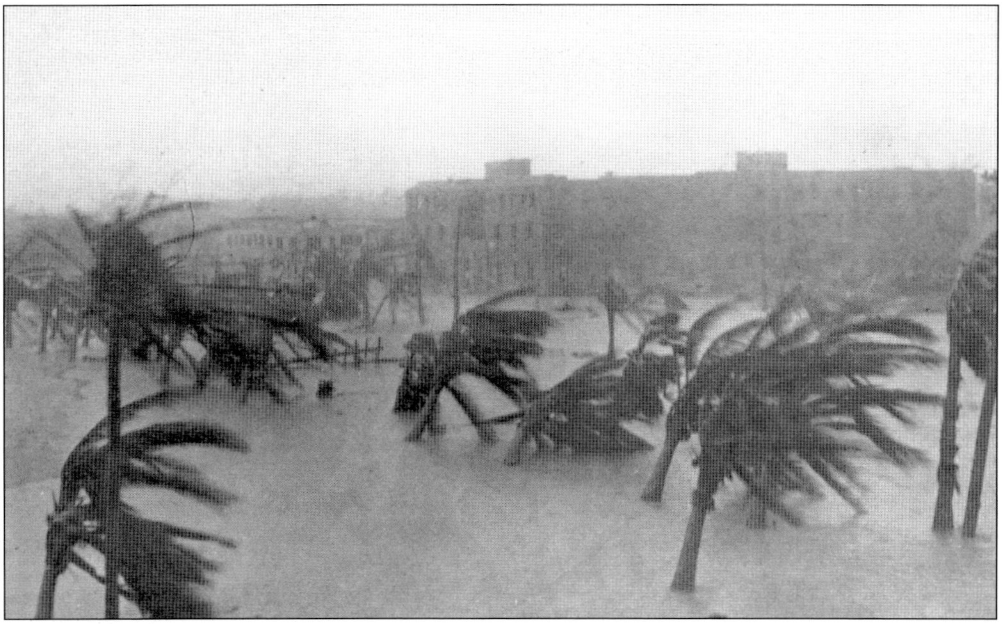

The awesome effect of the storm surge is evident in this scene of Miami Beach, where the ocean came in and met the bay. In this photo, waist-deep water and high winds pummel the city. (Courtesy of Florida State Archives.)

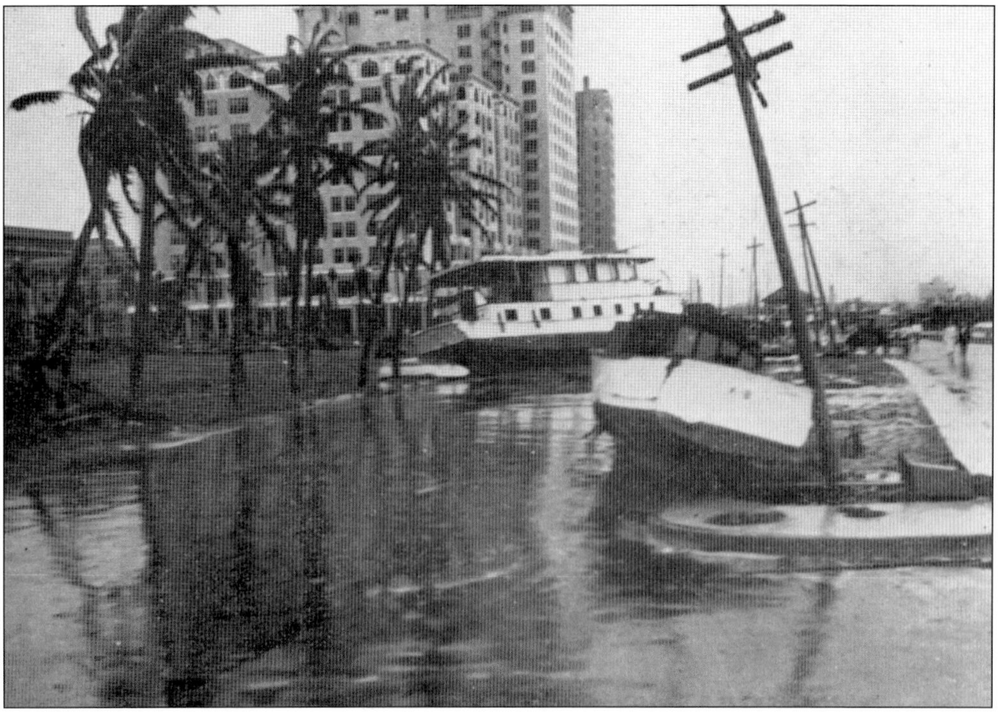

Boats left high and dry along the shoreline of Biscayne Bay give mute testimony to the ferocious power of the storm. (Courtesy of Florida State Archives.)

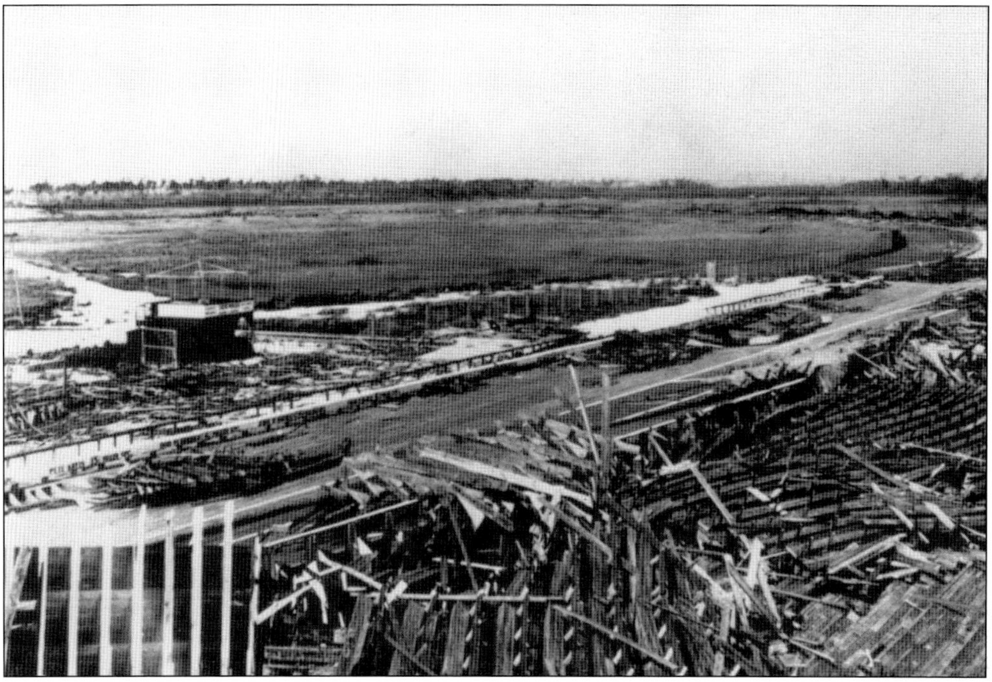

The Fulford Speedway, located in Fulford by the Sea, was completely destroyed and never re-opened. The lumber was salvaged to help rebuild the city. A sign marking the early community of Fulford by the Sea still stands off Northeast 163rd Street on the mainland in North Miami Beach. (Courtesy of Florida State Archives.)

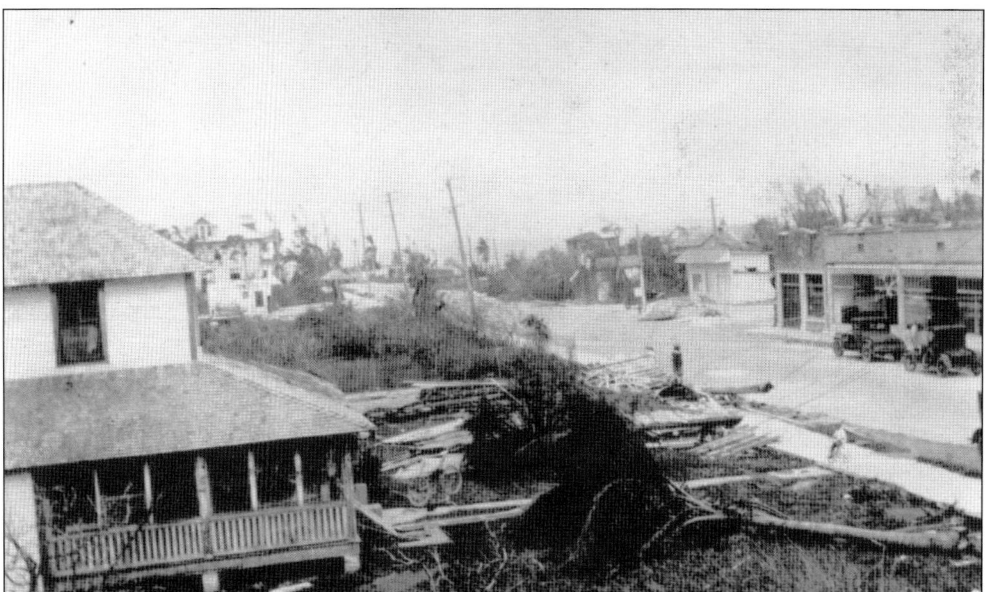

The high winds uprooted trees and caused extensive damage along Grand Avenue in Coconut Grove. In the true resilient Miami spirit, a small child is back on his tricycle after the storm. (Courtesy of Florida State Archives.)

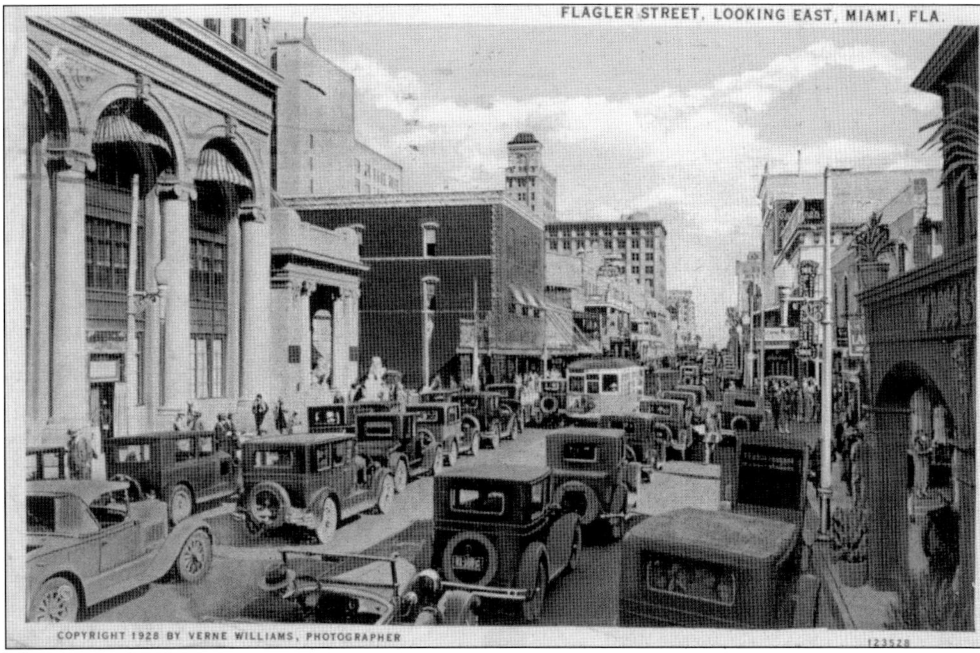

As a result of the hurricane, tourism fell off sharply in 1927. By the time of this photo in 1928, business was again flourishing and Flagler Street was packed with activity. The "good times" were short-lived however, as the stock market crash of 1929 also led to the collapse of Florida land prices. (Published by Curt Teich.)

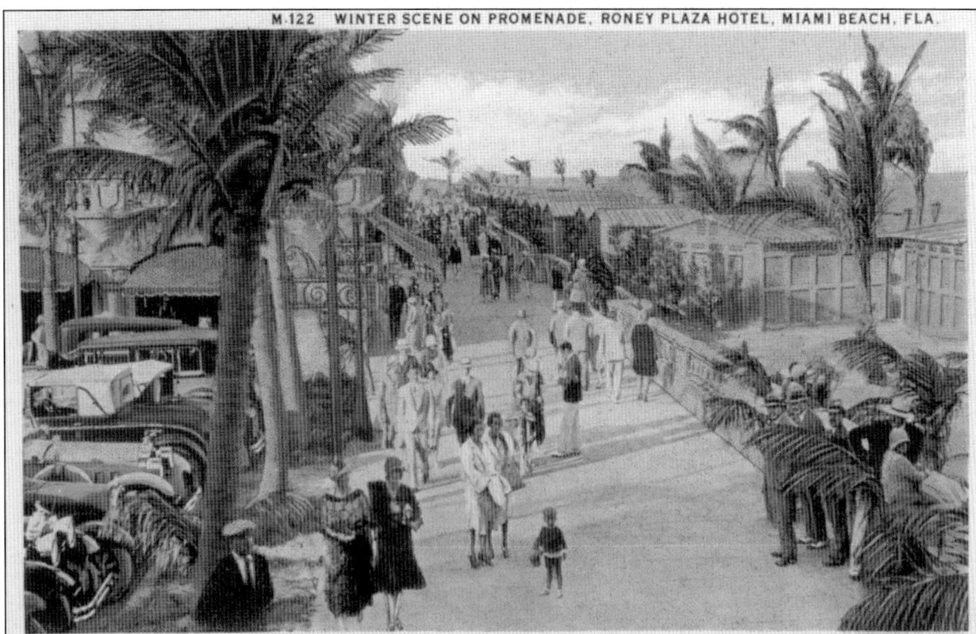

Tourists promenade in front of the Roney Plaza Hotel during the 1928–1929 winter season. Undoubtedly many did not return the following year as the Great Depression began. (Published by Curt Teich.)

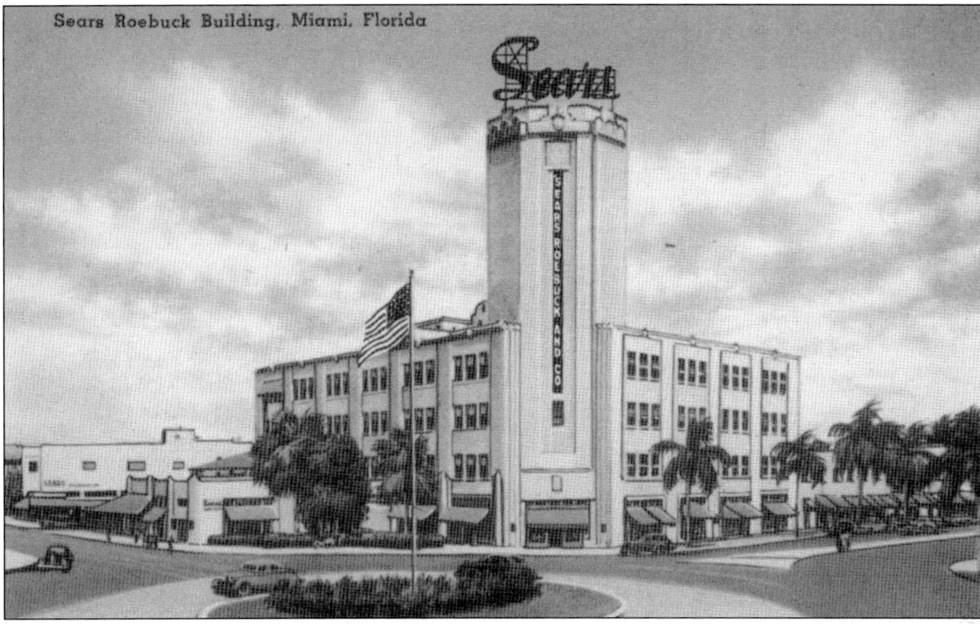

The Sears Roebuck building, built at the corner of Thirteenth Street and Biscayne Boulevard in 1929, is one of the earliest known Art Deco buildings in the Miami area. Originally, the company name was only displayed vertically on the front of the seven-story octagonal tower. By the time this *c.* 1940 postcard was made, the well-known logo at the top of the tower was added. (Published by Tichnor Bros.)

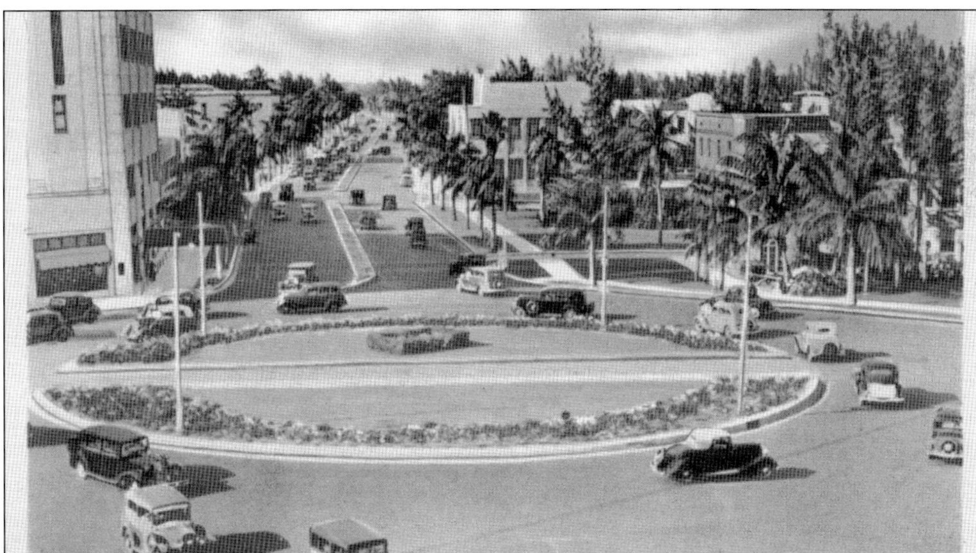

Biscayne Boulevard, shown above and with the Sears building to the left, connected downtown Miami with northeastern areas of the city as it does today. Trolleys, buses, and cars crossed through the traffic circle to go east to the beaches by way of the County Causeway (today's MacArthur Causeway), or westward along Northwest Fourteenth Avenue. The traffic circle, now gone, was one of the most important intersections in the city in the 1920s and 1930s. (Published by Tichnor.)

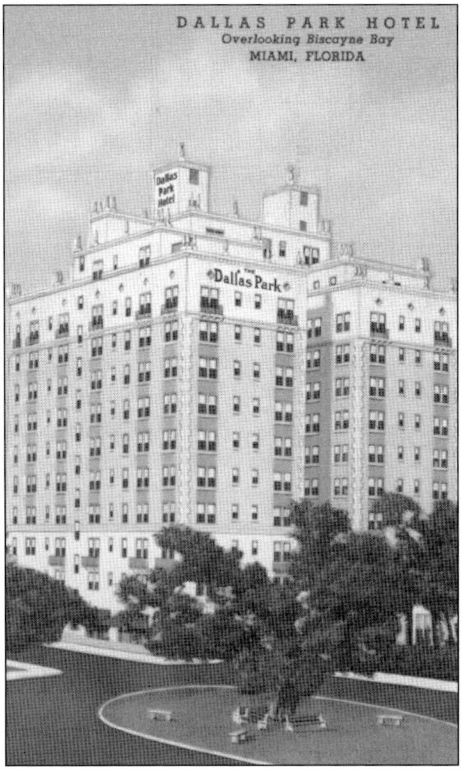

The Dallas Park Hotel was located at Southeast First Avenue at Third Street, on Julia Tuttle's former homesite. The luxury hotel offered furnished apartments and large penthouses. (Published by Curt Teich.)

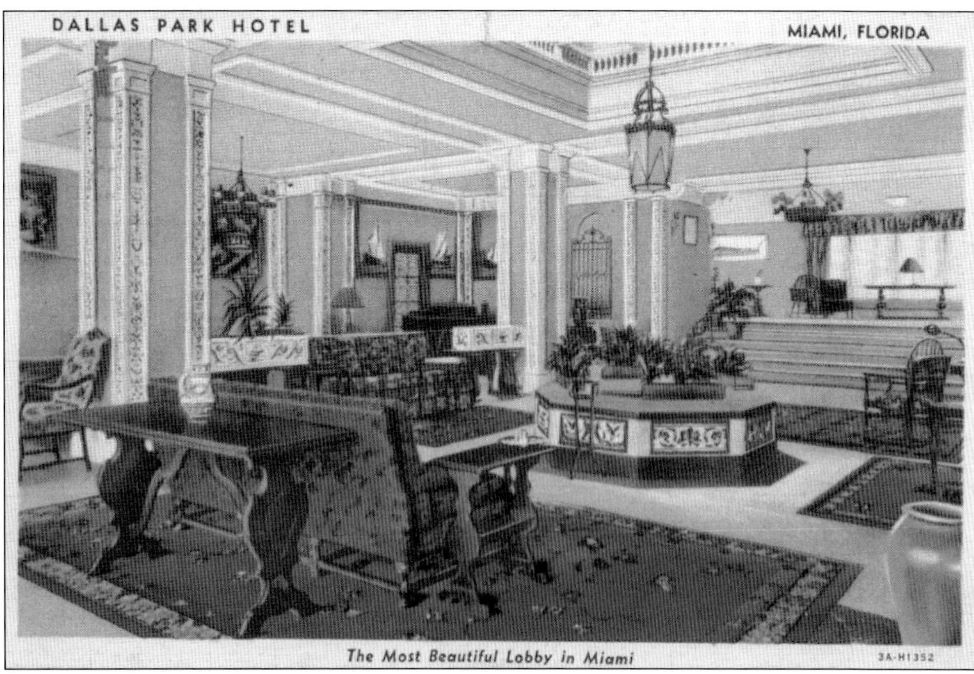

The lobby of the Dallas Park Hotel was considered to be the most beautiful in Miami. This 1933 postcard showcases the luxurious and spacious interior. (Published by Curt Teich.)

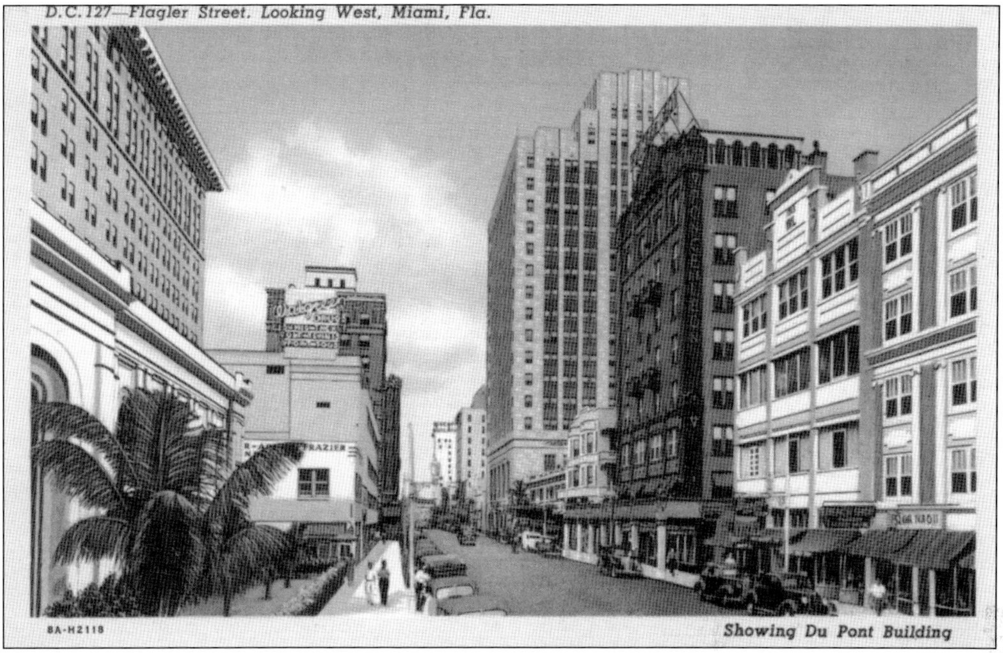

Flagler Street, in this 1930s postcard, seems unusually quiet compared with the bustling activity that characterized the 1920s land boom. (Published by Curt Teich.)

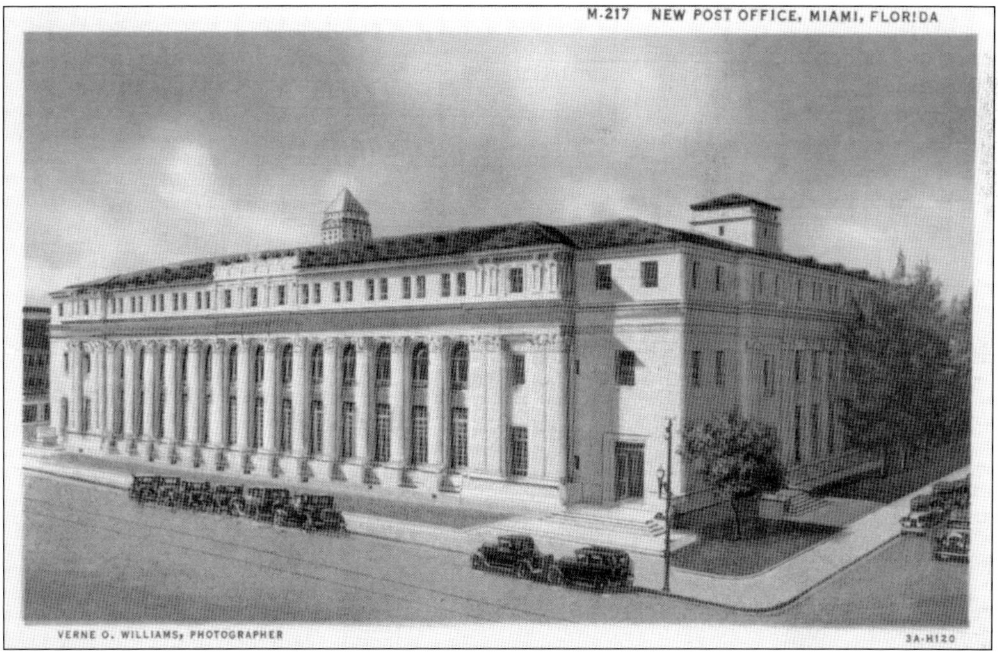

By 1933 a new, greatly expanded post office building was functioning in downtown Miami. The entire nation was struggling at the time to recover from the stock market crash, and the building symbolized efforts to rejuvenate the Miami area. (Published by Curt Teich.)

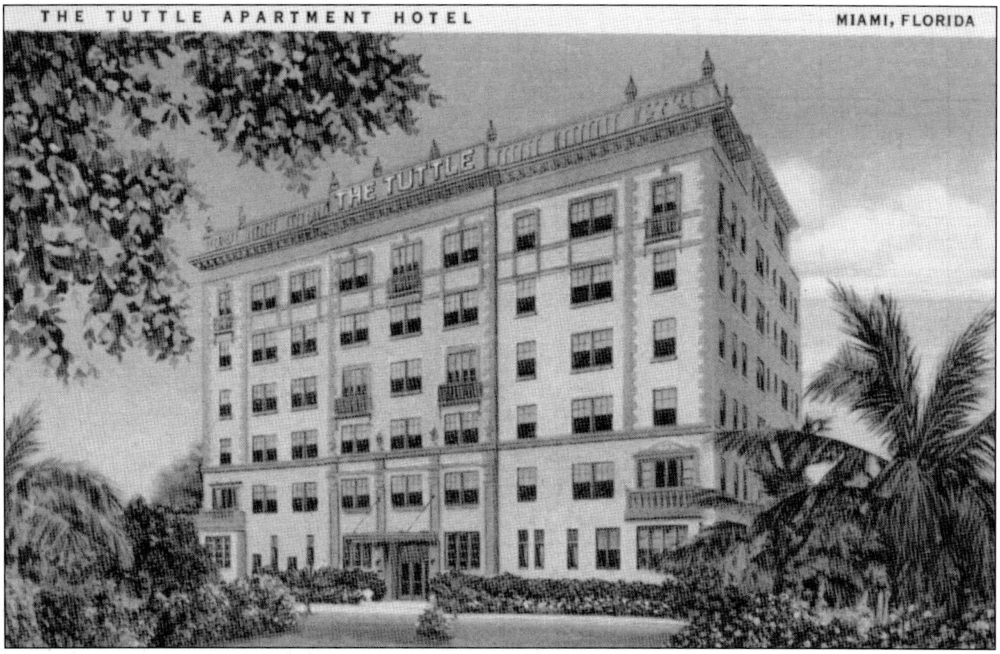

The Tuttle Apartment Hotel, featured in this 1934 postcard, was located in exclusive Dallas Park, the development begun by Harry Tuttle early in the century.

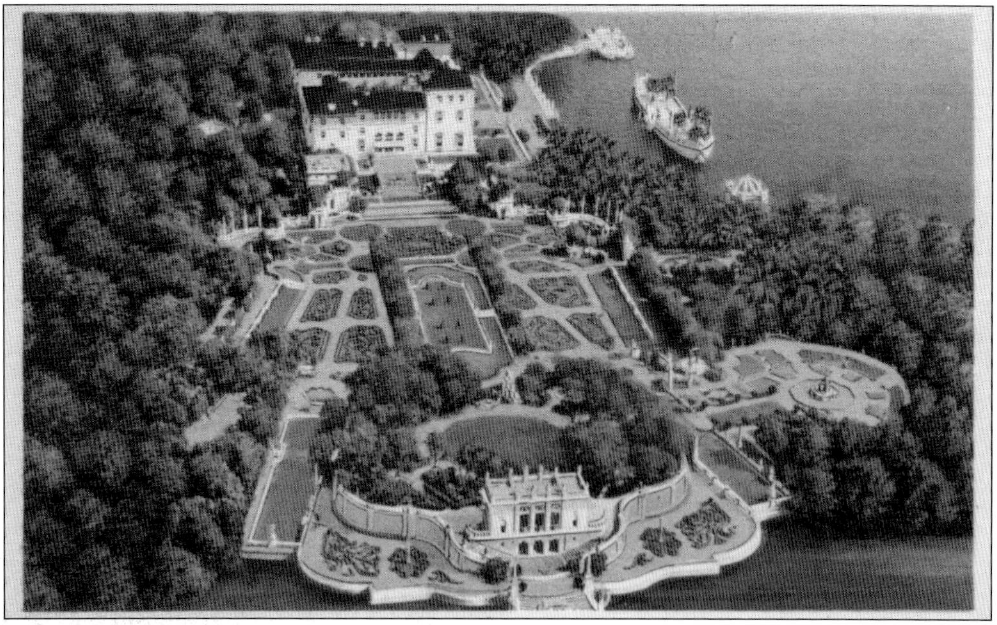

James Deering, heir to the International Harvester fortune, purchased land in 1912 from the Brickell family to build his 180-acre estate. Construction on Villa Viscaya, a 70-room mansion inspired by the great Italian villas, began in 1914 and was completed two years later. It remained Deering's winter home until his death in 1925. Dade County purchased Villa Viscaya, complete with furnishings from all over Europe and its Renaissance-style gardens, for $1 million in 1952 and opened it to the public. (Published by Curt Teich.)

The Ritz Hotel, shown here in the late 1930s, grew along with the city. The hotel had changed a lot since its earlier appearance on page 38. (Published by J.B. Sommers.)

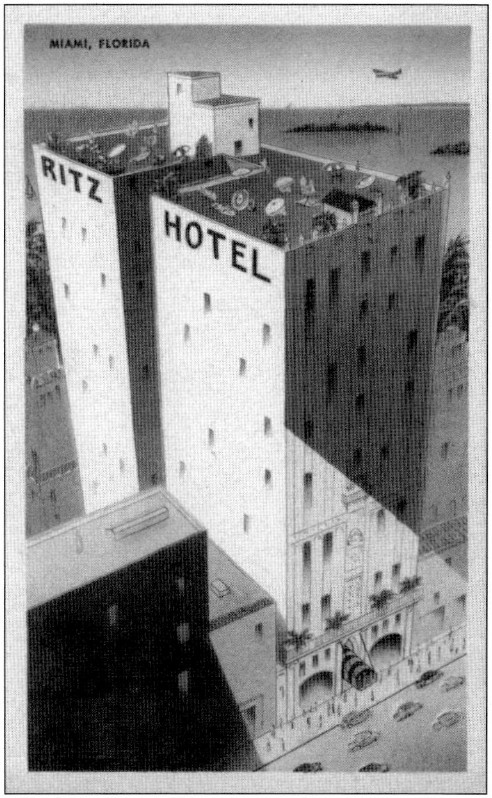

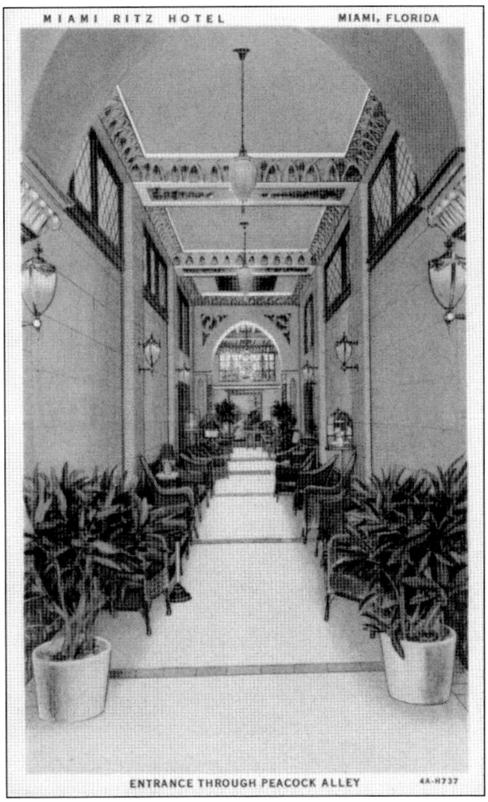

This postcard, printed in 1934, shows the entrance to the Ritz Hotel through Peacock Alley. (Published by Curt Teich.)

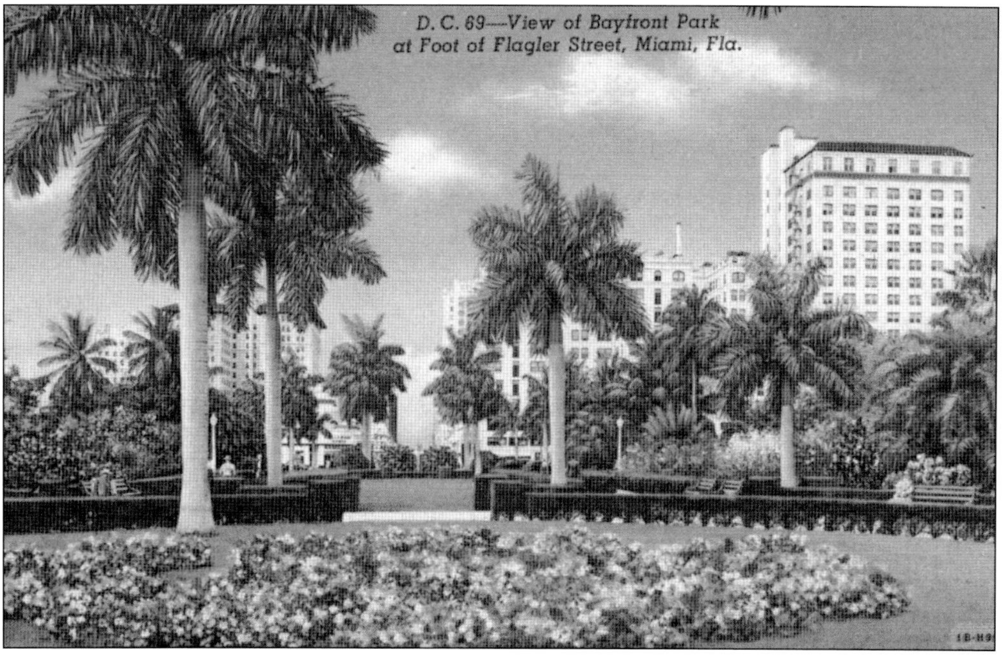

This 1941 postcard shows people sitting on park benches in the meticulously landscaped Bayfront Park at the foot of Flagler Street. Three decades had passed since early Miamians sat on park benches in Royal Palm Park in front of Elser Pier, also at the foot of Flagler Street (see page 55). (Published by Curt Teich.)

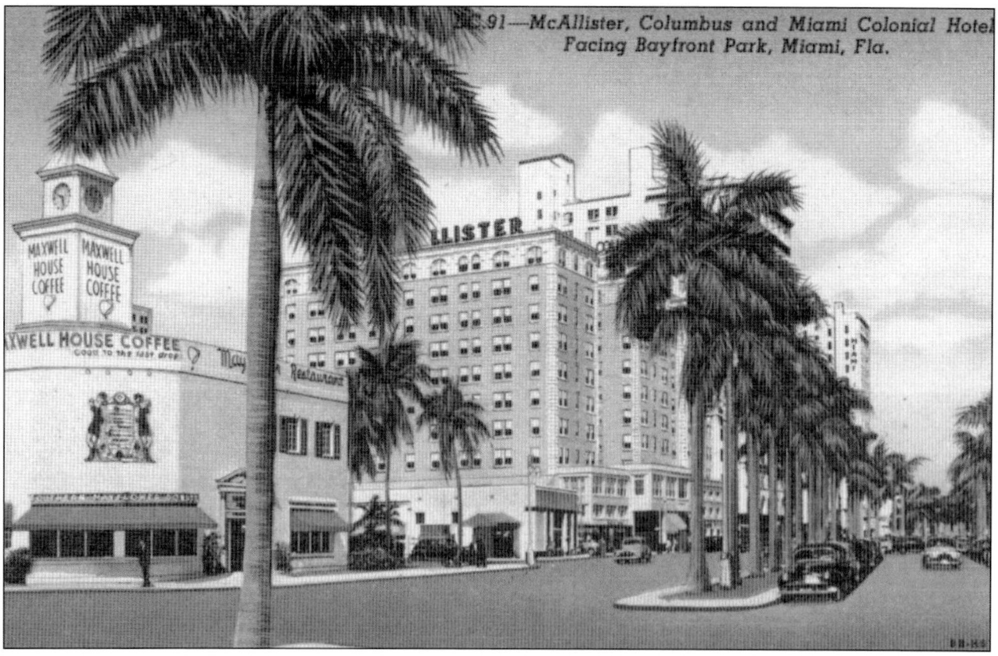

Majestic Royal Palms lead the way in this *c.* 1940 view of Biscayne Boulevard. Looking north on the left is the Mayflower Restaurant and the McAllister, Columbus, and Miami Colonial Hotels. (Published by Curt Teich.)

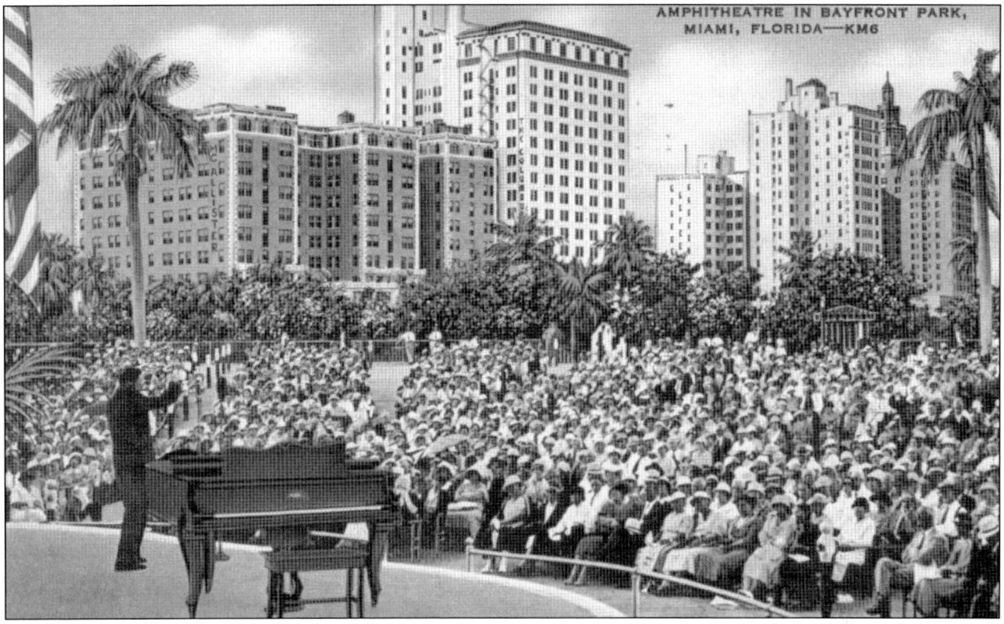

During the winter tourist season, concerts were held nightly at Bayfront Park. The message on this postcard, dated January 6, 1943, mentioned that the concerts were cancelled as a result of the blackouts necessitated by the outbreak of World War II. (Published by Thomas R. West.)

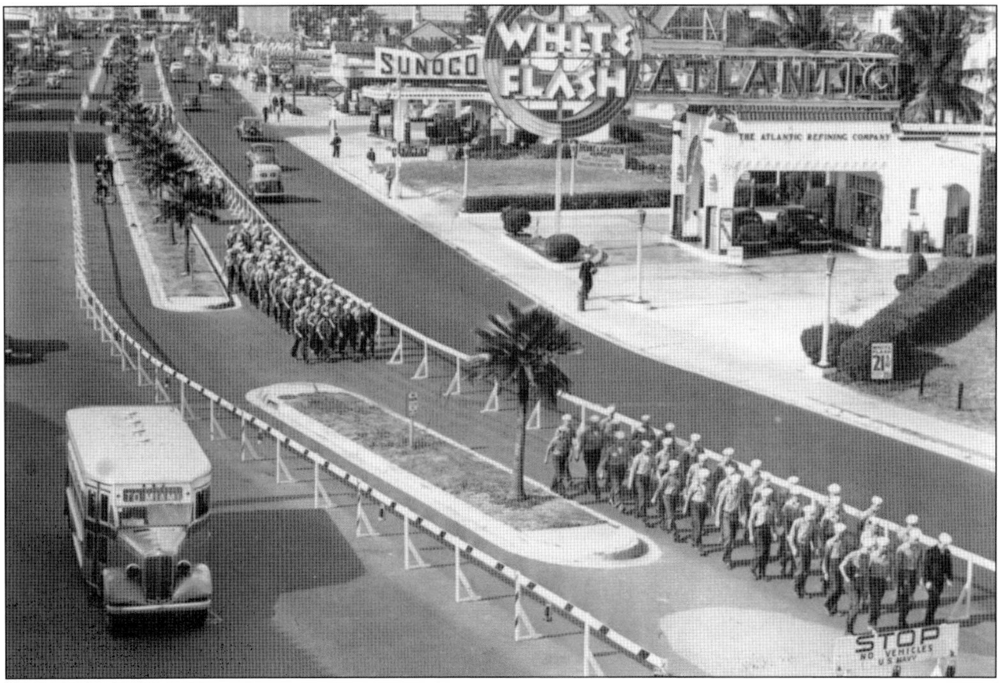

Naval units are seen marching down Biscayne Boulevard. During World War II, Miami was a major training center for all the branches of the service. (Courtesy of Florida State Archives.)

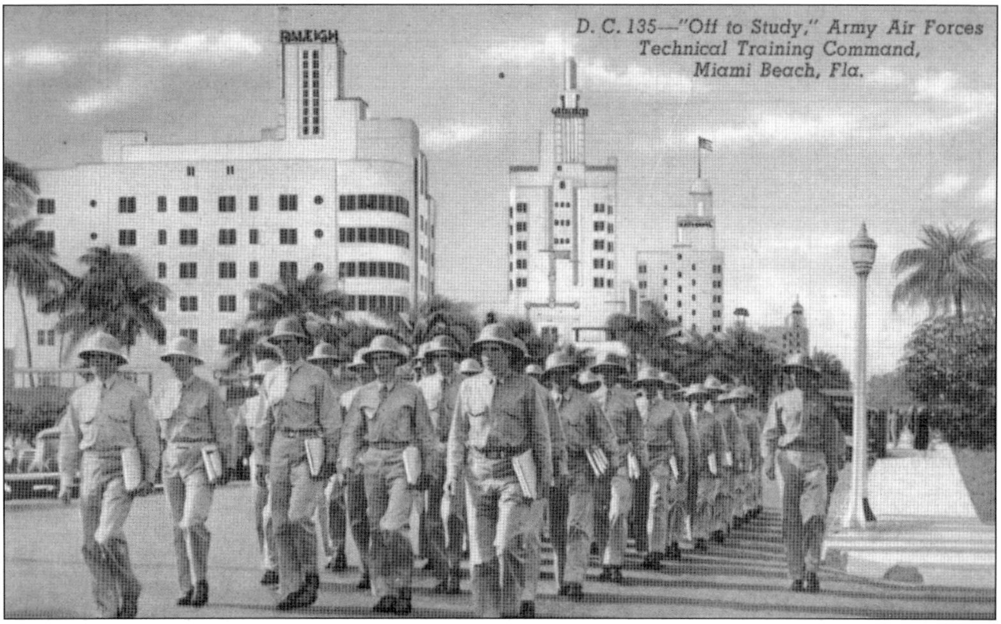

Miami Beach also served as a training center during the war. Most of the hotels became "barracks" for the trainees. By the end of the war, one-fourth of the officers and one-fifth of the enlisted men in the United States Army Air Corps had trained in Miami Beach. After experiencing the tropical weather, many servicemen returned after the war with their families for vacations and often relocated. (Published by Curt Teich.)

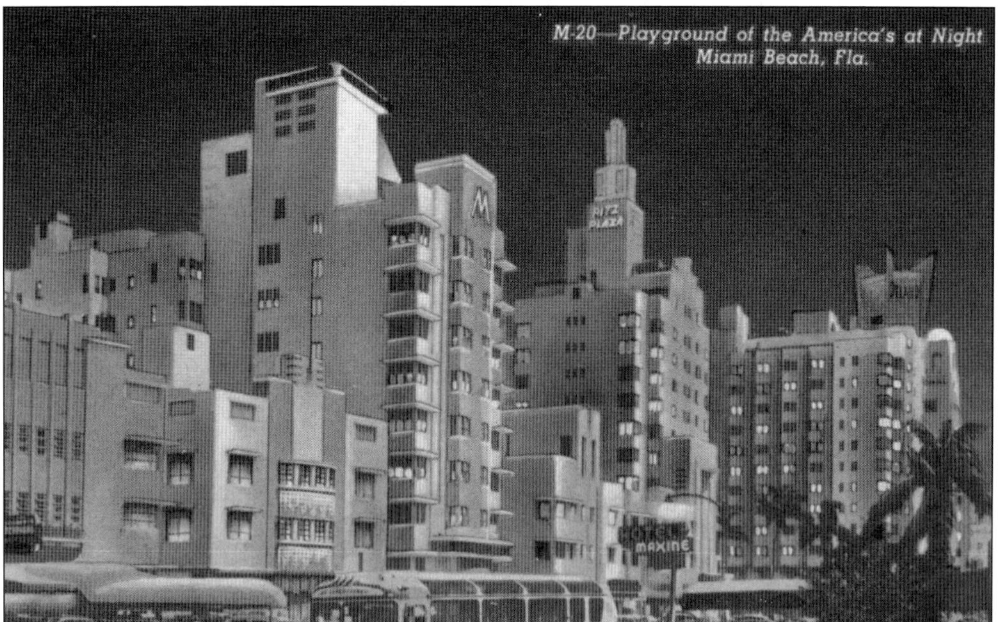

When the war ended, the Miami area continued to attract tourists and new residents. In the 1600–1700 block of Collins Avenue, glittering hotel towers provide the perfect setting for a night on the town. (Published by Curt Teich.)

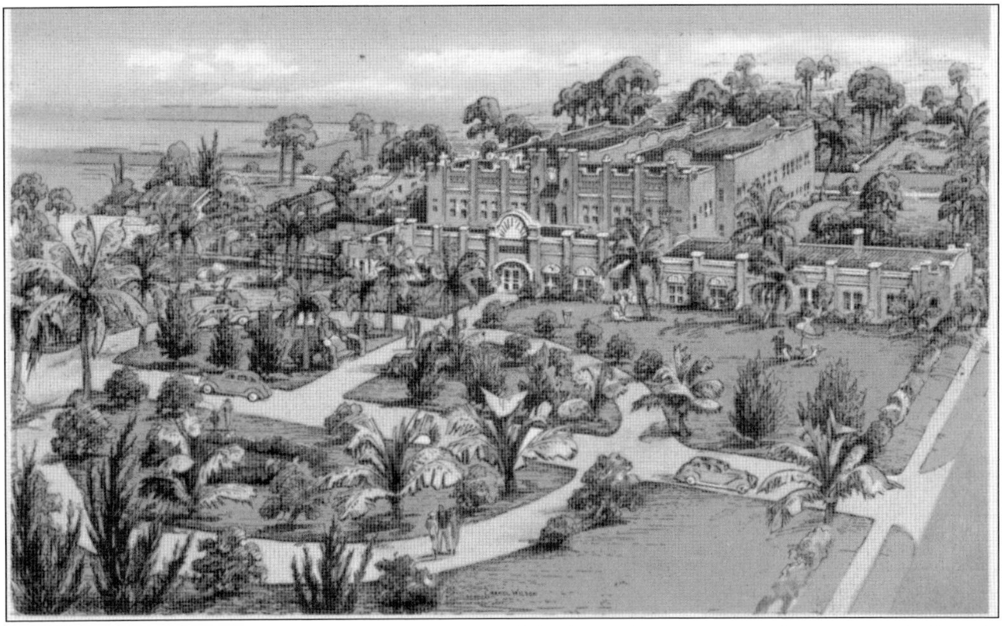

The Sun-Ray Park Health Resort, with "special facilities for rest, convalescence and chronic cases," was located at West Flagler Street and Thirtieth Avenue. In addition to a luxurious tropical setting, the resort offered excellent cuisine, a resident physician, nurses, a dietician, and treatments that are still popular as alternative medicine today. (Published by Curt Teich.)

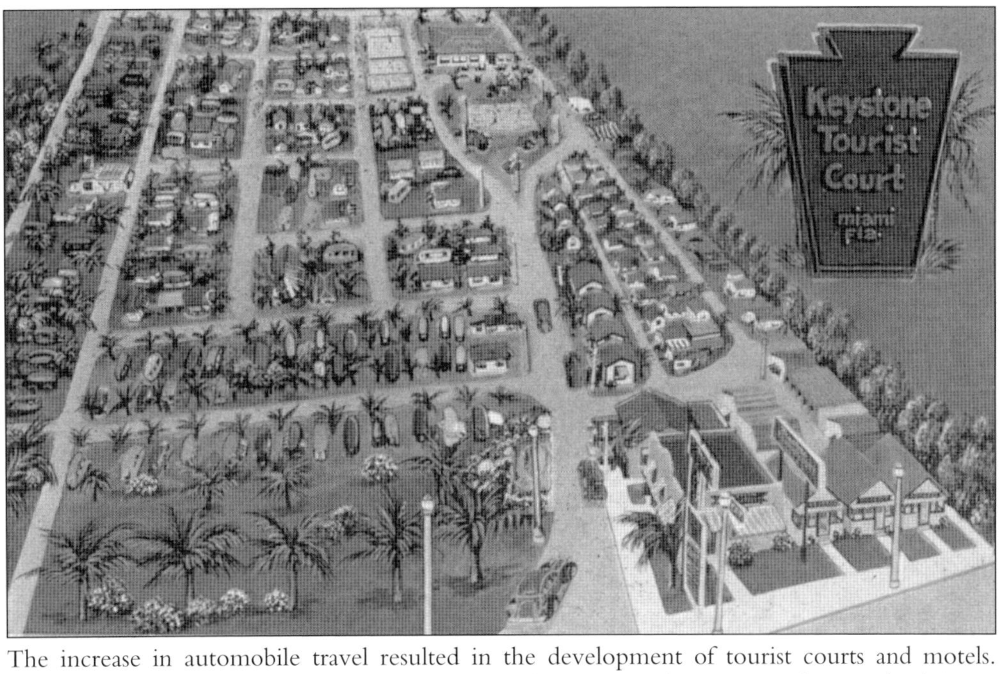

The increase in automobile travel resulted in the development of tourist courts and motels. George Lasche's Keystone Court, located at Northeast Second Avenue and Sixty-third Street offered one- to four-room cottages, 200 trailer spaces, and activities such as dancing, motion pictures, bingo, and shuffleboard. (Published by E.C. Kropp.)

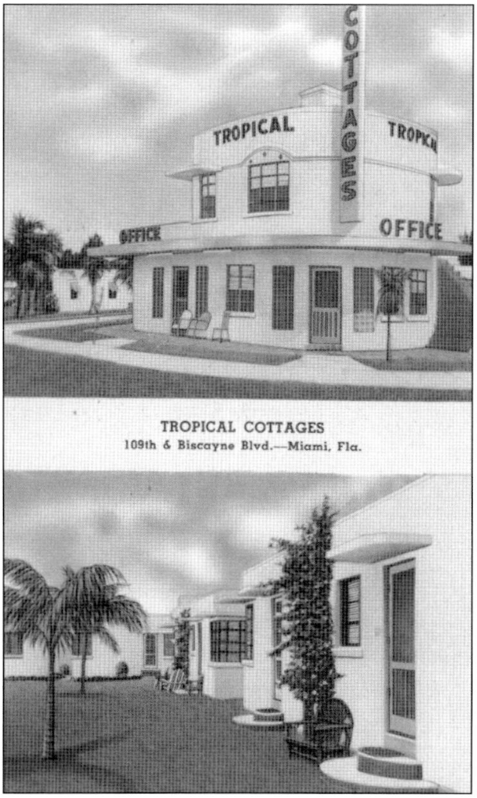

Charles Moore, owner of Tropical Cottages at 109th Street and Biscayne Boulevard, attracted customers with "kitchenettes with electric frigidaires" and maid service. Americans were being told to "See the USA in your Chevrolet," and were doing just that. (Published by Colourpicture.)

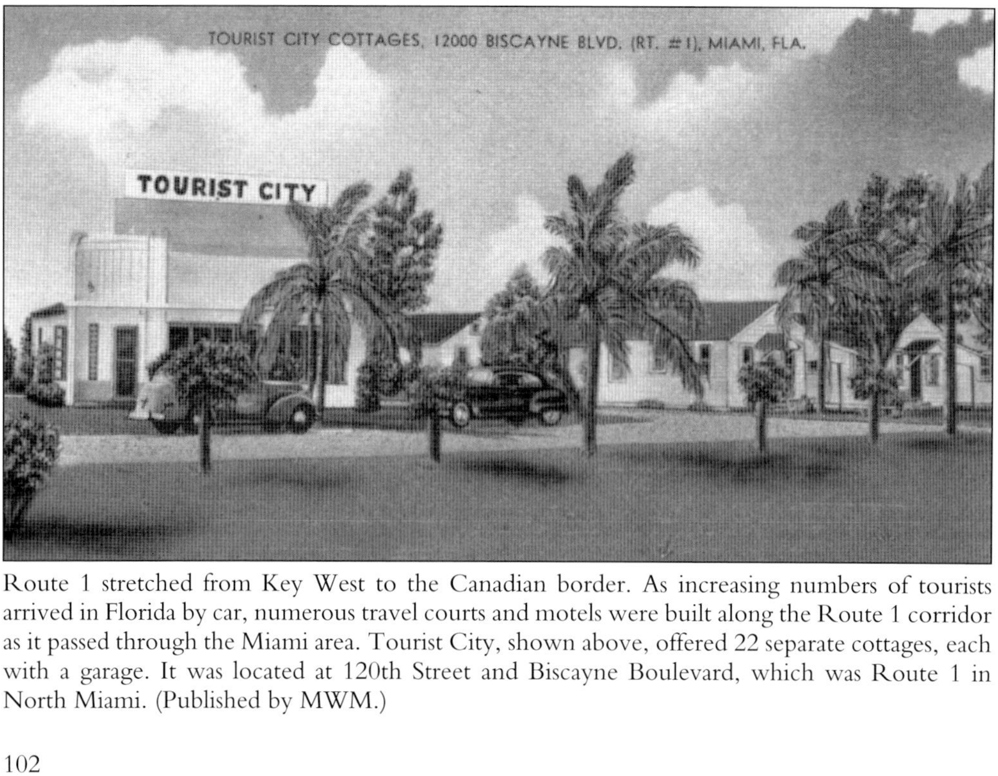

Route 1 stretched from Key West to the Canadian border. As increasing numbers of tourists arrived in Florida by car, numerous travel courts and motels were built along the Route 1 corridor as it passed through the Miami area. Tourist City, shown above, offered 22 separate cottages, each with a garage. It was located at 120th Street and Biscayne Boulevard, which was Route 1 in North Miami. (Published by MWM.)

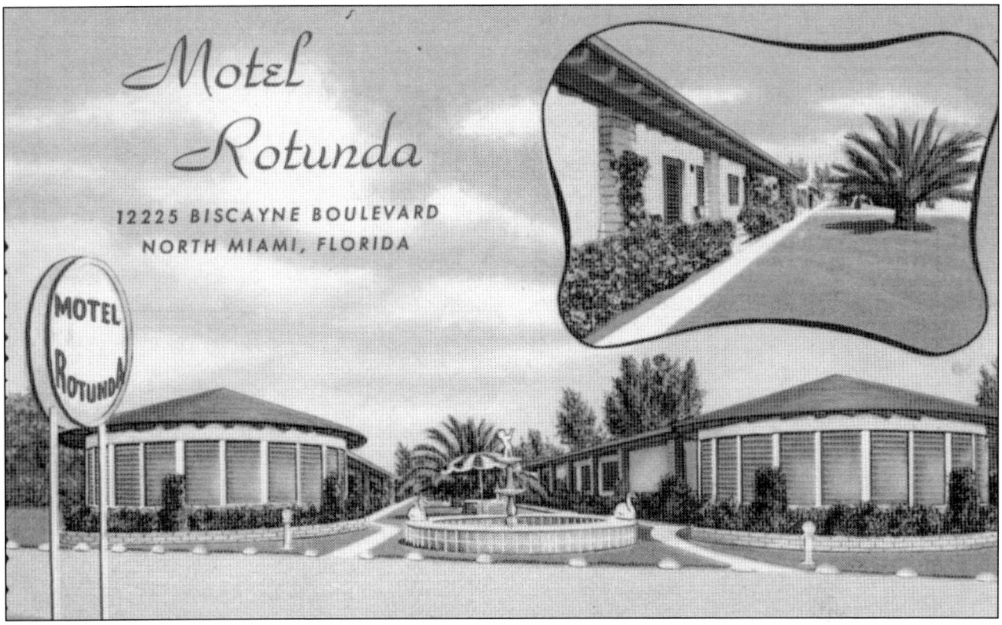

In addition to travel courts and cottages, many new and modern motels were built along Route 1. The Motel Rotunda was located at 12225 Biscayne Boulevard, two blocks north of Tourist City. (Published by Curt Teich.)

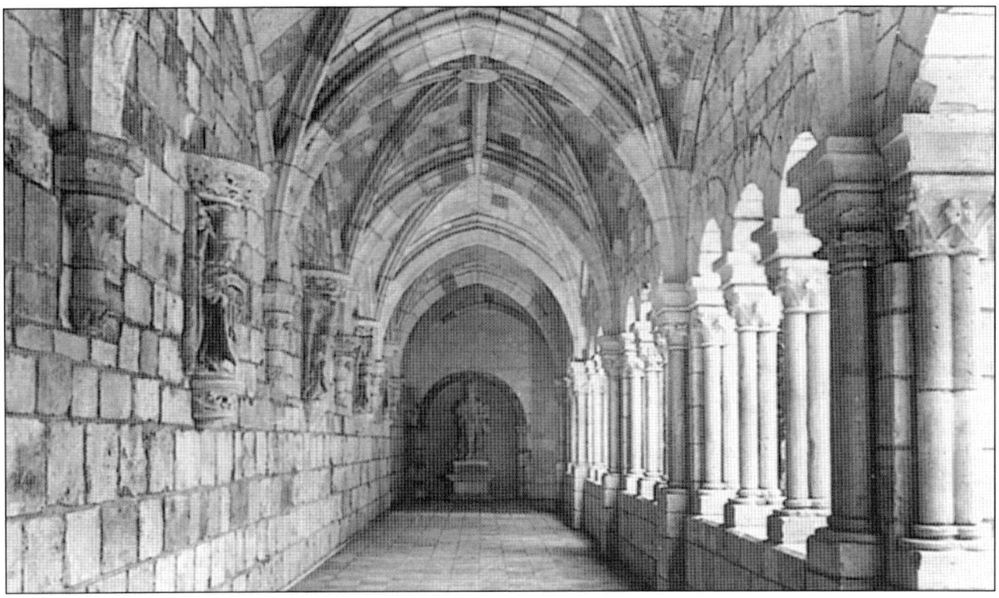

The Ancient Spanish Monastery, located at 16711 West Dixie Highway, was built in the 12th century in Spain. It was brought to America in 11,000 numbered crates by William Randolph Hearst, who abandoned his plan to reconstruct it after customs officials mixed up the crates. The crates remained in a Brooklyn warehouse for 26 years, until new owners reassembled the monastery at its present location in 1952. The Episcopal Church later acquired the monastery and now uses it as a place of worship and a museum. (Courtesy of Florida State Archives.)

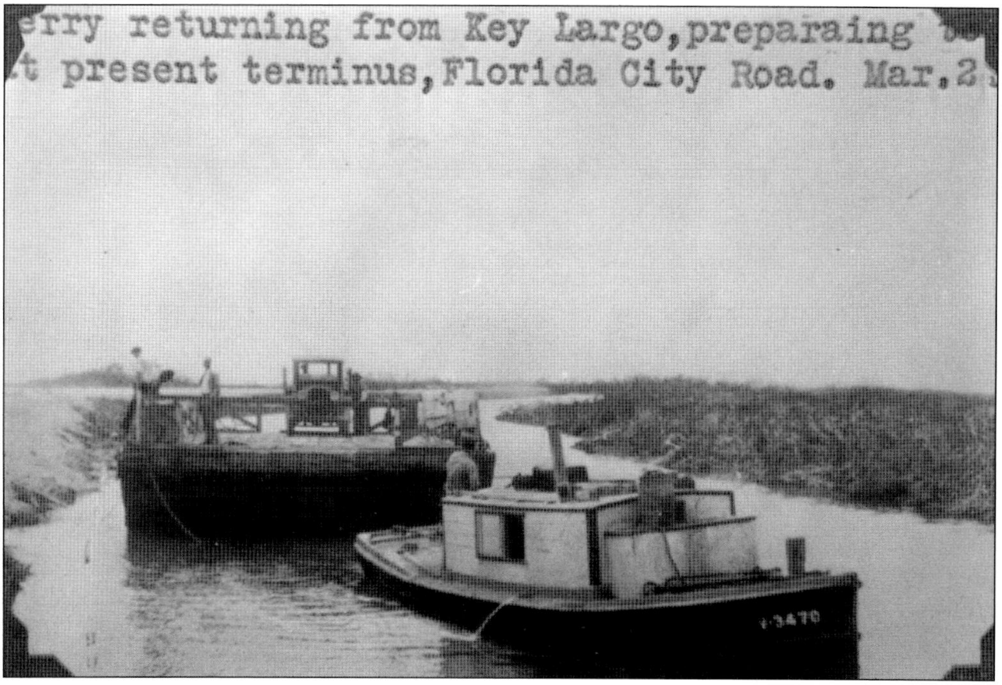

Visitors to Miami were increasingly drawn to the Everglades and the Florida Keys. In this early 1920s photograph, visitors to Key Largo return on a ferry that would take them to Florida City Road. (Courtesy of Florida State Archives.)

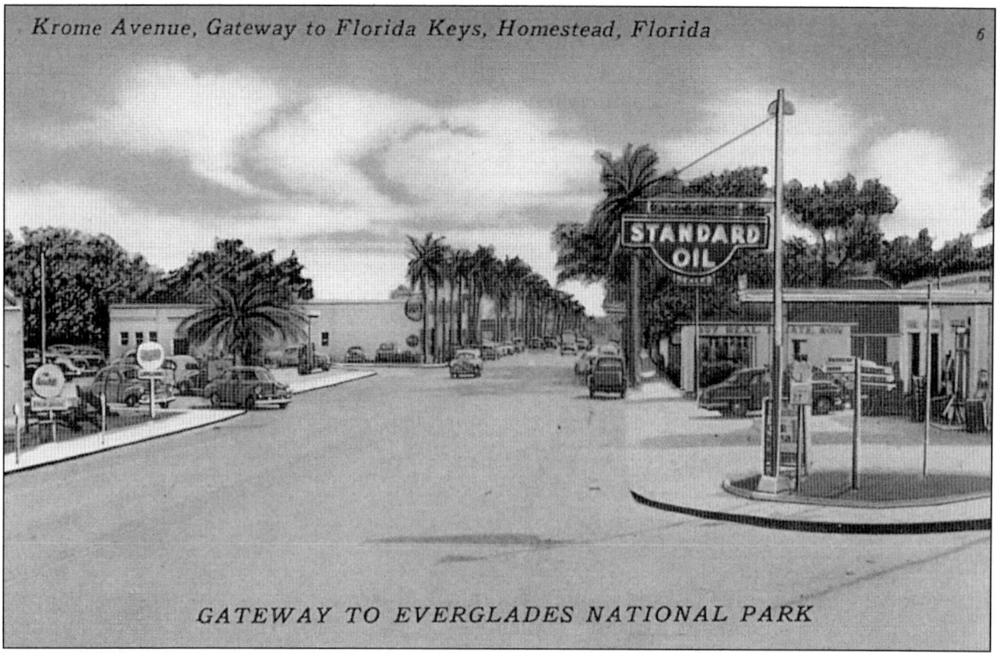

By the time of this *c.* 1940 postcard, it was much easier to get to the Florida Keys. Shown above is Krome Avenue in Homestead, labeled as the "Gateway to the Keys." (Published by Tichnor.)

Six

Sports and Recreation

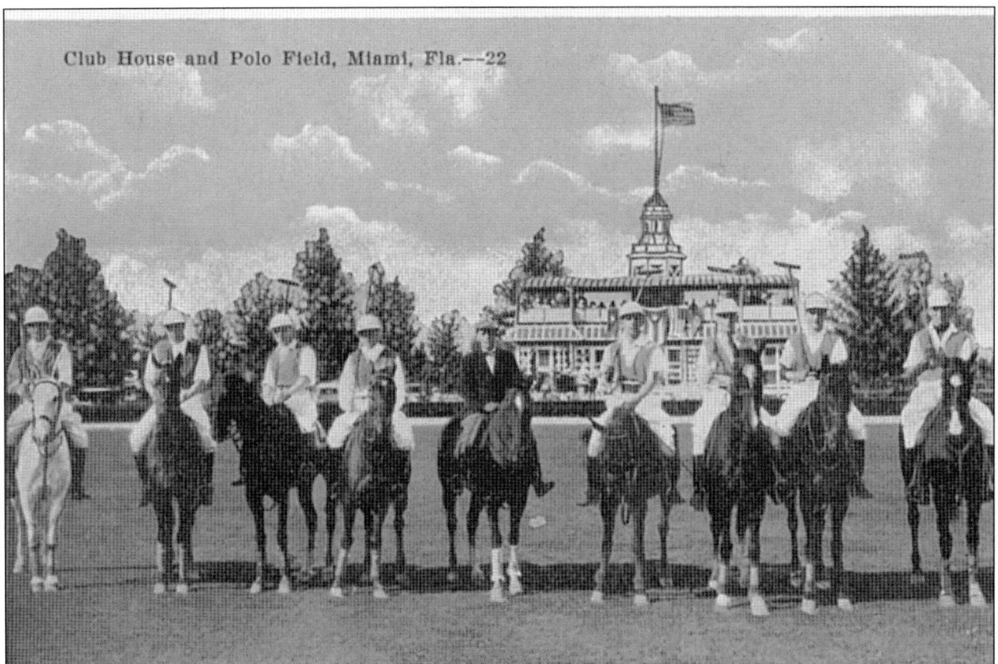

Seeing Miami's potential as a sportsman's paradise, Carl Fisher built the first polo field in the area and introduced polo to the new, thriving resort. This *c.* 1920 postcard shows players lined up in front of the clubhouse. (Published by E.C. Kropp.)

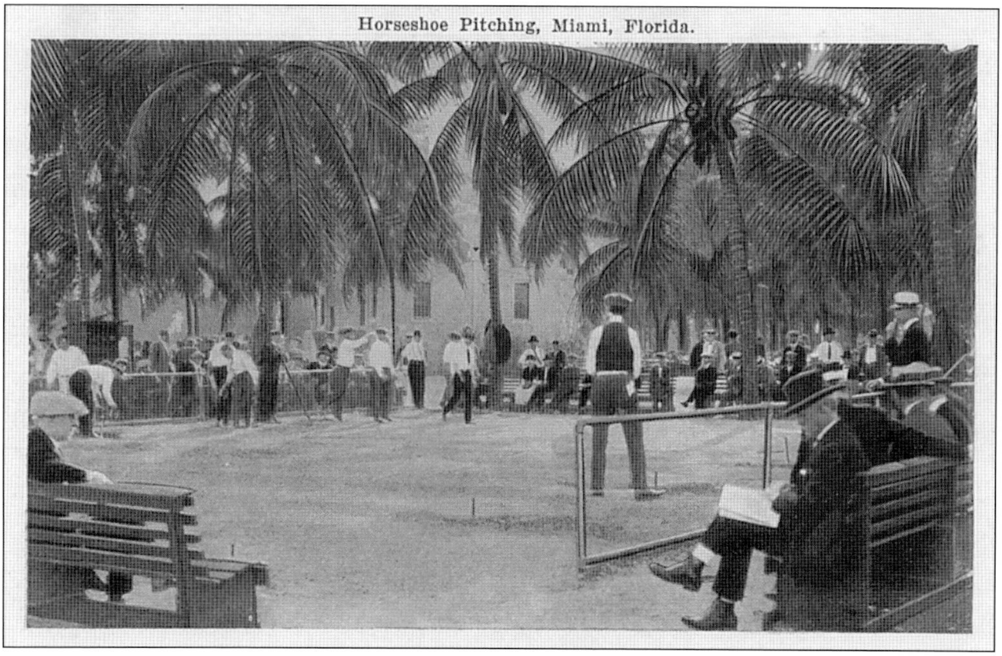

Pitching horseshoes was a widespread and very popular form of recreation in the early 1900s. Note how formally people were dressed, despite the warm weather. (Published by E.C. Kropp.)

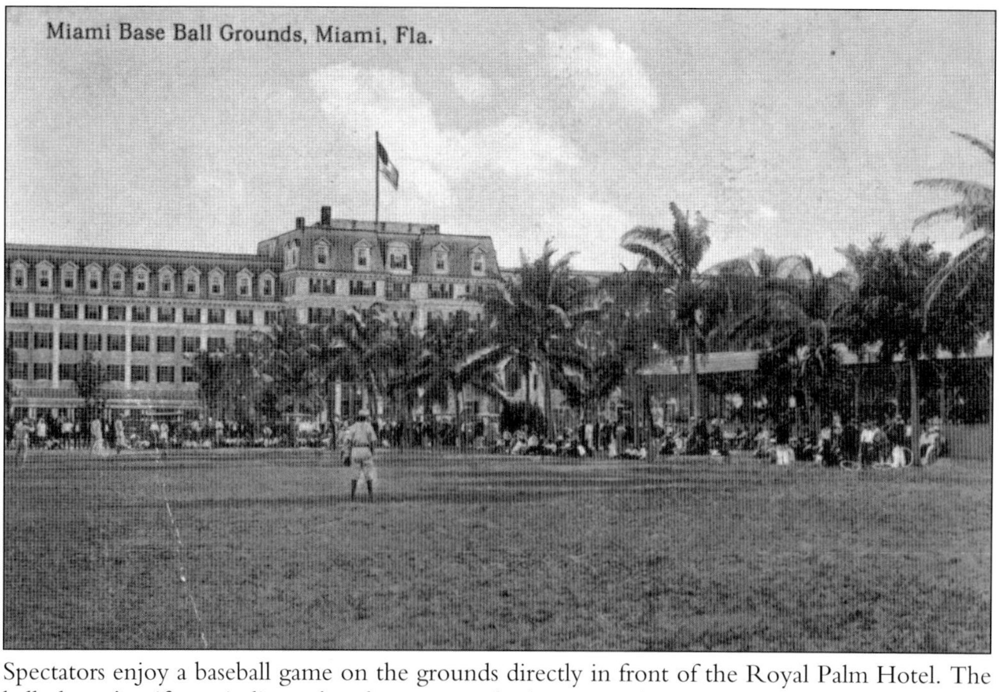

Spectators enjoy a baseball game on the grounds directly in front of the Royal Palm Hotel. The ball players' uniforms indicate that the game took place around 1900–1915. (Courtesy of Florida State Archives.)

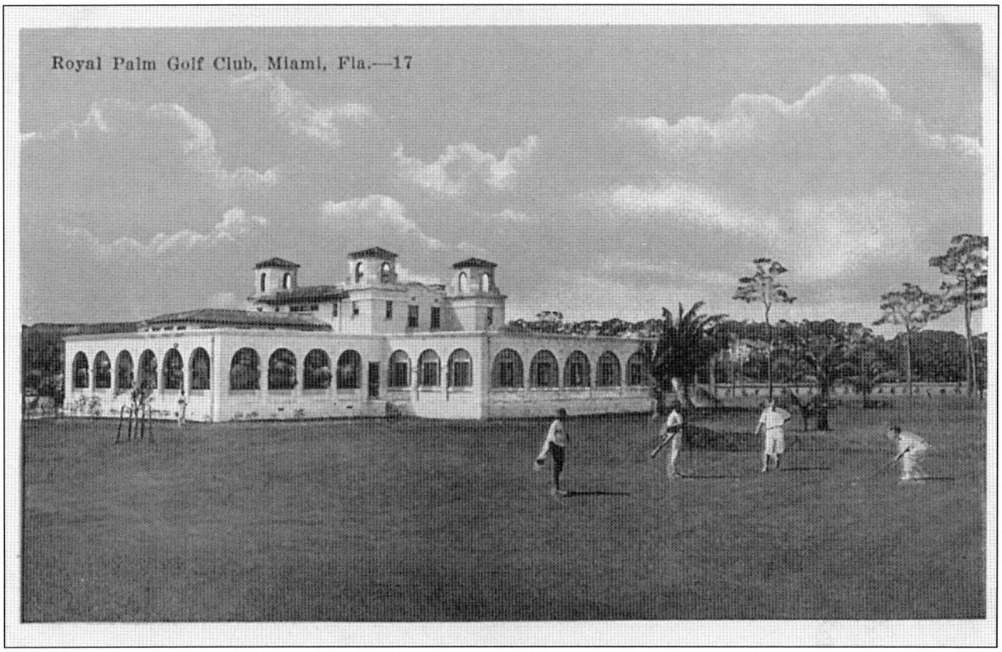

The Royal Palm Golf Club was a forerunner of the many elegant country clubs that dot the greater Miami area today. (Published by E.C. Kropp.)

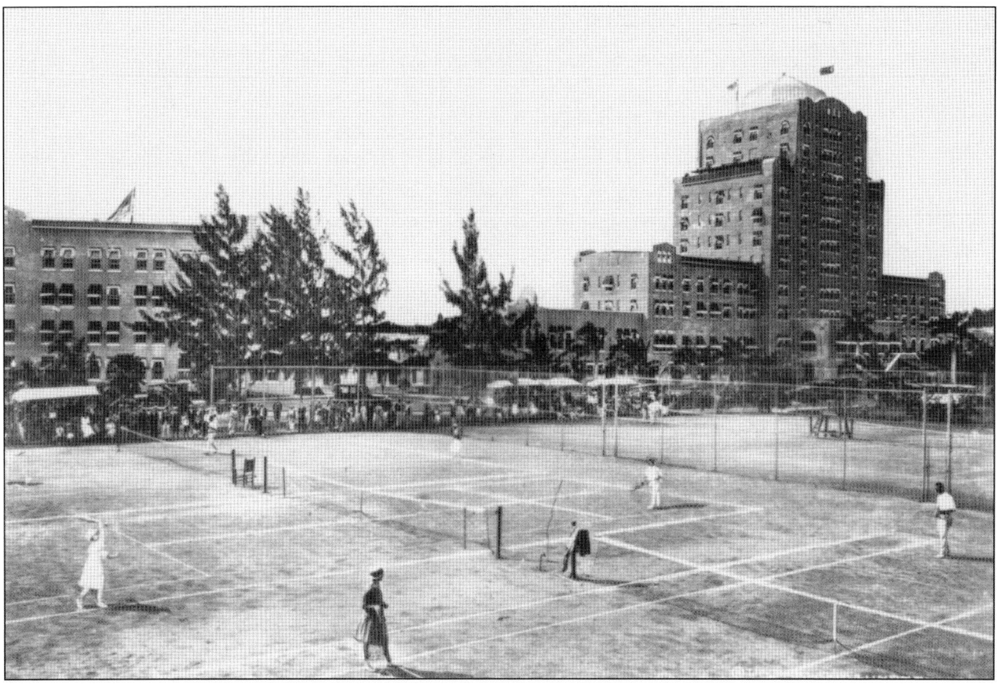

The tennis courts at the Flamingo Hotel in Miami Beach were rarely empty as tennis enjoyed a surge of popularity in the early 1920s. (Courtesy of Florida State Archives.)

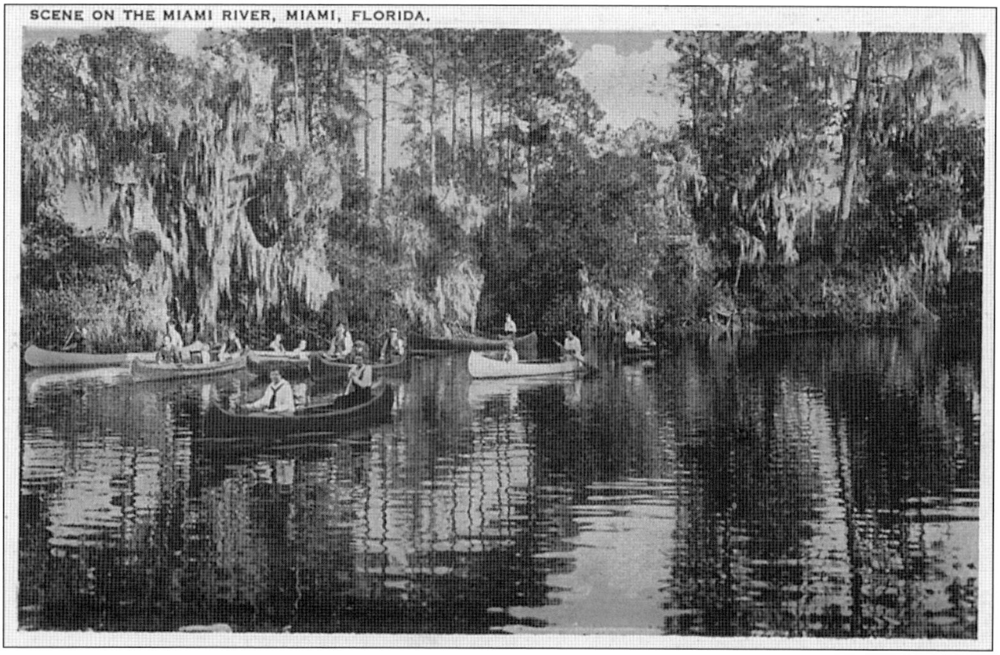

The Miami River resembles a sleepy lagoon as visitors canoe through its sparkling water in this *c.* 1920 view. (Published by Pictorial Centre.)

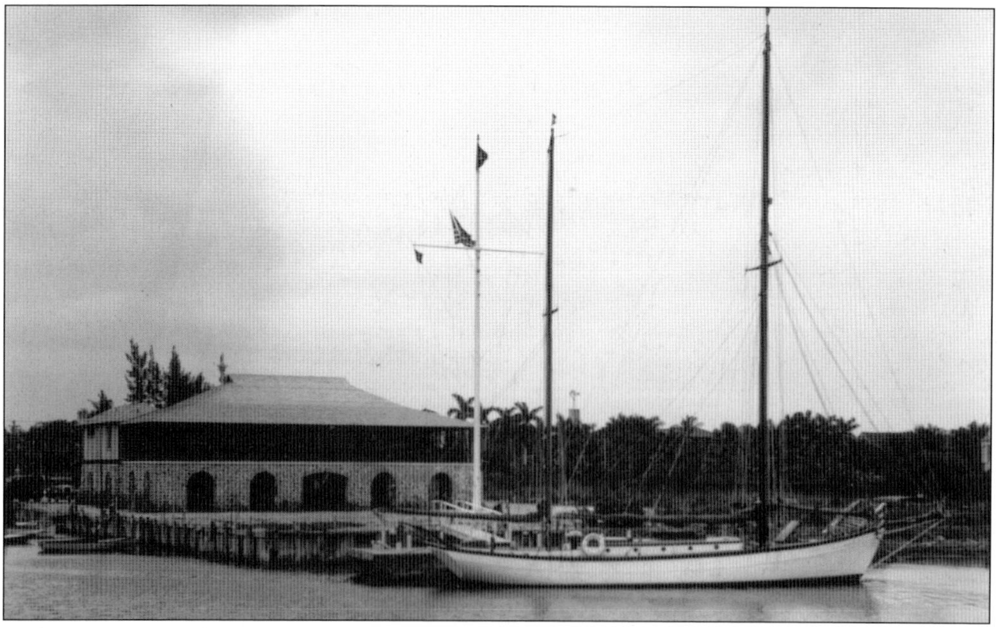

Kirk Munroe and Ralph Munroe (no relation) jointly established the Biscayne Bay Yacht Club. Ralph Munroe became First Commodore, a title he held for 22 years, while Kirk Munroe, an author of adventure stories, became the yacht club secretary. When the boathouse was destroyed by the 1926 hurricane, Ralph Munroe rebuilt it exactly as it had been before the storm. (Courtesy of the Romer Collection, Miami-Dade Public Library.)

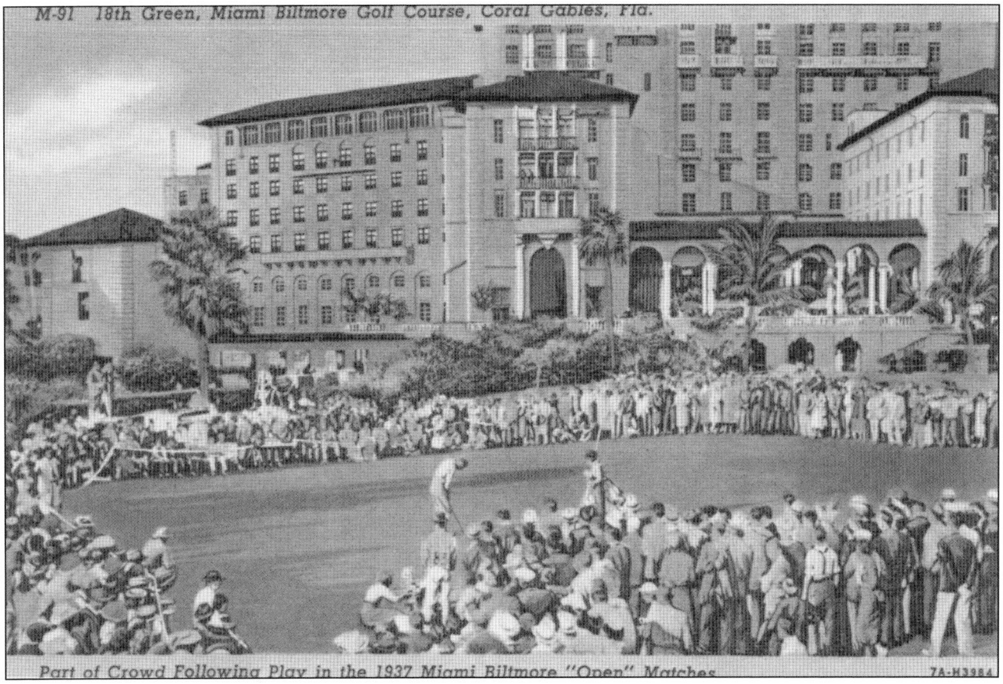

Crowds watch as a contestant prepares to putt on the 18th green at the 1937 Miami Biltmore Open Golf Tournament. (Courtesy of Florida State Archives.)

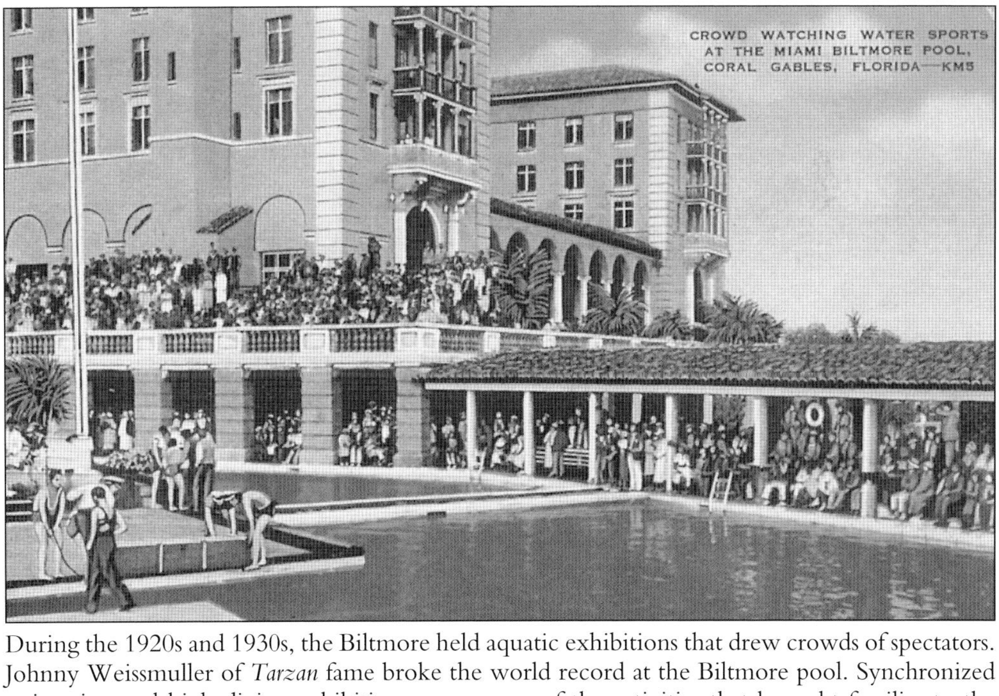

During the 1920s and 1930s, the Biltmore held aquatic exhibitions that drew crowds of spectators. Johnny Weissmuller of *Tarzan* fame broke the world record at the Biltmore pool. Synchronized swimming and high-diving exhibitions were some of the activities that brought families to the hotel. (Published by Thomas R. West.)

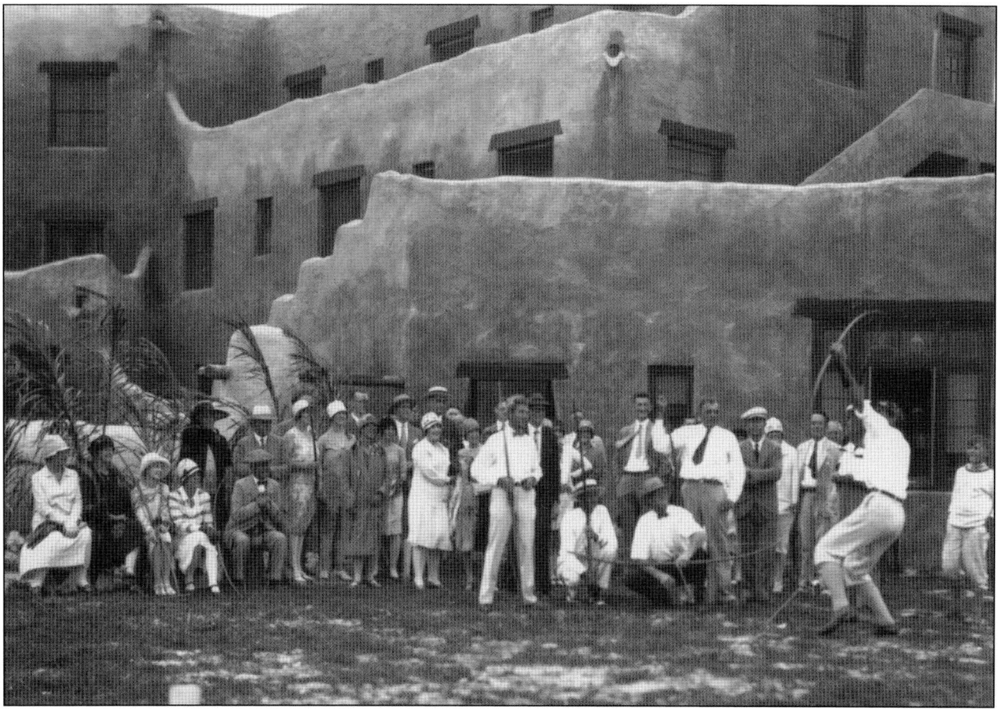

Spectators watch archery expert Howard Hill at a meet at the Pueblo Hotel in Miami Springs on February 26, 1928. (Courtesy of the Romer Collection, Miami-Dade Public Library.)

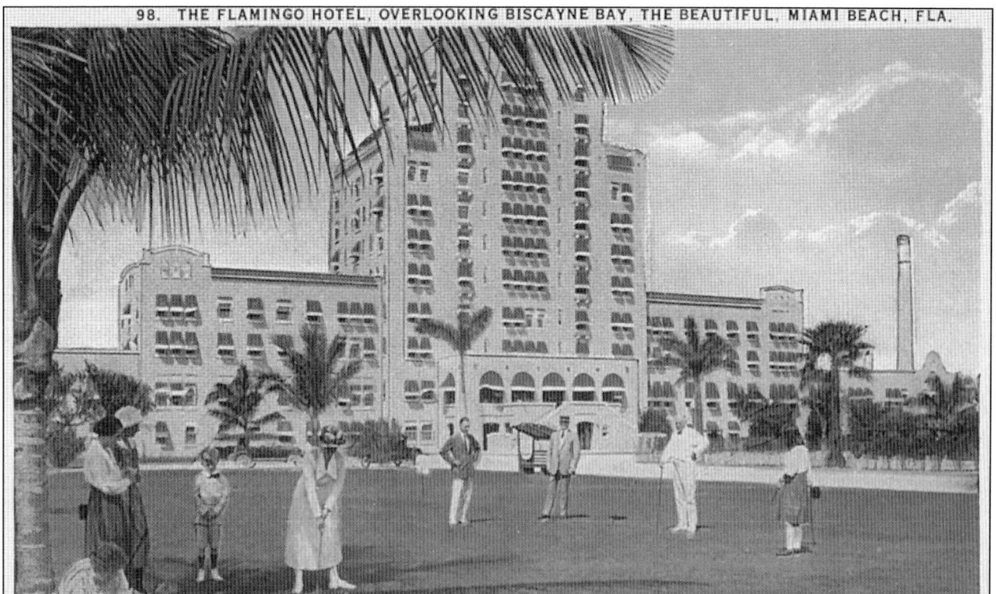

Family members enjoy a game of croquet at the Flamingo Hotel in Miami Beach while the baby and the grandmother sit in the shade of the palm tree. (Published by Curt Teich.)

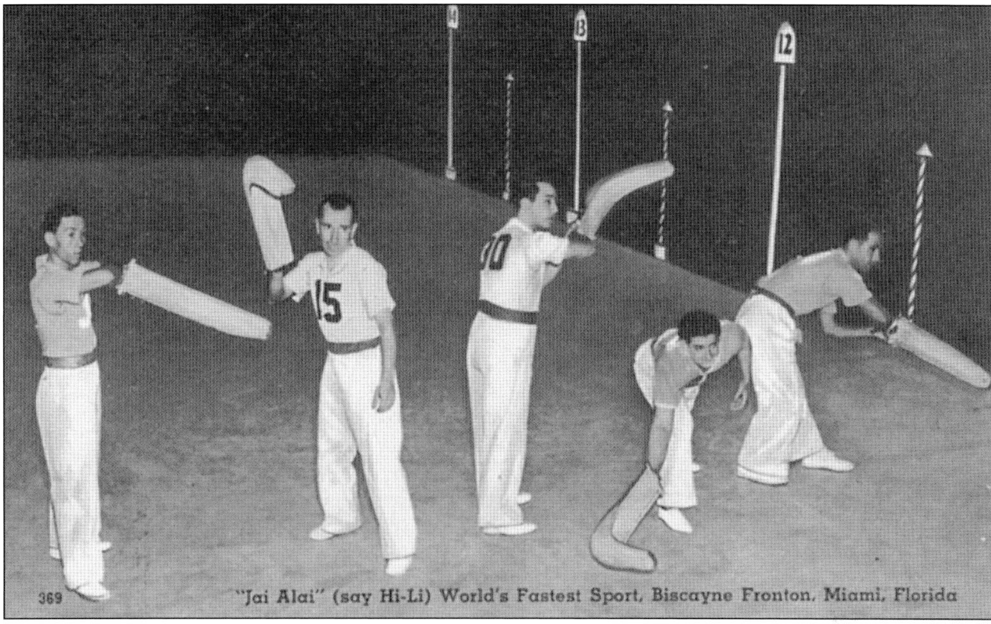

Jai-Ali, pronounced "HiLie," is one of the world's fastest sports. In this view, players are shown in various cesta positions for catching and throwing the ball, which travels in excess of 100 miles per hour. (Published by Tichnor Bros.)

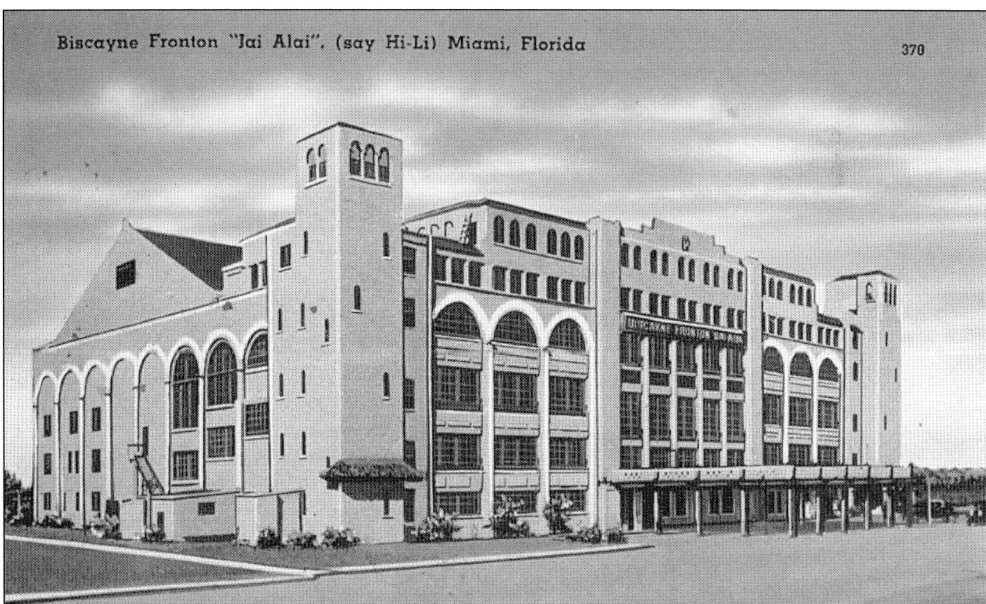

The Biscayne Jai-Alai Fronton opened in 1924 and was the first (and for many years the only) Jai-Alai Fronton in the United States. The legalization of parimutuel betting in the 1930s added greatly to the popularity of this exciting sport. (Published by Tichnor Bros.)

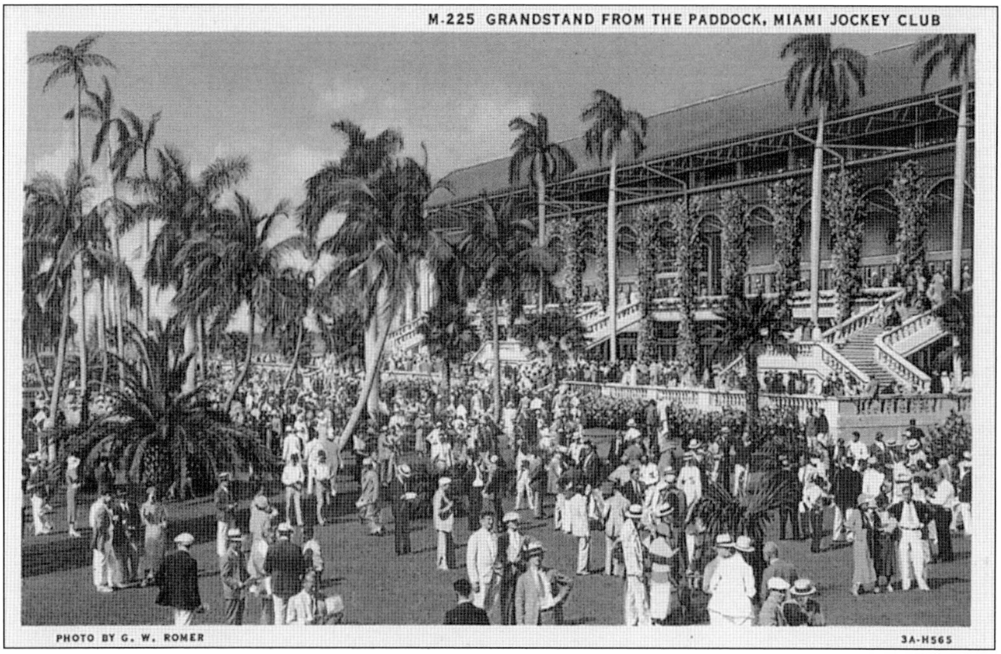

Well-dressed crowds fill the grounds of the Miami Jockey Club in this postcard. Parimutuel betting on horse races, dog races, and Jai-Alai games helped sustain the flow of tourists during the 1930s, and was of enormous benefit to the local economy. The Miami Jockey Club became Hialeah Race Track in 1932. (Published by Curt Teich.)

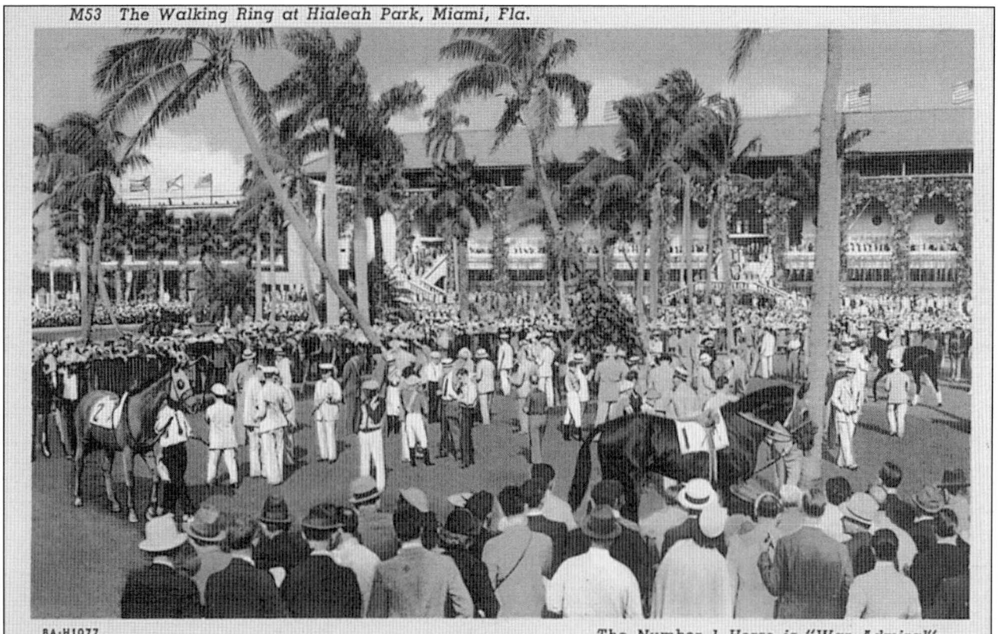

Horse Number 1 ("War Admiral") leads the other racing entries around the walking ring (paddock) at beautiful Hialeah Park. (Published by Curt Teich.)

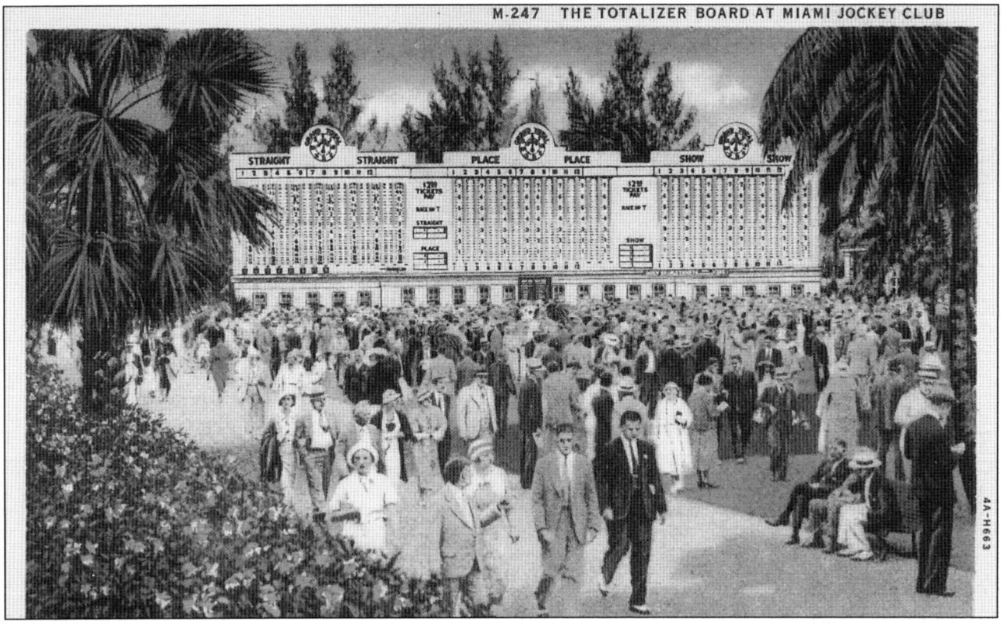

The 1930s presented few opportunities for legalized gambling. Horse racing was one of those outlets and was extremely popular. This 1934 postcard shows crowds in front of the totalizer board, which calculated and displayed the odds on all entries. (Published by Curt Teich.)

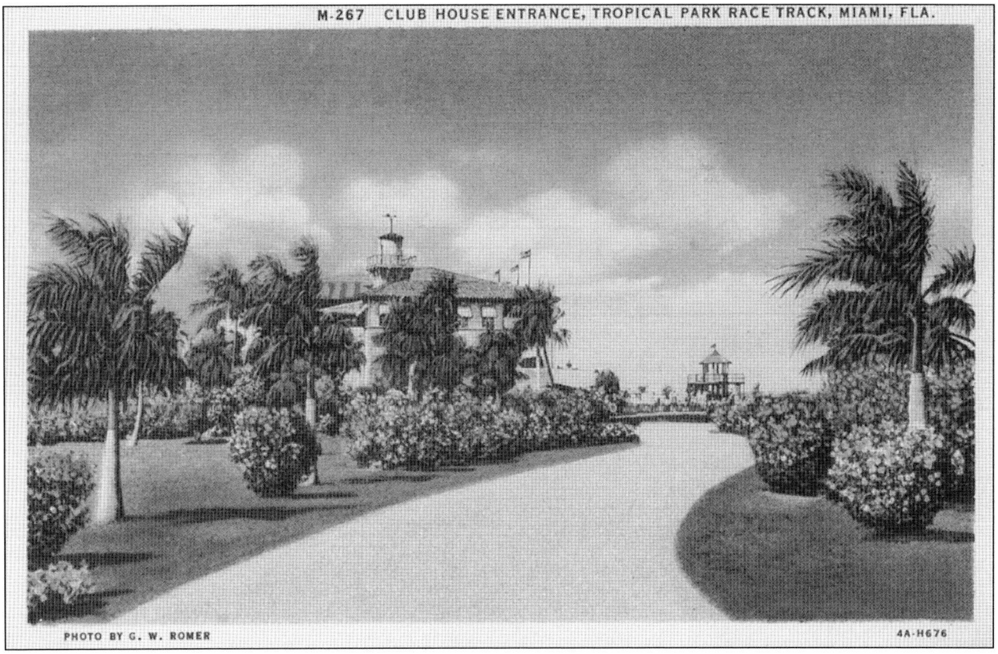

When the 51-day racing period at Hialeah was over, horse races were held at Tropical Park. Tropical Park shared the winter horse racing season with Hialeah Park. Shown here is the clubhouse entrance to the Tropical Park Race Track. (Published by Curt Teich.)

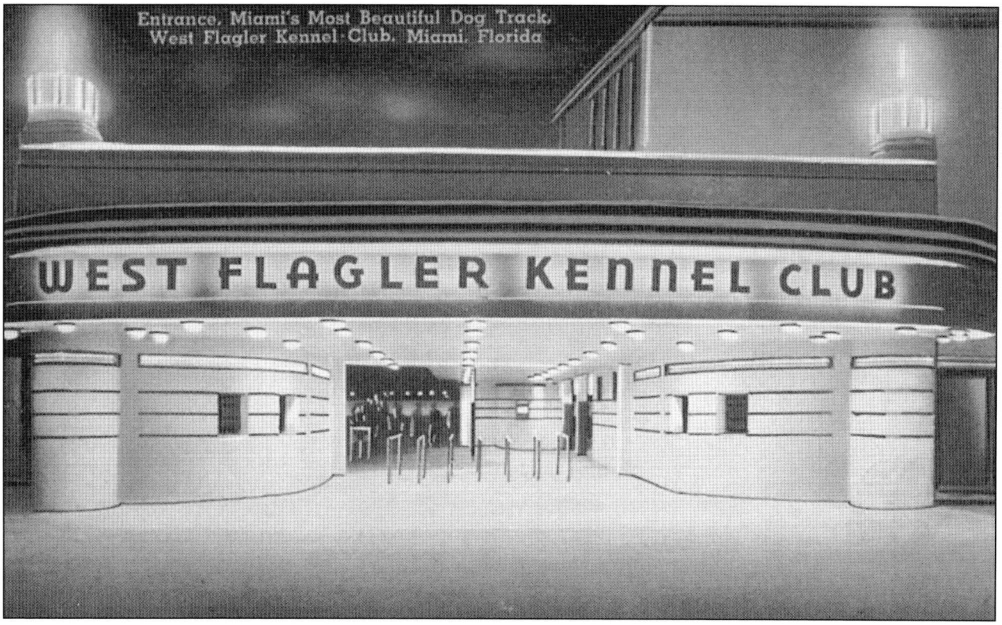

From its Art Deco entrance to the steam-heated grandstand, the West Flagler Kennel Club was considered Miami's most modern and beautiful dog track. (Published by Tichnor Bros.)

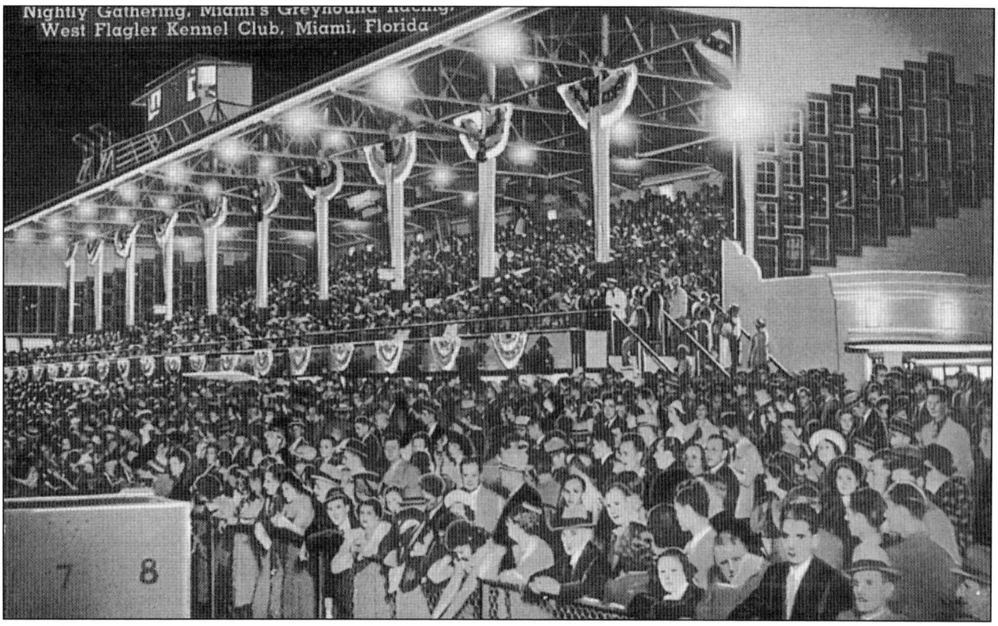

A large crowd fills the grandstand at one of the many greyhound races held nightly at the West Flagler Kennel Club. (Published by Tichnor Bros.)

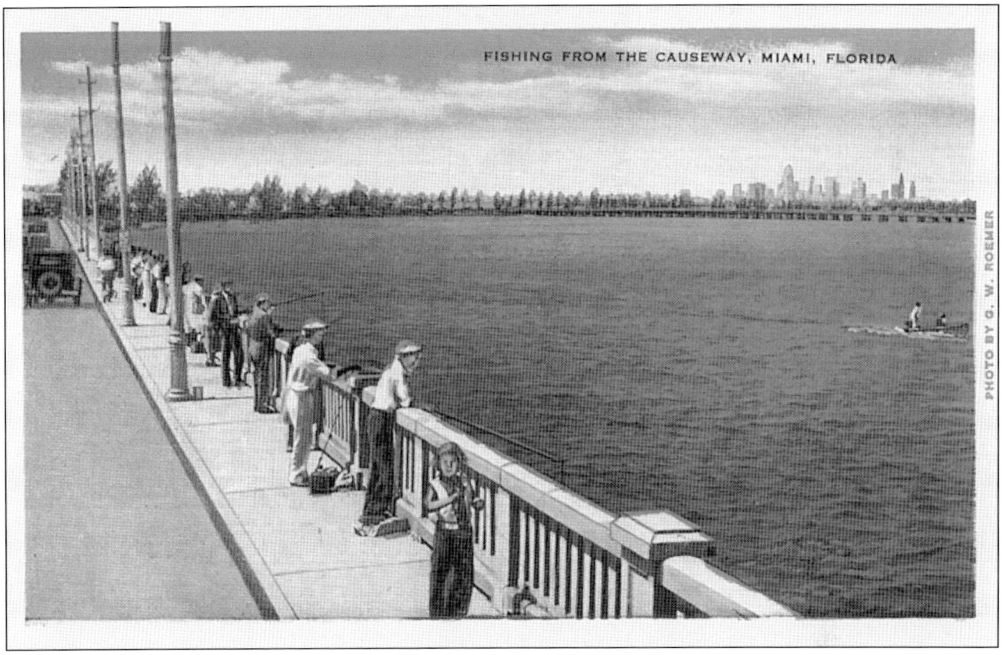

The Causeway provided an ideal location for fishing or just enjoying the warm breezes and beautiful waters of Biscayne Bay. (Published by E.C. Kropp.)

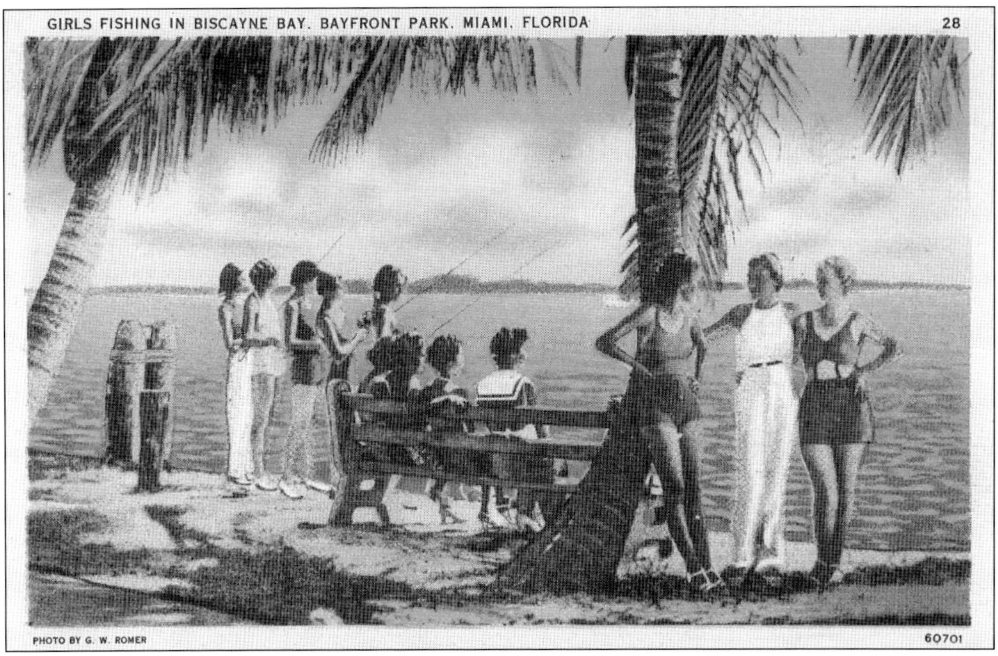

Girls enjoy the tropical weather and fishing in Biscayne Bay at Bayfront Park in this *c*. 1935 postcard. (Published by Tichnor.)

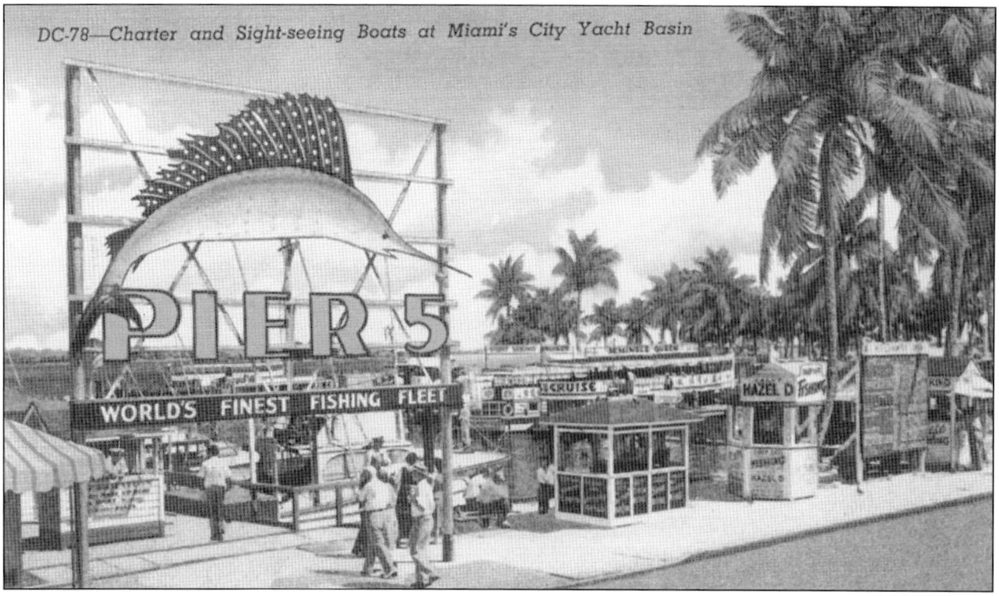

Pier 5 in Bayfront Park was a popular center for boating and fishing for over 30 years. Today, the Bayside Marketplace occupies the same site and contains numerous shops and restaurants. Included in that number is a "Pier 5 Marketplace," which pays homage to the original site. (Published by Curt Teich.)

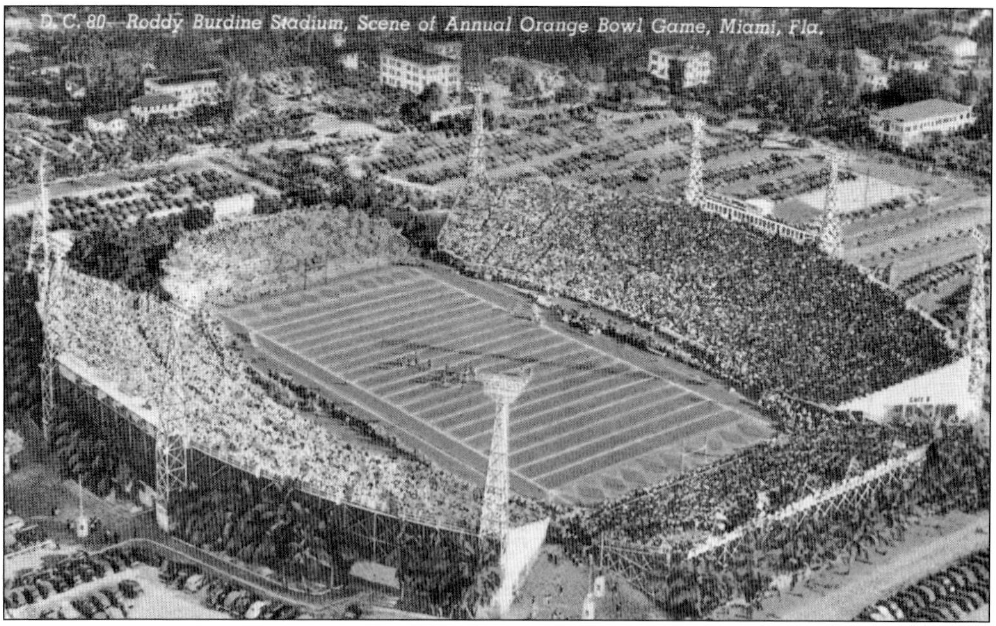

The Orange Bowl Stadium opened in 1934 and a year later hosted the first Orange Bowl game. In 1936, the City of Miami named it the Roddy Burdine Stadium, in honor of the man who ran the popular Burdine's department store from 1911 until his death in 1936. Mr. Burdine had been an outstanding and well-respected community leader. This 1941 postcard shows the stadium filled with spectators during the annual Orange Bowl game. (Published by Curt Teich.)

Seven

Planes and Boats and Trains

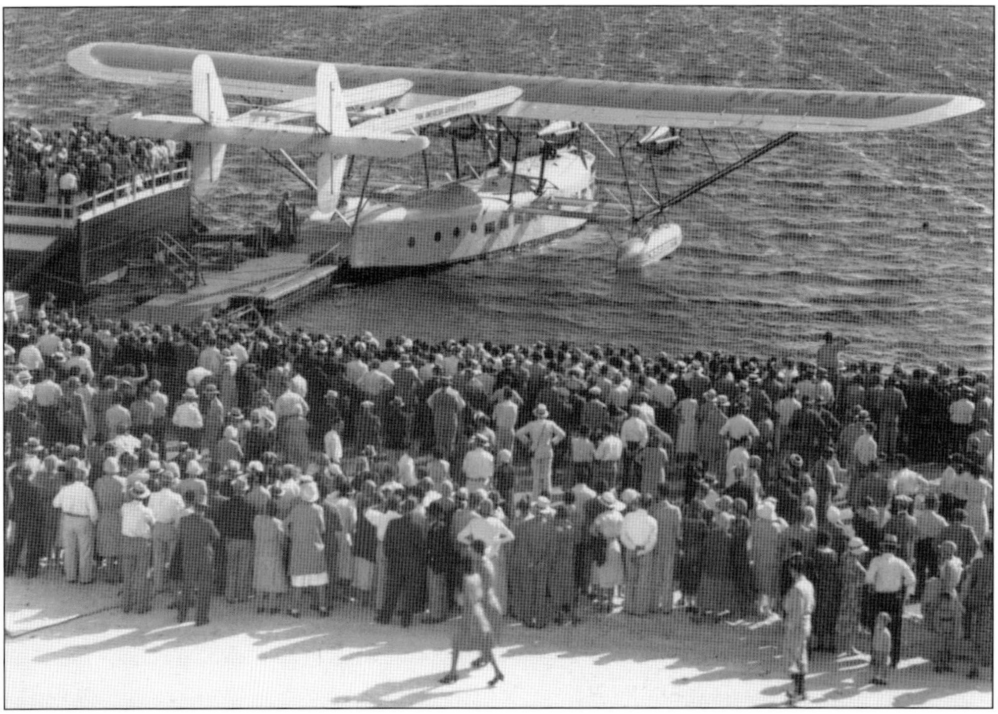

The departure of the Pan American *Clipper* on its December 1, 1930 maiden voyage attracted a huge audience. It marked the beginning of an era that captured the romance and intrigue of international travel. For the next 15 years, crowds enjoyed watching the "flying boats" take off and land on the shimmering waters of Biscayne Bay. (Courtesy of the Romer Collection, Miami-Dade Public Library.)

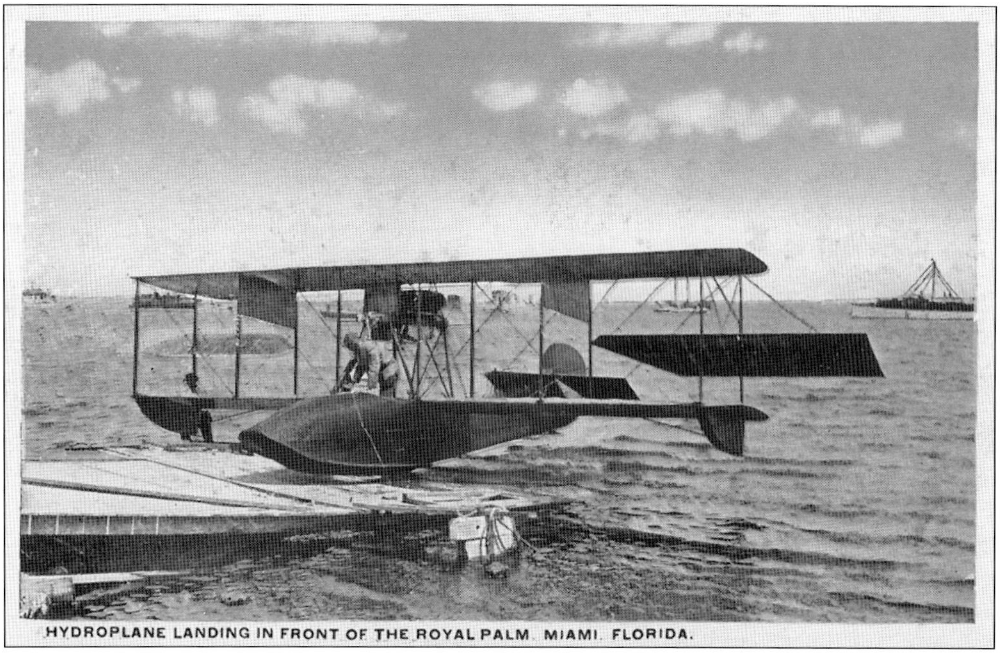

An adventurous pilot lands his hydroplane in front of the Royal Palm Hotel in this *c.* 1920 postcard.

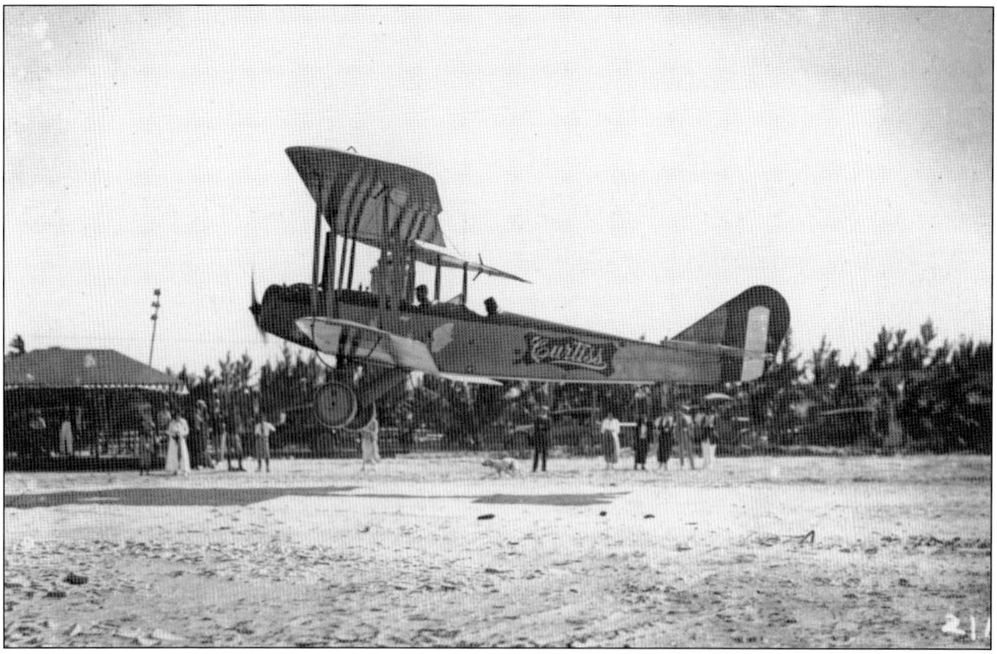

Glenn Curtiss played a vital role in the development of aviation over the early decades of the 20th century. Inventor of the world's fastest motorcycle and the first flying boat to cross the Atlantic, Curtiss also designed aircraft that trained most of the United States pilots who served during World War I. Seen above is an early Curtiss bi-plane taking off from the Miami Municipal Airport. (Courtesy of Florida State Archives.)

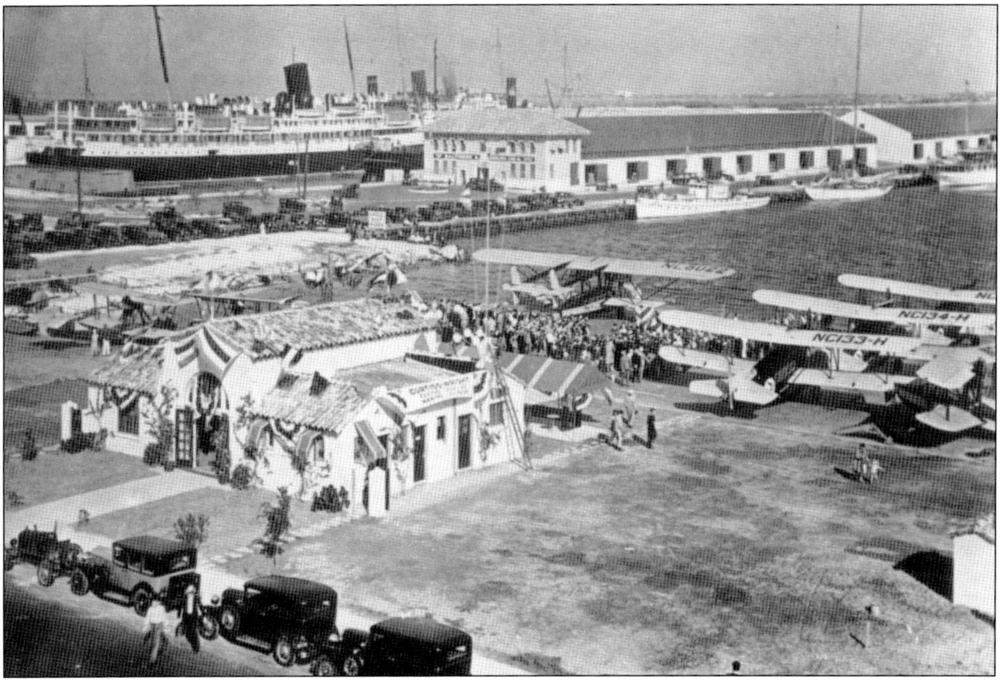

Chalk Airlines and Curtiss-Wright Flying Service shared Watson Island in Miami Harbor in this 1920s photo. A cruise ship passing the island can be seen in the background. (Courtesy of Florida State Archives.)

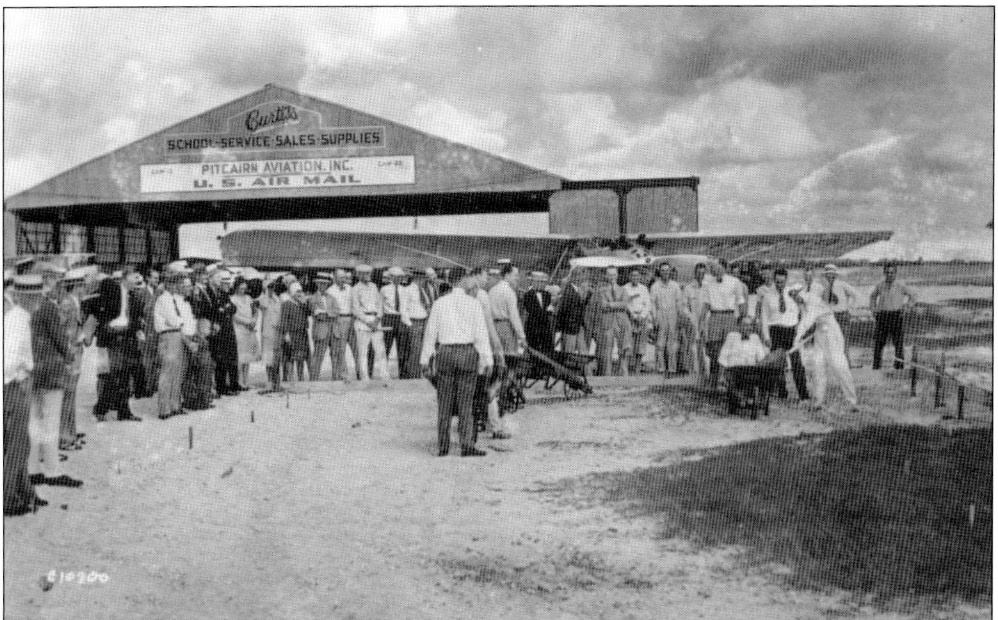

On November 4, 1929, officials from the city of Miami, Curtiss Flying Services, and Pitcairn Aviation gathered for the groundbreaking of the Miami Municipal Airport. (Courtesy of Florida State Archives.)

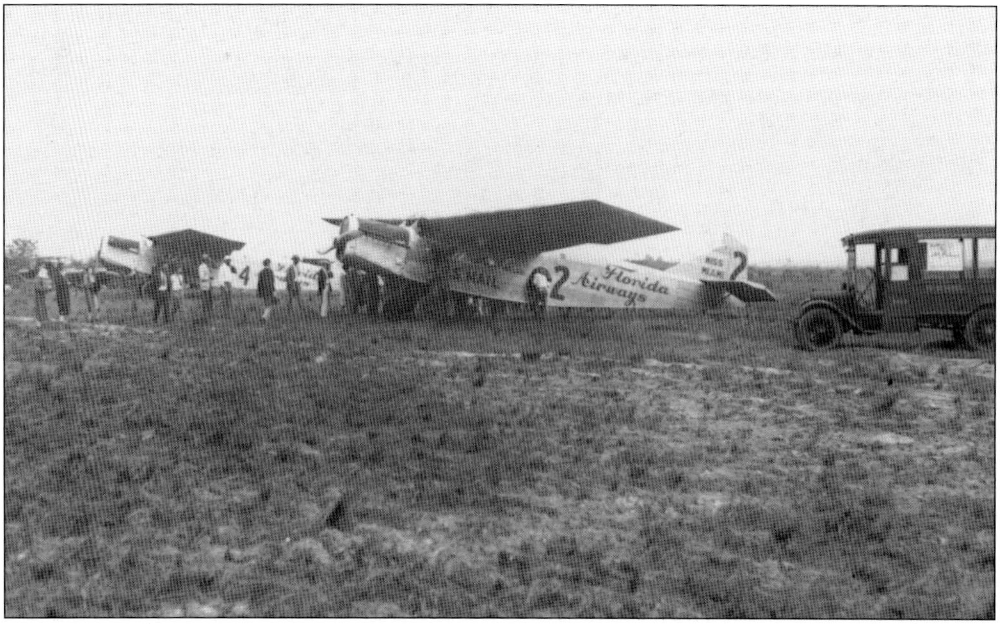

In 1926, the first airmail flight left Miami on a single engine aircraft operated by Florida Airways. The plane was appropriately named "Miss Miami." (Courtesy of Florida State Archives.)

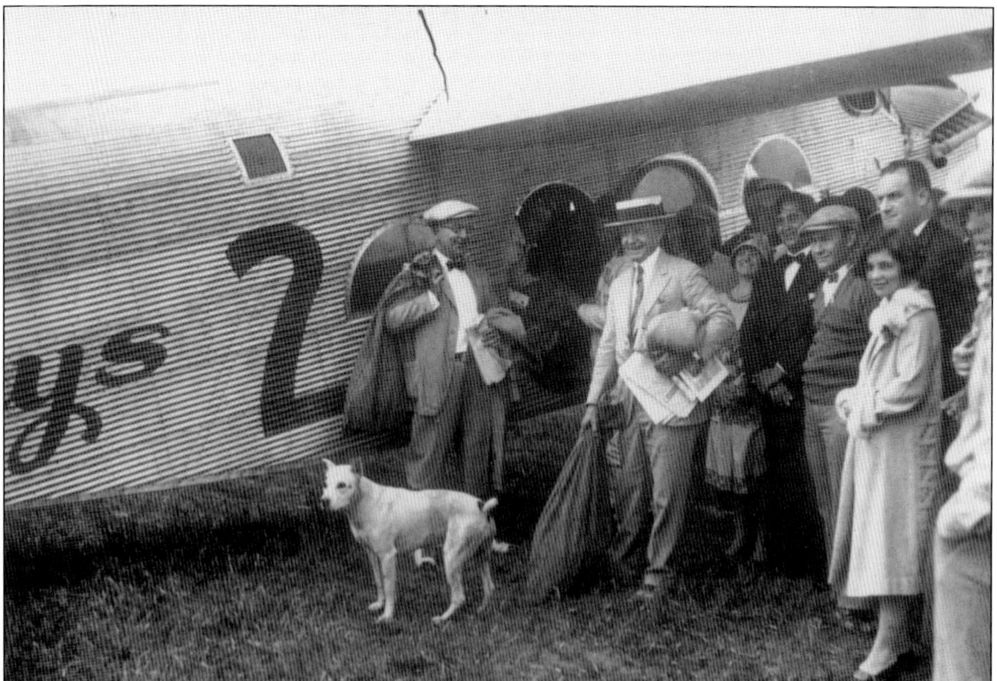

On June 1, 1926, Florida Airways began the first daily air passenger service in the United States, utilizing a previously established Federal Air Mail contract route. (Courtesy of Florida State Archives.)

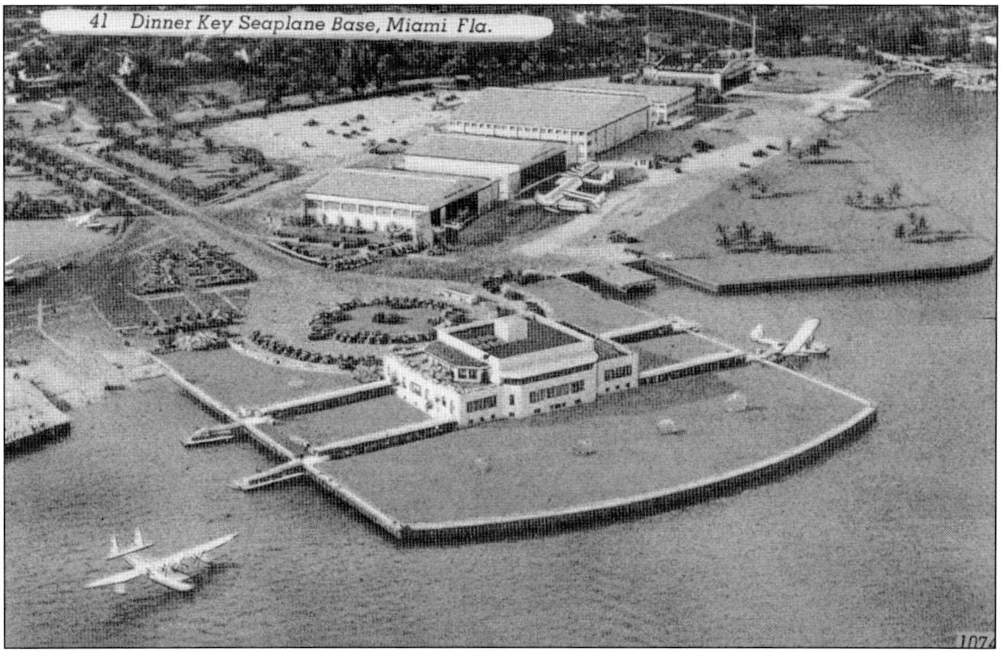

On September 15, 1930, Pan Am moved its operations to Coconut Grove to begin its Clipper "flying boat" service. Until the Dinner Key Marina (shown above) was completed in 1934, the airline operated from a two-story houseboat and barge. (Published by Colourpicture.)

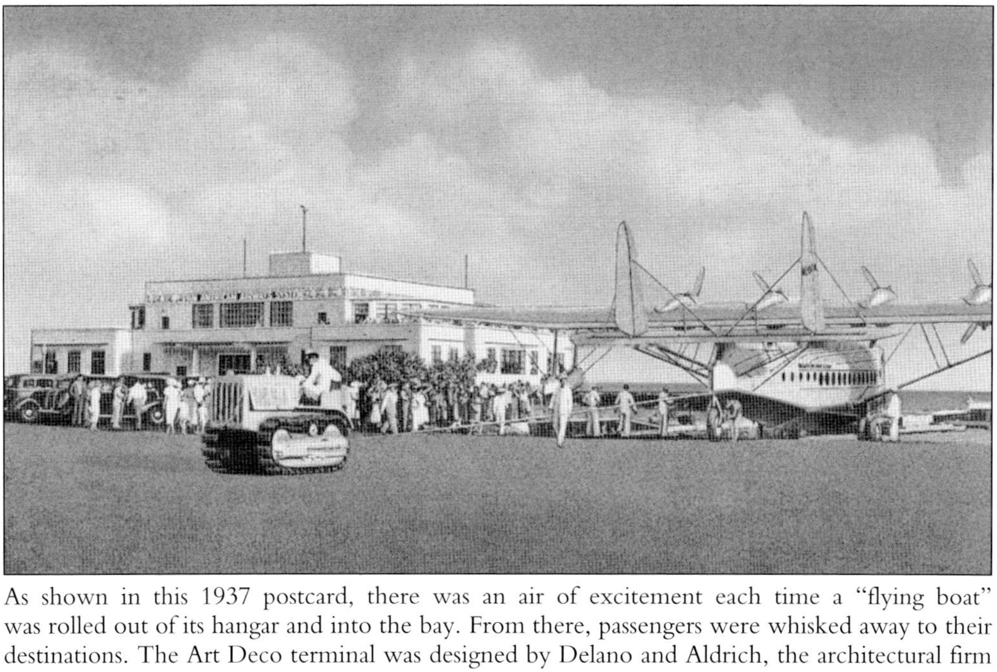

As shown in this 1937 postcard, there was an air of excitement each time a "flying boat" was rolled out of its hangar and into the bay. From there, passengers were whisked away to their destinations. The Art Deco terminal was designed by Delano and Aldrich, the architectural firm that created LaGuardia Marine Air Terminal.When Pan Am traded the clippers for faster land-based planes, the Dinner Key terminal became the Miami City Hall. (Published by Curt Teich.)

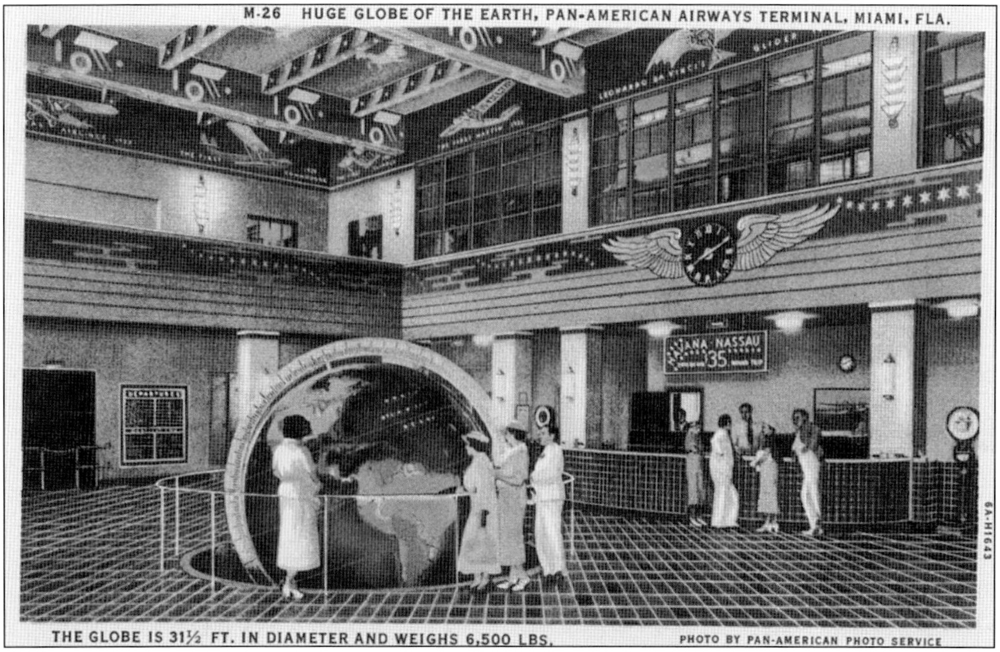

A huge 10-foot, full-color revolving globe was featured in the new Pan Am lobby. Rand, McNally and Company made the globe, which displayed all the airlines of the world. Although the last Pan Am flight left the terminal on August 9, 1945, the globe remained in the lobby until 1951. The globe is now in the lobby of the Science Museum on Bayshore Drive. (Published by Curt Teich.)

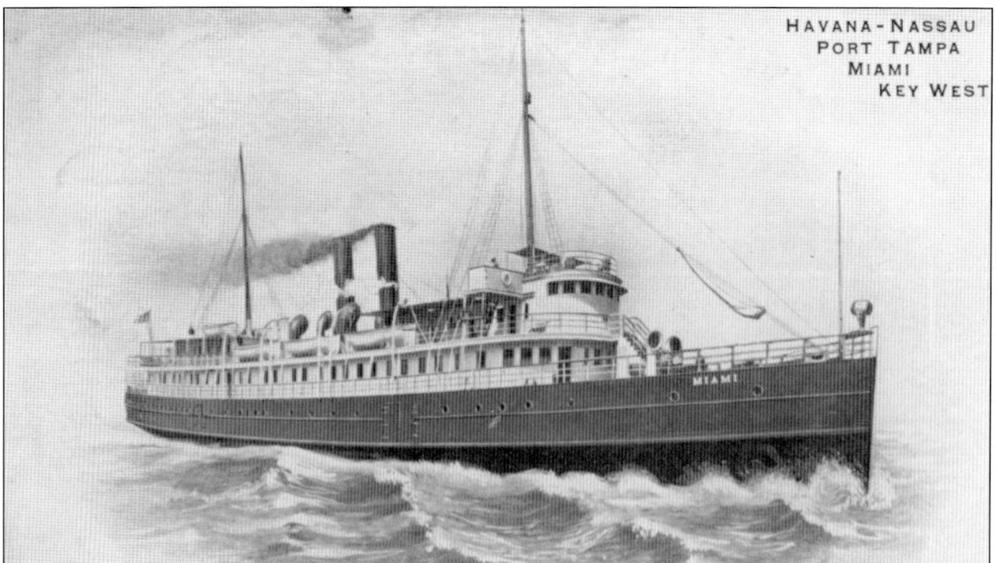

The ocean steamer *Miami* made three round trips a week between Miami and Nassau during the season. During the off-season, the ship operated in New England. The steamship line was controlled by Henry Flagler's Florida East Coast systems. (Courtesy of Florida State Archives.)

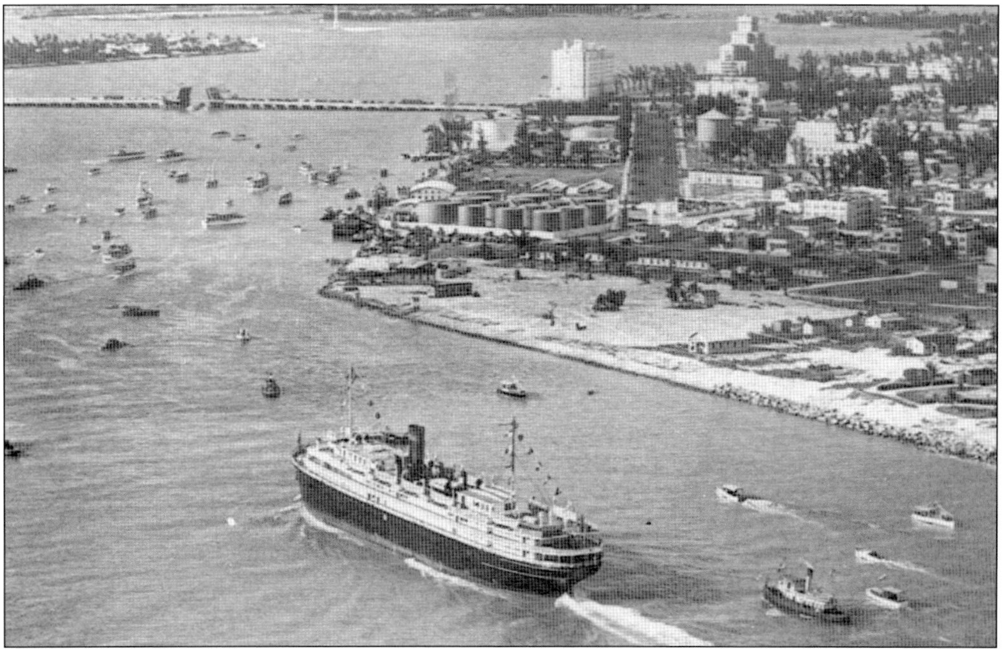

On December 13, 1927, the S.S. *Chatham* became the first large ship to pass through Government Cut, with its newly dredged 26-foot depth, into the Miami Harbor. Over 50 yachts, tugs, and pleasure boats greeted the ship. (Courtesy of Florida State Archives.)

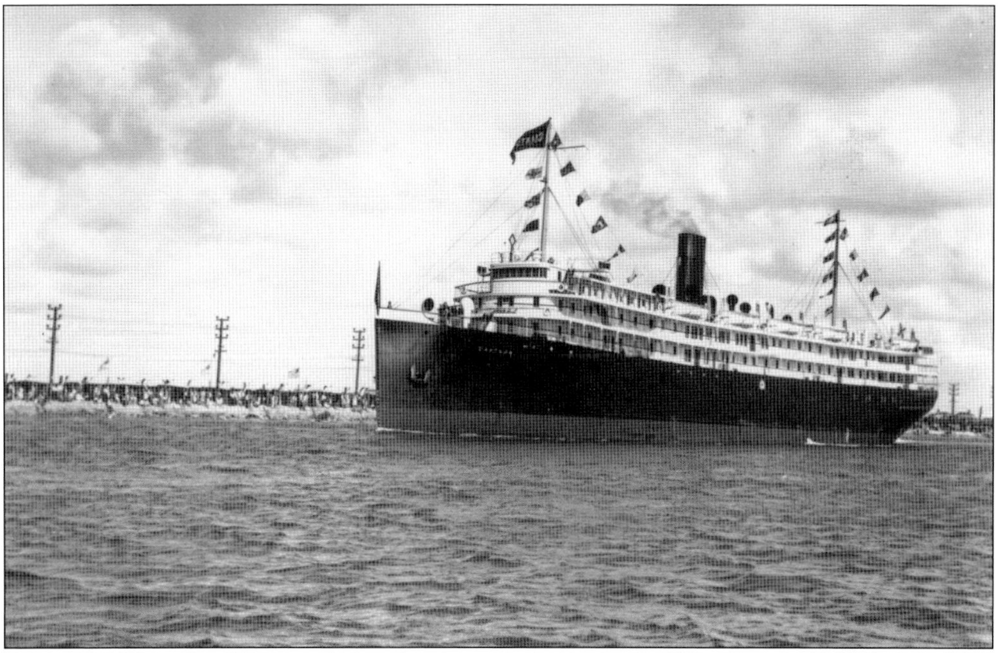

Enthusiastic Miami residents wave from County Causeway as the S.S. *Chatham* travels further into the Miami Harbor. The stage was set for the future busiest cruise port in the world. (Courtesy of the Romer Collection, Miami-Dade Public Library.)

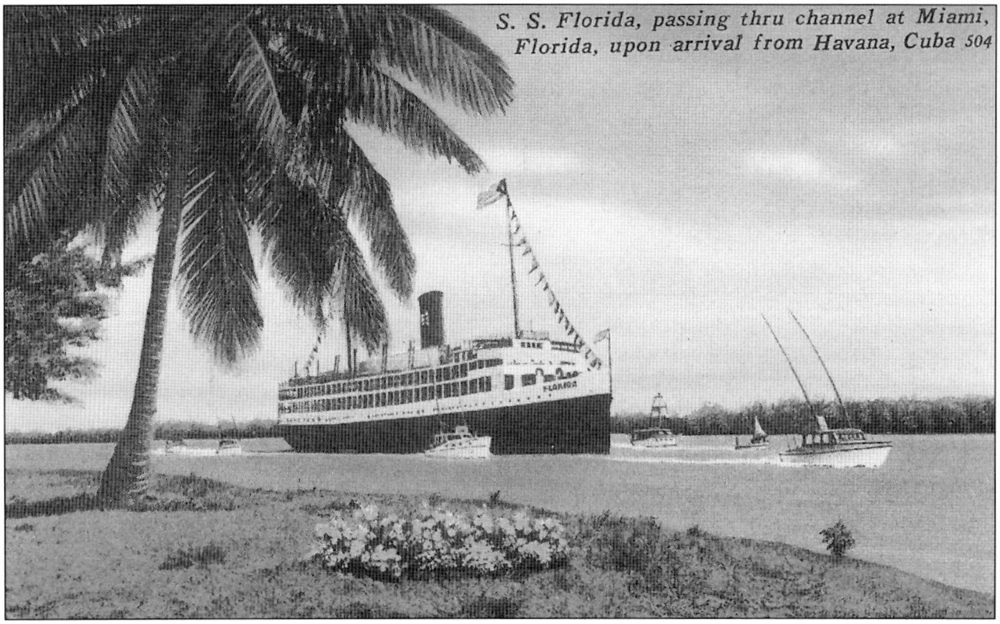

The S.S. *Florida* offered tourists a "Havana Holiday," an overnight cruise from Miami to Havana. Shown here, the ship is escorted by smaller boats as it enters the Miami Harbor. (Published by Tichnor Bros.)

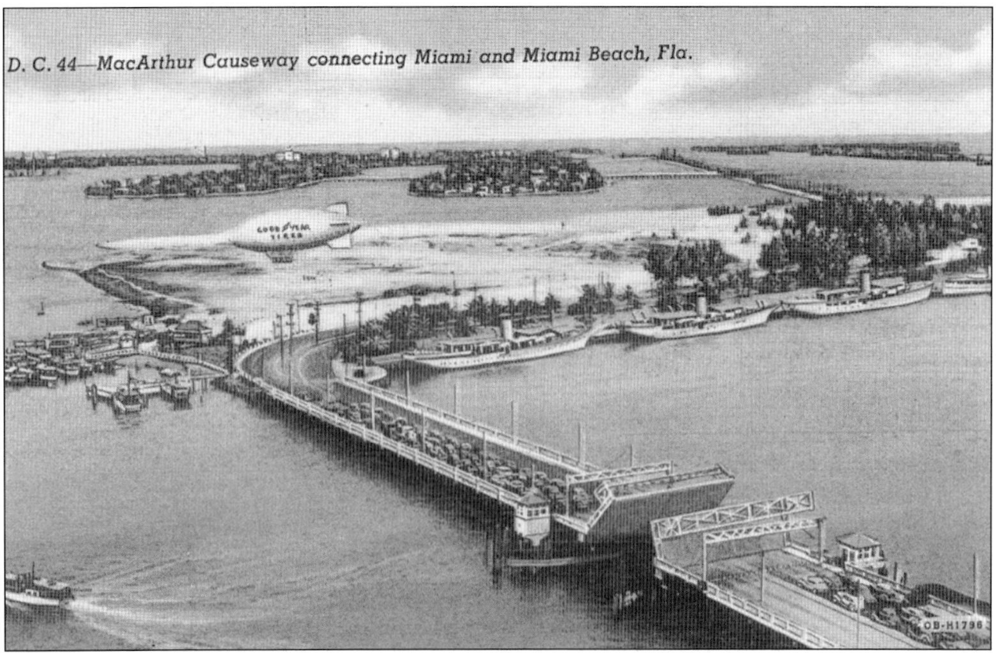

The County Causeway was renamed the MacArthur Causeway in honor of General Douglas MacArthur in 1942. (Published by Curt Teich.)

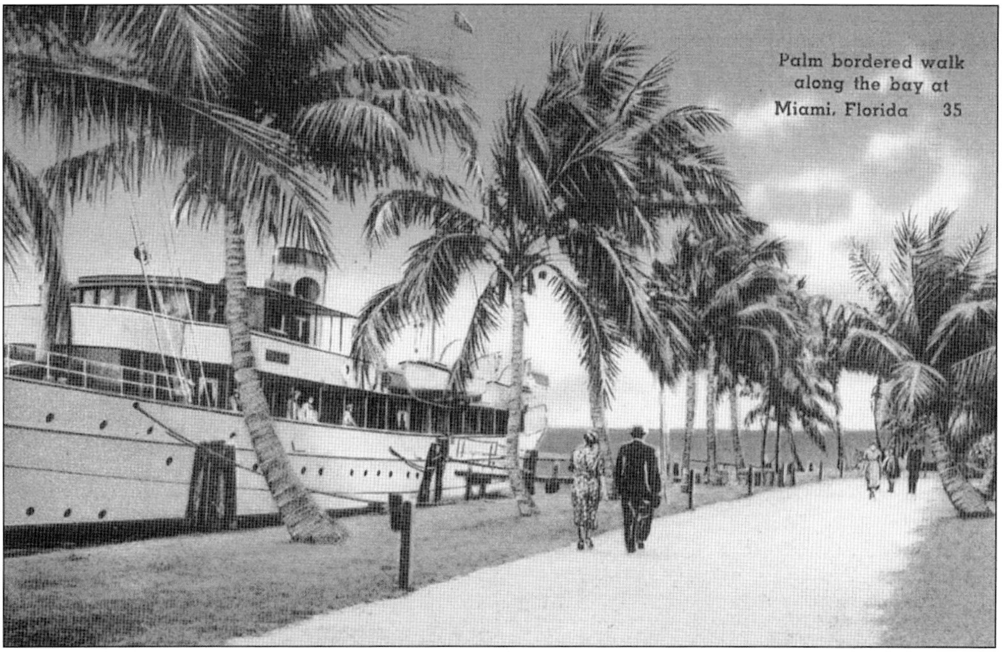

Miami became a mecca for yachtsmen. Beautiful ocean waters and a wide variety of land-based activities made an appealing combination. (Published by Tichnor Bros.)

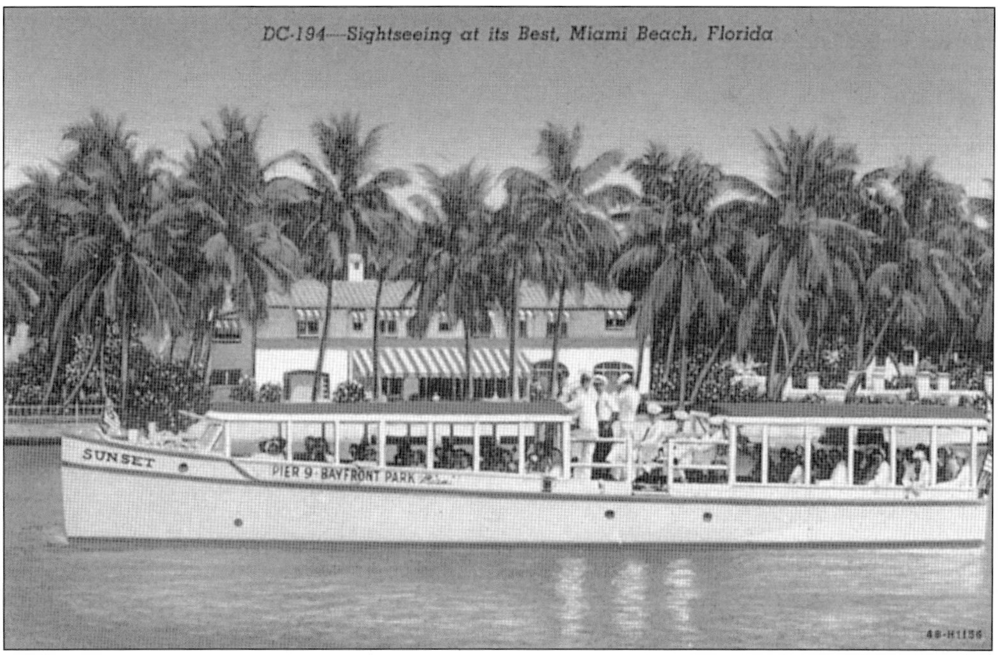

This 1944 postcard shows the tour boat *Sunset* cruising past elegant homes located on islands in Biscayne Bay. (Published by Curt Teich.)

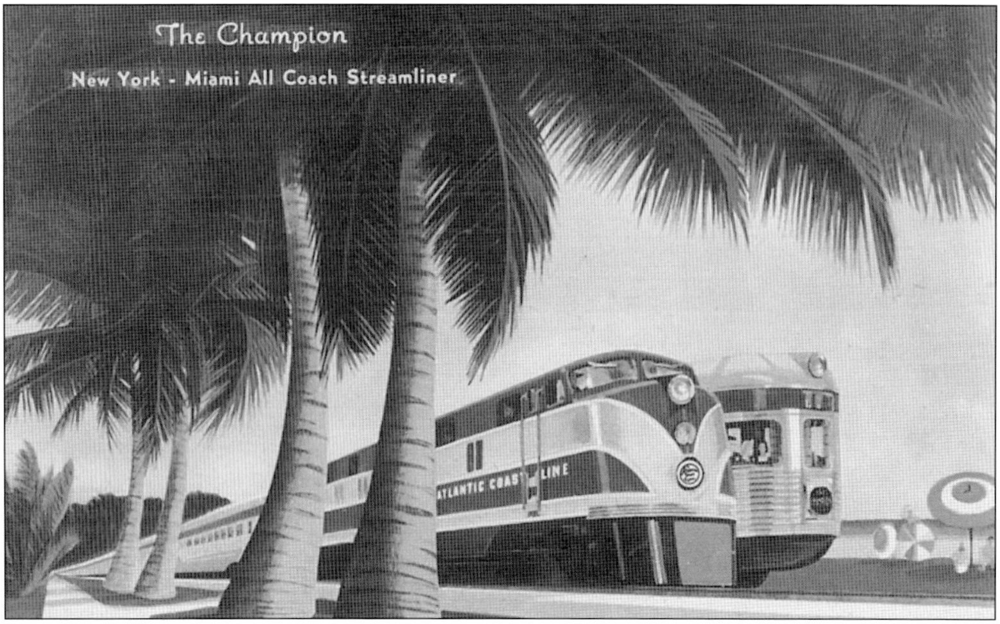

The *Champion* was the newest streamliner of Atlantic Coast Line Railroad and the Florida East Coast Railway. The famous all-coach train ran between New York and Miami daily. For the photo, the observation car, normally at the end of the train, is proudly displayed next to the new diesel engine. (Published by Colourpicture.)

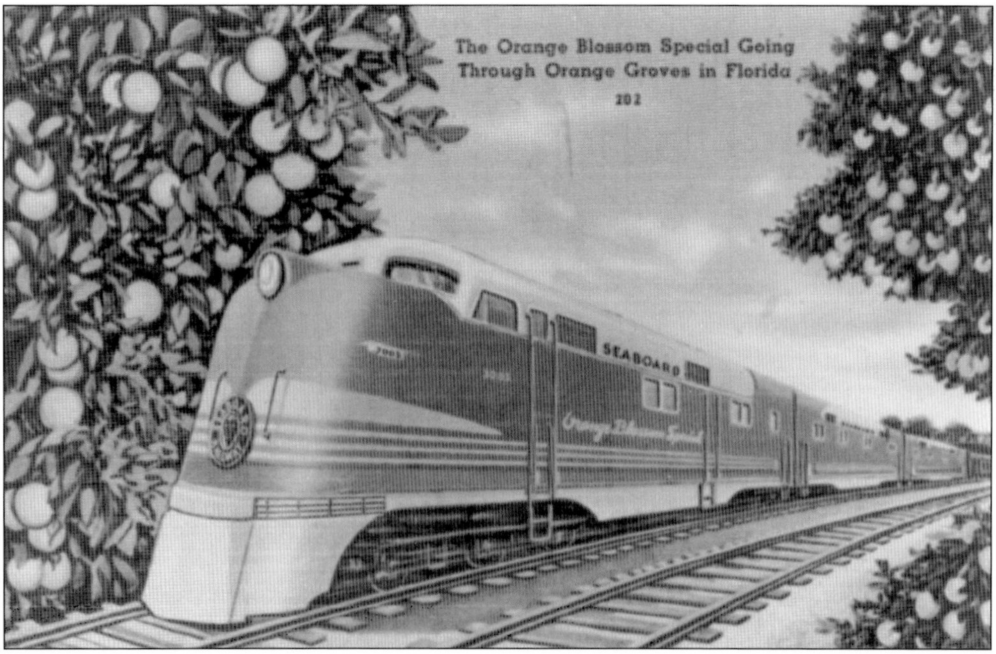

The *Orange Blossom Special* was the Seaboard Air Line Railroad crack flyer. The train made its inaugural run to Miami in January 1927. (Courtesy of Historical Museum of Southern Florida.)

This 1941 postcard aptly portrayed Miami's popularity as the "Winter Resort of America."

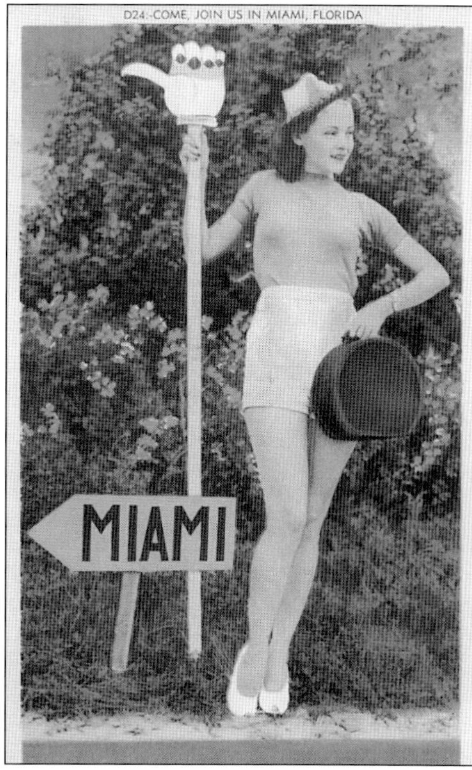

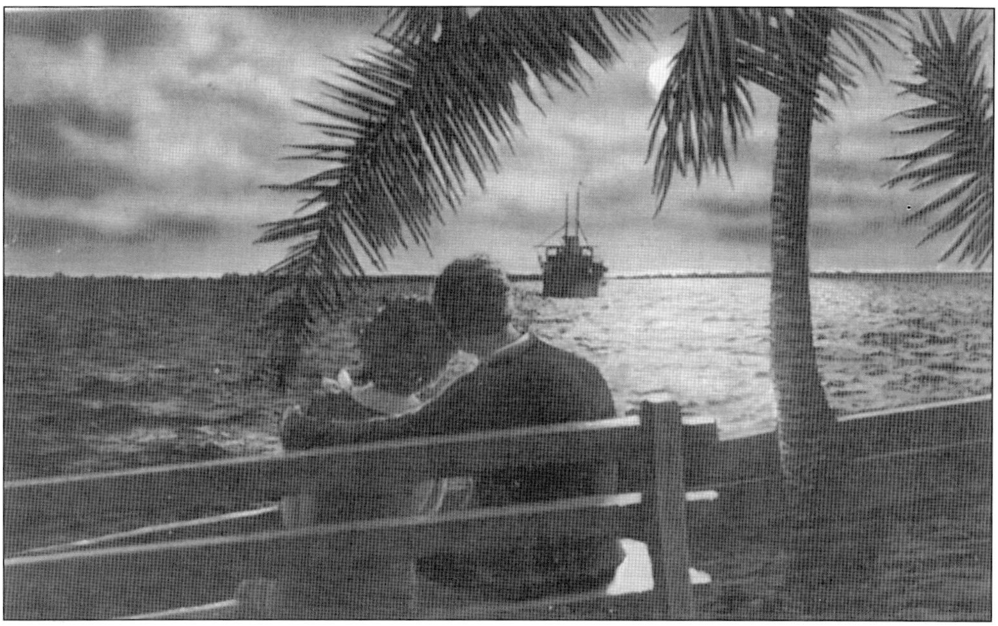

A balmy night, a magnificent moonlit bay, and palm trees that rustle gently in the warm evening breeze . . . Miami lives up to the caption, "Under the Miami Moon, Where Dreams Come True." At the end of this postcard journey , we reflect on the dreams that have come true for so many in Miami's first century and the ones that are taking shape now.

Bibliography

Blackman, E.V. *Miami and Dade County, Florida.* Washington, D.C.: Victor Rainbolt, 1921.

Bodek, Ralph. *Miami Poppycock.* Miami: Hallmark Press, 1994.

George, Paul S. *A Journey through Time.* Virginia Beach: Donning Company Publishers, 1995.

Hollingsworth, Tracy. *History of Dade County.* Coral Gables, Florida: Glade House, 1936.

Kleinberg, Howard. *Miami: The Way We Were.* The Miami Daily News, Inc., 1985.

LaRoue, Samuel D. Jr., and Ellen J. Uguccioni. *Coral Gables in Postcards.* Dade Heritage Trust, Inc., 1988.

Miami Herald Salute to South Florida's History. *Mostly Sunny Days.* Miami: Suniland Press, 1986.

Muir, Helen. *Miami USA.* Second edition. Coconut Grove, Florida: Hurricane House Publishers, 1990.

Parks, Arva Moore, and Gregory W. Bush. *Miami: The American Crossroad, A Centennial Journey.* Needham Heights, Massachusetts: Simon and Schuster, 1996.

Peters, Thelma. *Lemon City: Pioneering on Biscayne Bay 1850–1925.* Miami: Banyan Books, Inc., 1976.

Peters, Thelma. *Miami 1909.* Miami: Banyan Books Inc., 1984.

Rodriguez, Ivan A., Margot Ammidown, and Emily Perry Dieterich. *From Wilderness to Metropolis: The History and Architecture of Dade County (1825–1940).* Second edition. Metropolitan Dade County Historic Preservation Division, 1992.

Sewell, John. *Miami Memoirs: A New Pictorial Edition by Arva Moore Parks.* Miami: Arva Parks and Co., 1987.

Smiley, Nixon. *Yesterday's Miami.* Miami: E.A. Seemann Pub. Inc., 1973.